An Interview with Thomas Jefferson

Part of the Ten Program Video Podcast Series: 'They Are Here'

I0414071

By Paul Jefko

Paul Jefko

ISBN 978-1-540-42091-6

An Interview with Thomas Jefferson

Contents

Program # 1

Paul Jefko: Hello, Americans, welcome to the inaugural edition of 'They Are Here'. It is the chance for you to meet a person from our past through the Tempsecator, our Time Machine. Our first guest will be someone you all have heard about from your history books and whose image you see every time you purchase something with our nickel, or with our $2 Dollar Bill. Let me introduce the Third President of the United States, author of the Declaration of Independence, the Virginia Statute for Religious Freedom and founder of the University of Virginia, President Thomas Jefferson...

President Jefferson: Thank you very much for having me here.

PAUL: President Jefferson will be discussing in 10 programs what he thinks of our modern American government. We will look at 100 agencies that are quite different from or were not in existence when he was President and ask his opinion of their constitutionality as he sees them. We will also answer as best we can any questions he may have. The viewers should note that we took President Jefferson from his home at Monticello in the year 1819 when he was retired from politics.

Segment 1 – Department of Health and Human Services

Paul Jefko: Before we start, Mr. President, I know that the viewers would like to hear how you wrote what Americans consider one of its founding documents, the American Declaration of Independence. How did you go about writing that immortal document?

President Jefferson: Well, as you know, my good friend, Richard Henry Lee, proposed in the Continental Congress around the 7th of June in 1776, that the United Colonies be free and independent from the British Crown. There were several representatives of those colonies in the Continental Congress who had no authority to vote on such an issue. The chair had to give them time to consult with their colonial governments. While that was ongoing, it was decided to begin debate on the subject on July 1. In the meantime, a Committee of Five was delegated the responsibility to draft a statement stating the reasons for the

1

Congress taking such an action. Those five were John Adams, Benjamin Franklin, Roger Sherman, Robert Livingston and myself as its chairman. I wrote down some items that I thought should be included. When the Committee met the next day, I shared with them my observations and the Committee asked me to draft the statement. I consented and wrote it up but provided it to Franklin and Adams for their judgments. They provided three suggestions which I used to alter the draft. I wrote the final copy and gave it to the Committee. They approved it without adjustment for submittal to Congress.

PAUL: That is a wonderful story. All Americans can be proud of that document. But to begin our series of programs, Mr. President, the first organization we will look at in the Modern Federal Government is the Department of Health and Human Services. Even before you were president, the Congress created agencies to preserve and enhance Americans' health. For example, Congress established the Public Health Service under the Secretary of the Treasury in a 1798 law to care for sick and injured seamen.

JEFFERSON: I remember that law.

PAUL: The Bureau of Chemistry in the Department of Agriculture (a cabinet department established after your term) was set up to carry out the Pure Food and Drug Act, passed in 1906 to ensure food and medicine safety. The Department of the Interior (also a new cabinet department) and its Bureau of Indian Affairs Health Division had responsibility for providing Health Services to Indian Tribes.

JEFFERSON: Health Services?

PAUL: Hospitals were built and doctors went to Indian Reservations to provide health care to the Indians.

JEFFERSON: Reservations?

PAUL: Yes, Indians who did not assimilate into the American population were given federal land where they could practice their traditional way of life.

JEFFERSON: It was apparent George Washington's assimilation program would not work. Has the reservation system ended the constant wars with the Indians?

PAUL: Well, the wars have ended, but the reasons for that are complex. But we can discuss that later.

JEFFERSON: Please continue.

2

An Interview with Thomas Jefferson

PAUL: In 1930, Congress converted the Laboratory of Hygiene, set up to help handle a cholera epidemic in New York, to the National Institute of Health.

JEFFERSON: What is cholera?

PAUL: Like typhoid fever, contaminated drinking water is the main source of cholera. In our time, it occurs mainly in places like India, where people live in close quarters. It occurred in the late 1800's in New York City because of the large number of immigrants crammed into substandard housing.

JEFFERSON: So, the Congress took this small laboratory and made it into a National Institute to study cholera?

PAUL: It has grown into more than that, as we shall see.

JEFFERSON: Proceed.

PAUL: In 1935, Congress passed the Social Security Act and created a Social Security Board to implement it. The Act established a system of old age insurance.

JEFFERSON: I am familiar with fire insurance and life insurance, but old age insurance?

PAUL: Yes, in the 1930's the world went through a financial panic, referred to as The Great Depression, larger than anything before experienced. During that time, the President and Congress established programs called the New Deal transforming government's role. One program, Social Security, provided, at the time, a lump sum payment to every worker who reached the age of 65.

JEFFERSON: I assume we will get into the details of these issues.

PAUL: Oh, yes. Continuing, in 1938, Congress passed the Federal Food, Drug, and Cosmetic Act turning the Bureau of Chemistry into the Food and Drug Administration. In addition, in 1939, the President convinced Congress to create the Federal Security Agency to administer all the health, education, and insurance programs.

JEFFERSON: Tell me what programs these entailed.

PAUL: The Agency included the Social Security Board, the US Public Health Service, the Civilian Conservation Corps (no longer in existence), the Office of Education, the National Youth Administration (no longer in existence) and the Employment Service. The President reorganized this agency as the

Department of Health, Education and Welfare or HEW in 1953.

JEFFERSON: A cabinet department?

PAUL: Yes. In subsequent years, new programs were transferred or added to the Department. For example, in 1955, the Indian Health Service I already talked about moved to HEW from the Interior Department. A big program was established in 1965 as Medicare and Medicaid made health care available to poor and elderly citizens.

JEFFERSON: Did the elderly not save money for their later years? Moreover, what of their families? I sympathize with the poor, but weren't public relief or charities available to aid them?

PAUL: The Great Depression was so widespread, public relief agencies and charities were overwhelmed with the unemployed seeking help. Of course, that was not the case in 1965, when the US was prosperous. The problem then was that hospitals and doctor costs had increased greatly. One could purchase private health insurance for a monthly premium to pay for health care costs.

JEFFERSON: That sounds sensible.

PAUL: The problem is a healthy youngster paid less for health insurance because he rarely became ill, but older people naturally had more health problems, so insurance companies charged them higher fees. In 1965, fewer and fewer older people could afford the premiums the insurance companies charged and had to rely on public charities or their families. Without insurance, many families were bankrupted to pay for their parents' health care costs.

JEFFERSON: I will have more to say on this, but continue.

PAUL: In that same decade, Congress also passed the Older Americans Act to create programs administered today by the Administration on Aging. The Head Start Program educates poverty-stricken youngsters to enable them to compete with their more fortunate contemporaries. In 1979, the President reorganized HEW to establish a new Department of Education, and renamed HEW, Health and Human Services, HHS.

JEFFERSON: The federal government is involved in education, the proper province of the States?

PAUL: Yes, and since then, HHS has added more programs at the behest of Congress. In 1989, the Agency for Health Care Policy and Research was created. In 1997, the Children's Health Insurance Program was established, and, in 2003, Congress created a Medicare Prescription Drug Benefit.

JEFFERSON: Prescription drugs?

PAUL: Since the 1930's, federal law has mandated certain medicines must be prescribed by a physician before they can be purchased. A person took this written prescription to an apothecary, now called a pharmacist who dispensed the medicine. The original Medicare Act did not pay for medicine. However, we will get to this in detail later.

JEFFERSON: I look forward to it.

PAUL: Finally, in 2010 the Affordable Care Act was enacted providing health insurance to all citizens.

JEFFERSON: We now come full circle. We start with Indians, then the elderly, then youth, and finally everyone.

PAUL: Well, that ends the history of this department. We will be looking in detail at the major programs of this Department later. For now, let us move on to one of the largest of the federal agencies, the Social Security Administration.

Segment 2 – Independent Agencies: The Social Security Administration

Paul Jefko: The idea for this program, Mr. President, began with a Democratic Party Senator from Louisiana, Huey Long, who touted his "Every Man a King" program in 1930. Long suggested every person receive an old age pension at the age of 60. In 1934, the President's Committee on Economic Security sponsored a town hall meeting on this idea and drafted a law for Congress to consider.

President Jefferson: What prompted the Senator to come up with this bad idea?

PAUL: As I mentioned in the last session, the nation, and the entire world, experienced the Great Depression. The entire financial system collapsed. People's life savings dissipated in a matter of days. Banks closed because they could not refund their depositor's money. In effect, the entire market system collapsed. No one was exempt. The unemployment rate reached over 20%. President Roosevelt was elected in 1932 in a landslide promising a New Deal for the American people.

JEFFERSON: Speculators and banks, the fruits of Hamilton's dangerous financial system. It serves them right if they lost everything.

PAUL: I guess I did not make myself clear. Even those who were honest, law-abiding workers suffered.

JEFFERSON: I am familiar with financial panics. A great one started last year, in 1819, that still has not abated. That damned National Bank brought that about. The suffering fell on the ones least likely to bear it. Until we curb bank speculation, our country will always have these problems.

PAUL: In any case, the President proposed numerous programs to resolve the resulting problems. But, back to Social Security. President Roosevelt got his version of the program established in law in 1935 via the Social Security Act. It provided a lump sum payment to those who reached 65.

JEFFERSON: Every person in the US who reached the age of 65 got a sum of money from the federal government?

PAUL: Only if they worked a minimum number of years. Certain workers did not receive benefits, such as government workers, farm laborers, and domestic servants. Lump sum payments at the time averaged $58.06, not much to provide economic security even during those times.

JEFFERSON: A common laborer earned less in my time.

PAUL: In 1932, a construction worker made about $907 a year, so $58 was welcome, but it did not cover many expenses. Anyway, the program began to expand. In 1939, Congress made spouses and children of workers eligible for Social Security upon the death of the worker.

JEFFERSON: How many persons were 65 or older at the time?

PAUL: Over 6 million. In 1942, monthly benefits were established and, in the 1950's, benefits were increased for the first time. In 1953, Congress placed Social Security under the newly created Department of Health, Education and Welfare.

JEFFERSON: As you stated in the last session.

PAUL: Yes, and in 1956, Congress allowed disabled workers to receive benefits at age 50 and in later years opened it up to workers of all ages who were disabled. In 1961, Congress lowered the retirement age to 62 with a reduced benefit. In the 1970's, cost of living adjustments were added to keep up with inflation.

JEFFERSON: What does that mean?

PAUL: As a general economic rule, the value of a dollar drops as the supply of money increases in the marketplace.

JEFFERSON: You mean we debase our coinage?

PAUL: No. The US does not use silver or gold coinage as legal tender much anymore. The Treasury prints paper money as legal tender. (Shows Jefferson a dollar bill)

JEFFERSON: Is this paper money issued by the National Bank?
PAUL: No, Congress abolished the National Bank you are familiar with after your time. During the Civil War, the US Treasury began to print paper money constituting legal tender for all debts to help pay for the war. However, as a rule, the increase in the supply of money over and above specie will decrease the worth of the dollar.

JEFFERSON: Is that why the laborer we talked about earlier only made $50 in my time and almost $1,000 in your time?

PAUL: Yes, and no. A number of things affect the costs of labor. In your day, a free laborer, competing with slave labor, received lower wages. Labor unions tended to increase wages.

JEFFERSON: Labor unions?

PAUL: Yes. In our day, workers can collectively bargain with their employer for wages and benefits.

JEFFERSON: What if the employer refused to bargain?

PAUL: The unionized workers can strike the business, that is, refuse to work and not permit others to work in their place.

JEFFERSON: That is not legal. The workers would be arrested.

PAUL: No, but I will explain why later. However, to return to Social Security, Congress became concerned about the financial state of the program.

JEFFERSON: Yes, we have not discussed that. Who pays for this?

PAUL: We will get to that in a minute, Mr. President, but let me continue with the history of the program. President Reagan established the Greenspan Commission to recommend Social Security financing improvements. Changes were made to include taxing social security benefits, adding federal employees

7

to the program and raising the retirement age.

JEFFERSON: How could you tax these benefits? The Constitution does not permit a direct tax on a person.

PAUL: The nation amended the Constitution in 1913 allowing direct taxation via an individual and corporate income tax. As for Social Security, all these funding ideas were designed to increase social security reserve funds. In the late 1990's, non-citizen benefits were scaled back.

JEFFERSON: Are you saying non-citizens received these benefits?

PAUL: Yes, as long as they fulfilled the work requirements we will discuss in a few minutes. Later, President George W Bush recommended the private market take over Social Security, a plan falling flat with Congress and the American public. That covers the history.

JEFFERSON: How much does this cost?

PAUL: The cost of the program in a recent year was $773 Billion.

JEFFERSON: Each year?

PAUL: Yes. Funding comes through a system of taxes on wages. Employees are taxed 6.2% of their pay and employers must match that amount. A self-employed individual is taxed 12.4% of his income.

JEFFERSON: So, I must pay 12% of my agricultural earnings each year?

PAUL: Yes, but only on your profit. Moreover, you have to pay 6.2% of the wages you pay your laborers.

JEFFERSON: My servants are not paid, but they receive free housing, food, and medical attention.

PAUL: Slavery is no longer legal, so ...

JEFFERSON: What did you say?

PAUL: The Northern and Southern States fought a war resulting in the abolishment of slavery.

JEFFERSON: What compensation did the slave owners receive for their property?

PAUL: None, because they lost the war.

JEFFERSON: That certainly was not fair. Nevertheless, tell me, where are all the freed slaves now? Were they shipped back to Africa?

PAUL: No, most of the descendants of former slaves are still here, working as other Americans do in various businesses, or as teachers, doctors, lawyers and other professions.

JEFFERSON: You jest. How could a Negro ever become a lawyer?

PAUL: By going to law school. African-Americans, the term we use today, are a vital part of our society, and have contributed much since the days of slavery. In fact, the current US President is African-American.

JEFFERSON: What?

PAUL: Yes, his name is Barack Obama. His mother was a white anthropologist and his father was an economist for the government of Kenya in Africa. (Shows Jefferson a picture of President Obama)

JEFFERSON: Ah, he must have received his intelligence from his white mother.

PAUL: Continuing...on the taxes supporting Social Security, there is a maximum. The taxes are levied only against the first $97,500 of wages or earnings each year or a maximum annual payment of $6,045 per worker, with the same amount matched by his or her employer.

JEFFERSON: So, if I understand this, the money workers and their employers pay every month goes to the Social Security Administration who distributes it to persons over 62 and those who are disabled. Is it taking in more than it is paying out?

PAUL: Currently, the program runs a surplus. However, beginning in 2023, the amount of money coming in will be less than the amount going for benefits, and by 2036, all the previous savings will be exhausted. So, Mr. President, what about this program?

JEFFERSON: Simple. Preparing for old age is an individual and family responsibility, not a federal responsibility. As it does not provide for the general welfare of the US, but only for the elderly, the program is unconstitutional. The program should be turned over to the States if they wish to continue it, but no federal funding should be provided.

PAUL: But how do we abolish it?

JEFFERSON: Obviously eliminating this program will cause problems. Current recipients contributed to the program with the promise of receiving the benefits. Current contributors nearing retirement expect to receive the payments. To resolve the issue, I suggest the following plan to phase out this program at the federal level.

1. On a date that Congress determines, any state wishing to continue the program for their citizens can do so if their state constitution permits it and they notify Congress. Those wishing to continue the programs will:

A. On a date to be determined by Congress, begin to receive Social Security taxes currently received by the Social Security Administration for their citizens who work in their State.

B. On that same date, the State will begin to send benefit payments to those citizens residing in their State who received payments from the federal government at the time of transfer.

C. The Social Security Administration will provide funds out of current surpluses to the States for no longer than one year to make up for any shortfalls.

2. A state at any time can revise benefits and contribution rates or eliminate the program after the transfer date.

3. If a state declines to accept the responsibility for the program, halt social security benefits to their citizens and contributions from their citizens, effective on the transfer date.

4. Two years from the date of transfer, the Social Security Administration will be abolished.

PAUL: Thank you, Mr. President. We will return to our interview with President Jefferson after this message.

Commercial Break

Segment 3 - Department of Defense

Paul Jefko: Let us proceed to the next costliest federal program, Defense. As you know, the US started out with two cabinet departments dedicated to Defense: The Department of War and the Department of the Navy. After the Spanish-American War in the late 19th century, a review was made of our operations.

President Jefferson: We had a war with Spain?

PAUL: Yes, the outcome was our obtaining the Spanish possessions in the Pacific and the Caribbean. With these new territories, we became a world power and to defend them, Congress reorganized the Department of War and established a general staff to coordinate US ground forces in the same way other European armies were organized at the time.

JEFFERSON: Are you saying we have a permanent standing army?

PAUL: As we go through this, believe me, you will see we have much more than a standing army...Later, during the First World War, the War Department was given supervision of the National Guard, the successor to the state militias.

JEFFERSON: The 'First' World War?

PAUL: Yes, we got involved in a major war that began in Europe over the killing of the Austrian Archduke.

JEFFERSON: We got into a war over a worthless noble in a backwater country?

PAUL: We will discuss the war later when we talk about the Army...Back to where we were, the former State militias were reorganized into the National Guard as a reserve force for the army in 1903. During the First World War, the Secretary of War took control of the National Guard. How it works is that the National Guard of each state is normally under the State governor's control, unless the President declares them to be under his authority. That happened during the First World War.

JEFFERSON: Your adjective 'First' implies there was more than one 'world war'. How many have there been?

PAUL: Just two...Anyway, by 1941, when we entered World War II, over 24,000 civilian and military persons worked in Washington DC on War Department activities. And, although we won the war, the disputes between the Navy and Army during the war led Congress to pass the National Security Act that merged the Departments of War and the Navy into one Cabinet Secretary of Defense, with subordinate Departments of the Army and the Navy.

JEFFERSON: That seems sensible. After all, I never understood why there were two separate cabinet members dedicated to war in my administration.

PAUL: Also, a new Department of the Air Force was added as a coequal with the Army and Navy.

JEFFERSON: An Air Force? You mean we have soldiers shooting at the enemy from balloons?

PAUL: A little more sophisticated than that, but the principle remains the same. We have aircraft that travel faster than sound and bombs that can level an entire city. (Shows picture of F-16 Fighter plane)

JEFFERSON: You are joking.

PAUL: I am deadly serious. One aircraft manned by a 12-man crew dropped one bomb from 6 miles above the city of Hiroshima, Japan that killed 160,000 people. (Shows picture of H-Bomb mushroom cloud test and City of Hiroshima after the A-Bomb was dropped)

JEFFERSON: (Staring speechless)

PAUL: During the Cold War...

JEFFERSON: I though you said there were only two world wars.

PAUL: Well, this was a Cold War because there was no actual fighting between the two antagonists.

JEFFERSON: A war without fighting?

PAUL: Well, there was fighting but it was done between surrogates. The Cold War was a struggle against worldwide Communism, an ideology spread by totalitarian and militant states in Russia and China. Besides the traditional army and naval forces and equipment, we developed bombs and airborne delivery weapons that could annihilate a country in minutes. The US also developed counterinsurgency forces to conduct guerrilla warfare against Communist allied states.

JEFFERSON: Guerilla warfare?

PAUL: You recall the type of warfare that was fought by irregulars like Col Marion in the American Revolution that ambushed and harassed the British regulars? That is guerilla warfare...Eventually, the internal contradictions of Communism led to its collapse that ended the Cold War. Under President Clinton, less emphasis was placed on defense, as new weapon systems designed for use against the Communists were no longer needed.

JEFFERSON: So, with the Cold War's end, we do not have a standing army?

PAUL: Well, no, we just made a change in strategy. The new threats we faced were small-scale conflicts that required rapid deployment of conventional forces. Therefore, we needed a modern force with top-notch weapons and highly trained warriors, in other words, a standing army...Anyway, that sums up how the Department of Defense evolved. As we did for Health and Human Services, we will be looking at the largest parts of the Department later. It is now time to discuss one of the largest entitlement programs: Medicare.

Segment 4 - Medicare

Paul Jefko: You may recall, Mr. President, we touched on this program in our first segment on the Department of Health and Human Services. In 1945, President Truman proposed legislation for a national health insurance program to provide medical care for all Americans.

President Jefferson: I thought the Medicare program was solely for the elderly.

PAUL: The current program is for the elderly. However, the Democratic Party has tried for many years to provide health care for all Americans. Congress and the nation debated the issue. Those opposed to the idea said it was Socialism and contrary to American values.

JEFFERSON: What is Socialism?

PAUL: Socialism is an economic system that encourages group action and public ownership of the major means of production. It arose in the mid-19th century as a reaction to the abuses of the free market system. Medicare is socialistic, but setting these ideological arguments aside, Medicare solved the problem the elderly faced. Because the elderly need more medical care as their health deteriorates, paying for such care could bankrupt a person, and even purchasing health insurance on the open market was too costly or even unavailable.

JEFFERSON: I understand doctors are not cheap, but how much money are we talking about here?

PAUL: Quite a lot. The federal government uses the Gross National Product, a measure of the market value of all the goods and services produced by a country. Health care is 15% of our economy today.

JEFFERSON: I cannot believe doctors provide services equal to 15% of the national economy. That is absurd.

PAUL: It may sound that way, but I'll just give you a sample of where these monies go. First, Research. We have private and government laboratories conducting research leading to cures for diseases that killed many people in your time. Examples include Scarlet Fever, Catarrh, Consumption, Bloody Flux, and Enteric Fever.

JEFFERSON: Consumption is curable?

PAUL: Very few cases of what we call tuberculosis occur in the US. Second, diagnostic tools such as X-Rays, Cat Scans, and Magnetic Resonance Imaging are available to look into the body and discover health problems such as cancer, heart disease, and broken bones.

JEFFERSON: You can cure cancer?

PAUL: We can cure some cancers but the disease is so complex that in most cases, we can only control its spread. However, the diagnostic tools we have can locate it sooner to help control it. Third, drugs that control but not cure diseases such as diabetes.

JEFFERSON: How can you control sugar diabetes?

PAUL: Research discovered how sugar is used in the body and developed the missing link, insulin, which is injected daily by diabetics who cannot produce it.

JEFFERSON: Injected?

PAUL: Yes, after your time, a scientist invented a hollow needle with a hole in the tip. (Shows illustration of hypodermic needle) You insert the needle below the skin or into a vein and then administer any drug you wish. Fourth, heart surgery, where a machine replaces the heart by pumping blood while the heart is stopped to correct an abnormality.

JEFFERSON: This is exciting. I now understand why the costs are so high.

PAUL: I am not finished. Fifth, treatments for cancer involving radiation therapy and chemotherapy to kill cancerous tumors. Sixth, blood banks to store blood to be used to replace blood loss during surgery or accident.

JEFFERSON: You mentioned this in our earlier session on Health and Human Services. These blood banks store blood? Where do they get it?

14

PAUL: People voluntarily donate blood in campaigns sponsored by a charity called the Red Cross. The blood is stored in a cold environment and used as needed. Seventh, antibiotic drugs to kill the bacteria causing disease.

JEFFERSON: You mentioned a disease called cholera in an earlier session. You did not mention the term bacteria.

PAUL: Bacteria is a term after your time. I assume you know about Leeuwenhoek's studies on animalcules. Well, these animalcules are actually tiny animals and plants we call bacteria, some of which are helpful, and others harmful. Bacteria cause many diseases. Now we inject antibiotics into the body to kill the harmful bacteria. In addition, vaccines like the smallpox vaccine you are familiar with have been developed for diphtheria, measles, and poliomyelitis.

JEFFERSON: I am unfamiliar with the diseases diphtheria and poliomyelitis.

PAUL: In your day, diphtheria was a common childhood illness called "The Strangling Angel of Children." Eighty percent of children under 10 who contracted it died. Various doctors in your day referred to poliomyelitis as "a debility of the lower extremities," or "Infantile spinal paralysis." So, because of these advances in medical care, plus sanitation, and worker safety, people were living longer.

JEFFERSON: How long are they living compared to my day?

PAUL: Life expectancy in the US in your time was about 39 years, compared to our time of about 75 years.

JEFFERSON: That is quite a step up.

PAUL: Quite right. Consequently, the rapid growth of the elderly population led to a point where only 1 in 8 seniors had health insurance because these high-risk individuals were excluded from obtaining private health insurance. To meet this need, Congress passed Medicare under President Johnson. On July 1, 1966, over 19 million individuals registered for the program. In 1972, Congress added to Medicare those persons under 65 who had long-term disabilities and end stage kidney disease.

JEFFERSON: What is end stage kidney disease?

PAUL: The kidney removes the body's waste products accumulating in the blood and excretes them as urine. When kidneys fail, the person dies, as they did in your day. Today, we can hook up a person to a dialysis machine to remove the waste products.

JEFFERSON: How does that function?

PAUL: I am not a medical expert, but it involves inserting a tube into a vein and pumping the blood into a machine taking the kidney's place. Done regularly, the cost is expensive. That is why Congress determined the federal government could pay for this. To continue, Chiropractors and Speech and Physical Therapy were also added to the benefits available.

JEFFERSON: What is a chiropractor?

PAUL: A chiropractor is a health professional who believes spinal misalignment causes many health problems. Many people use them to solve back pain problems other methods have not been able to cure. As you can see, Congress continued to add pieces to the program raising its costs so that today, Medicare spends more than it receives in revenue.

JEFFERSON: How are these costs funded?
 PAUL: The funding process is the same as Social Security: wage taxes. To increase revenue, Congress added federal employees to the program in the 1980's. In 1985, Congress passed a law that created higher health care costs for everyone. The law required hospitals that accepted Medicare payments to provide emergency care to anyone even if they could not pay or did not have insurance.

JEFFERSON: So, if I break my leg, the hospital has to set it gratis?

PAUL: Yes. However, the hospitals had to pay for this some way so they increased the bills of other patients who had health insurance or could pay to cover these costs.

JEFFERSON: That does not seem fair to those who can pay or who buy insurance. Why did Congress do that?

PAUL: I am not sure, but leaving a person to bleed to death on the hospital doorstep because he could not pay for treatment sounded cold hearted. Anyway, to control some costs, Congress established a Medicare fee schedule in 1989 to control doctor fees. In 2003, a further costly program was added to Medicare when President Bush requested Congress to pass a prescription drug benefit to Medicare beneficiaries.

JEFFERSON: We discussed the need for prescriptions in a previous session.

16

PAUL: Correct. That covers the history; now here is how the system works. There are four parts of the program: Part A – Hospital Insurance. Throughout a person's work life, the government taxes his or her wages to fund this program. Three months before you reach 65, you can sign up for Medicare. You will get a Medicare card you show when you need hospital treatment to pay for a hospital room, meals, nursing services, and even hospice and home health care.

JEFFERSON: A hospice; a place for those dying?

PAUL: Yes, they used to be managed by Catholic religious orders in Europe. Today we have a hospice system where a dying person can still receive care to make them comfortable. Part B – Doctor and Medical Services and Supplies. When a person becomes 65, they can purchase this coverage, deducted from Social Security payments. It pays for doctors and for medical services such as lab fees and medical supplies.

JEFFERSON: If a person chooses not to purchase this when they become 65 years of age, can they change their mind and purchase it later?

PAUL: Yes, but the longer they wait, the higher are their monthly fees. Continuing...Part C – Medicare Advantage. There are some companies called Health Maintenance Organizations (HMO's) or Preferred Provider Organizations (PPO's) that do it all. They provide hospital care, doctors, and even prescription drugs for a standard monthly charge. However, you are limited to using only doctors and hospitals within the HMO or PPO network.

JEFFERSON: This seems to be the optimum. They provide everything.

PAUL: Some people do not like them because you cannot choose your doctor. They provide one to you and you must accept him or her. Finally, Part D – Prescription Drugs. The participant pays a fee for this coverage, provided by the private sector. The government subsidizes the person's payment by paying the pharmaceutical company directly. Finally, Medicare does not cover all health care costs for the elderly and disabled.

JEFFERSON: How much does it cover?

PAUL: Normally, Medicare covers only 80% of medical costs, the remaining 20% covered by either private health insurance or personal funds. Health Care costs are increasing for everyone and Medicare is no exception. Payments will exceed revenues in 2018. The current program cannot be sustained. So, Mr. President, what do you think about this program?

JEFFERSON: Quite simply, Medicare is unconstitutional, because it provides benefits to a select group, the elderly. It would be constitutional under the general welfare clause if Congress provided health care to everyone and not just the elderly. As currently structured, however, no federal dollars can be used for this program.

PAUL: How do we eliminate this program?

JEFFERSON: I realize the elderly depend on this program and it is cold hearted to end it abruptly, but I see no alternative to using the same process I suggested for undoing the Social Security program. Maintain the program for one year at the federal level while implementing the following changes:

1. All citizens will be notified that on a date to be determined, the federal government will disestablish the program.

2. Any state wishing to assume the program from the federal government for their citizens can do so if their state constitution permits it.

3. On a date to be determined, send Medicare payroll taxes currently sent to the federal government to each state's organization established to manage the program for those states assuming the program.

4. On that same date, the state organization established to manage the program will assume responsibility for benefit payments for their citizens eligible at the time of transfer.

5. The federal Medicare organization will assist States with financing until a sufficient surplus is available to pay benefits but for no longer than one year from the date of assumption.

6. A state at any time can revise benefits and contribution rates or eliminate the program after the transfer date.

7. If a state declines to assume the program, Medicare benefits will be halted to citizens of that state and taxes will not be collected from their citizens on the date to be determined.

8. Two years from the date of transfer, abolish the Medicare federal organization.

PAUL: Thank you, Mr. President. We will move on to Medicare's sister program: Medicaid.

Segment 5 – Medicaid

Paul Jefko: Mr. President, our next program is Medicaid. Like Medicare, Congress created Medicaid in the Social Security Act of 1965. Originally designed for the health care needs of the disabled and elderly poor, it expanded quickly to become a health care system for anyone in poverty. In its early beginnings, it applied to only 15 million, but now provides for over 50 million people.

President Jefferson: Health seems to be a major issue with Congress. Obviously, the votes of 50 million people are a strong incentive to comply with their wishes. I understand in our democracy, people, through Congress, establish the laws they wish to have. However, it must be done within the constraints of the Constitution.

PAUL: The Supreme Court has decided these programs are constitutional.

JEFFERSON: That does not mean they are correct in their interpretation. Members of the court have a political viewpoint coloring their judgments. But, go on...

PAUL: Through the years, Congress has also increased services provided through Medicaid. Although the federal and state governments jointly fund the program, they must follow federal rules in administering the program. In some cases, waivers have been granted to states to modify the general rules if it would be more efficient. For example, some states use the funds to purchase private health insurance for enrollees.

JEFFERSON: The process seems so woefully inefficient and byzantine. You provide free health care for children, the poor, and the elderly. It must be horrifically costly to administer.
 PAUL: Actually, Medicaid is less costly than private insurance. Some services provided include dental services for those less than 21 years of age...

JEFFERSON: So, we cover the pulling of teeth?

PAUL: The services provided by dentists these days are quite different from your day. In your day, they pulled decaying teeth and provided dentures for those with no teeth. Today, they can seal teeth to prevent decay and fill decaying teeth with metal to preserve them. In addition, they have other methods besides dentures to replace missing teeth.

JEFFERSON: Question. Is a State able to refuse participation in the program?

PAUL: Yes, but all states participate.

JEFFERSON: The efforts of those who want to tap the largesse of government have always been with us. That is why we have a Constitution to prevent these raids on the Treasury.

PAUL: Continuing on...a recipient of the program must be a US citizen or legal resident, and must be poor, based on a formula determined by family

19

income, age of the recipient and his or her residence. Hospital services, laboratory and x-ray work, pediatric and nurse consultations, nursing services, medical screening, diagnosis, and treatment, physician services, and dental services as described earlier are provided to those qualifying.

JEFFERSON: X-Ray Work?

PAUL: Yes, a diagnostic device allowing a doctor to see inside the body to detect fractures and tumors. (Shows photo of X-Ray image of chest)

JEFFERSON: Amazing, a wonder anyone dies anymore.

PAUL: Also, home health care, midwife, and postpartum services are provided for mothers. Some states also allow optometry services, transportation, prescription drugs and artificial limbs, plus rehabilitation and physical therapy.

JEFFERSON: What is optometry?

PAUL: Optometry is a branch of medical science dealing with vision problems. In summary, the cost for this program is $203 Billion in a recent year, most of the money going to the States for their further distribution. How do you see this program?

JEFFERSON: From your description, the program only benefits a portion of the American public, the poor, and therefore cannot be supportive of the general welfare. Therefore, federal participation is unconstitutional. Since the States administer the program and the only federal involvement concerns funding and setting of standards, it should be easy to eliminate the federal funding and involvement in setting standards.

PAUL: Thank you, Mr. President.

Segment 6 - Department of Agriculture

Paul Jefko: We now have a cabinet department devoted to something dear to your heart, Mr. President, Agriculture. The Department started as a Division of the US Patent Office in 1839, to review the new imported seed, plant, and animal varieties. The initial law establishing the office also required the Division to collect agricultural statistics. Later President Lincoln raised it to a Cabinet department during the Civil war in 1862.

President Jefferson: Why was it elevated to a Cabinet position?

PAUL: Probably because he believed its importance would be emphasized if it were in the cabinet. The first efforts by Congress on agriculture were focused on food safety. In 1865, diseased livestock arriving at a US port encouraged Congress to pass an act requiring quarantining of imported animals. In 1884, Congress created the Bureau of Animal Industry and tasked them to prevent diseased animals entering the food supply.

JEFFERSON: Why weren't the States doing this?

PAUL: I assume the States did some inspections, but it did not seem to work well. Their failure was highlighted in a novel, The Jungle, written by Upton Sinclair, describing the disgusting details in the Chicago meatpacking industry. These revelations led to passage of the Food and Drug Act of 1906 and the Meat Inspection Act. With its authority, President Theodore Roosevelt directed government inspectors to inspect slaughterhouses.

JEFFERSON: Where is Chicago and what is meatpacking?

PAUL: Chicago is now the third largest city in the US, located in Illinois. Meatpacking is an industrial operation for slaughtering cattle and swine and processing them for food shipped to other areas. Chicago became the center of this industry after the Civil War. To continue...during the Great Depression, President Franklin Roosevelt created the Rural Housing Service and the Rural Utilities Service to help develop poor farming communities.

JEFFERSON: The federal government was building houses?
PAUL: Well, during the 1930's, 40% of farms were operated by tenant farmers or sharecroppers who did not maintain the housing they lived in because they did not own it. Similarly, the farm owner did not have an incentive to maintain the housing as long as he could get someone to live in it.

JEFFERSON: I am familiar with tenant farming in England where the nobility owned the land and the farmer did the work. Tenant farming never occurred in my day. What happened to generate this occupation?

PAUL: The emancipation of slaves in the South after the Civil War left many plantations without adequate labor. Landless white farmers rented the owner's land and paid him after harvest. This was tenant farming. A sharecropper usually was an emancipated slave who farmed the property and received a share of the crop to compensate. Most housing on these farms for both tenants and sharecroppers was in very poor condition.

JEFFERSON: So these sharecroppers just lived in the house and did nothing to better themselves?

PAUL: Usually the share the farmer received was at a subsistence level

21

and any money obtained was barely enough to feed him and his family until the next harvest. In reality, most tenant farmers and sharecroppers were poorly educated, and were probably cheated by the landowner out of part of the crop.

JEFFERSON: What are Rural Utilities?

PAUL: A modern home in the 1930's had running water available for use inside the home; some homes had electricity or gas and indoor bathrooms.

JEFFERSON: I have heard about the central water works in Philadelphia that extracted water from the Schuylkill River and distributed it through the city. I am also familiar with electricity, but what use is it?

PAUL: The water system in Philadelphia you are familiar with has spread throughout US cities. (Shows a modern home kitchen) Most every US town takes water either from wells or from rivers or lakes, cleans, chlorinates and fluoridates it, and then pumps it to those who pay a monthly fee for the service.

JEFFERSON: Chlorinate and Fluoridate?

PAUL: Chlorine is added to the water at a low concentration to kill bacteria. They also add fluorine to prevent tooth decay.

JEFFERSON: How can fluorine stop tooth decay?

PAUL: Fluoride compounds harden the teeth and make them resistant to bacteria that cause tooth decay. When a person drinks fluoridated water, the fluoride binds with the teeth.

JEFFERSON: Electricity? I know about static electricity and Franklin's proof that lightning was electricity, but what use does it have?

PAUL: In your time, electricity had not been harnessed as an energy source. For home use, specifically in the era we are talking about, electricity powers many things, the most common of which is lighting, and heat for cooking and comfort. (Shows photo of electric streetlights) However, to get back to the Rural Utilities Service, the agency gave money to local communities to establish water companies and electric companies.

JEFFERSON: Why did the government need to do this?

PAUL: To provide the water service, the company had to lay the hollow pipe underground from the facility to the home. The electric company had to hang copper wire from their facility to the home on poles anchored to the ground. Laying pipe or wire miles into the country was costly, plus the homeowner could not afford the monthly fee, especially tenant farmers and sharecroppers. Therefore, the federal government inserted itself in building the systems. Continuing on...concerns over pesticide and drug use in animals led in 1958 to the Food Additive Amendment to control the use of additives in food.

JEFFERSON: Drugs in animals?

PAUL: Yes. They give livestock antibiotics to control disease and increase weight gain, allowing them to come to market faster and save feed and medical care costs.

JEFFERSON: Isn't that a good thing?

PAUL: No, because antibiotic overuse lessens its effectiveness as the bacteria become resistant to the antibiotic.

JEFFERSON: Explain.

PAUL: Science has discovered that an organism fitter or better suited to its environment will survive over others not so blessed and later transmit this fitness to its offspring.

JEFFERSON: What evidence is there for this?

PAUL: In your time, have you not grafted buds from one tree to another?

JEFFERSON: Yes, I grafted cherry trees at Monticello to combine the characteristics of say a tree with a sweet fruit with one more resistant to drought.

PAUL: What you did was transfer the properties of one tree to another. The same process occurs naturally. For example, some cherry trees will survive a particular pest and others will not. Those surviving trees transmit this mechanism to its seeds and the offspring will have this ability. Similarly, some bacteria will survive the onslaught of an antibiotic and transmit that ability to its offspring. If we take too many antibiotics, we will not get mild bacterial illnesses but major ones will likely kill us, because no other antibiotic would be effective.

JEFFERSON: I understand.

PAUL: Continuing...Congress passed the Wholesome Meat Act of 1967 requiring States to conduct better meat inspections.

JEFFERSON: I thought the federal government conducted inspections.

PAUL: The federal government only inspects those establishments engaging in interstate commerce. The States and local communities are the ones conducting the inspections of those companies doing business within the state.

JEFFERSON: So, we tell the States what to do in their inspections?

PAUL: Yes, because the law empowered the federal government to set inspection standards. Continuing...in 1972, the Animal and Plant Health Inspection service was created to take over the regulatory functions of the Agriculture Research Service. Congress later transferred these duties to the Food Safety and Inspection Service (FSIS). When four people died in 1993 after eating at a public restaurant, the FSIS developed the Pathogen Reduction/Hazard Analysis and Critical Control Point System, making the food industry and restaurants required to prepare food according to federal standards.

JEFFERSON: From what did they die?

PAUL: E. coli poisoning. E. coli are bacteria living in human waste. They are inside your colon right now.

JEFFERSON: I have deadly bacteria in my body?

PAUL: In your large colon, they serve a useful purpose in digesting other harmful bacteria.

JEFFERSON: So, some bacteria are helpful?

PAUL: Yes, for example, bacteria in the nodules of legumes convert nitrogen in the air to proteins in the plant. E Coli, though, are found in the guts of all warm-blooded animals. During slaughtering, there may be some contamination on the carcass. The meat must be cooked to a certain temperature to ensure all the E Coli are killed. At the restaurant under discussion, the people ate contaminated beef.

JEFFERSON: Dreadful.

PAUL: That concludes a quick summary of what has happened in food safety, and farm assistance but the Agriculture Department does a lot more. We will look into that in future programs. This concludes our first program in this Series with former President Thomas Jefferson. On behalf of President Jefferson and myself, Paul Jefko, we will see you next time on 'They Are Here!'

Program # 2

Paul Jefko: Hello, Americans, welcome to the second program of 'They Are Here'. It is the chance for you to meet in actuality a person from our past through the Tempsecator, our Time Machine. This program continues our discussions with President Thomas Jefferson. Let me reintroduce the Third President of the United States, author of the Declaration of Independence, and the Virginia Statute for Religious Freedom, President Thomas Jefferson...

President Jefferson: I am looking forward to our discussion.

Segment 7 – Department of Defense: Department of the Army

Paul Jefko: Before we start this segment, Mr. President, not many people know that you authored the Virginia Statute for Religious Freedom or even what it entailed. Could you provide us an explanation of why you think it was one of your greatest achievements?

President Jefferson: Certainly. In the Virginia colony and in many other colonies of Great Britain, the Church of England was supported by taxes collected by the colony. This, in my mind, gave preference to that church over other churches at the time, such as Baptists, Presbyterians and Methodists, who had their own congregants who were forced to support a religion that they did not espouse. I believe that God has given us the freedom to believe or disbelieve in any manner we wish. That is why I thought it important to introduce this law into the Commonwealth of Virginia after we had declared our independence from Great Britain.

PAUL: And our viewers may not know that that law was the inspiration for our First Amendment separation of Church and State. But to continue on our quest...As you know, Mr. President, the Continental Congress disbanded the Continental Army after the American Revolution because they did not like to have standing armies around with nothing to do as it supposedly encouraged tyranny. Consequently, although we fought wars against the British in the War of 1812, fought Mexico, and Spain and even had a huge Civil War, we always disbanded the Army at the end of the conflict.

JEFFERSON: A sensible approach.

25

PAUL: When US leaders decided to enter World War I, we sent over a million troops to Europe in a war assisted by the Industrial Revolution. Tanks, chemical weapons, and machine guns heralded the new modern age of war.

JEFFERSON: What is the Industrial Revolution?

PAUL: Beginning in the latter 18th century, there were tremendous changes in agriculture, mining, transport and manufacturing, which changed the entire social character of the world. These changes were abetted by technological advancements such as steam engines, to make things cheaper and faster. Although the changes started in England, the US made the most use of it until we became the world manufacturer in the 20th century.

JEFFERSON: What are these tanks, chemical weapons, and machine guns?

PAUL: Tanks are armored, self-propelled vehicles with guns. (Shows a picture of M-1 Abrams tank) Germany in WW I placed chemical weapons like chlorine gas in hollow artillery shells and shot them at the enemy. When inhaled, the chlorine gas combined with the water in the lungs to produce hydrochloric acid killing many by slow strangulation. A machine gun shoots bullets at the rate of 120 a minute. One gun can decimate an entire attacking regiment.

JEFFERSON: Please continue.

PAUL: Although that war indicated our national defense in the modern age could not rely on quickly trained volunteers and a peacetime return to a small defense establishment, we disbanded the Army again. After the attack on Pearl Harbor, the Army faced a two-front war, one in Europe, and the other in the Pacific. After this war, the threat from the Soviet Union ended any attempt to downsize and in fact, we integrated our armed forces into NATO and permanently stationed some troops in Europe.

JEFFERSON: What is NATO?

PAUL: NATO is the North Atlantic Treaty Organization. It binds the US with Europe in a treaty assuming an attack on one is an attack on all.

JEFFERSON: So, we get involved in all those petty wars the Europeans have from time to time?

PAUL: Most of the countries formerly warring against each other are now in NATO. NATO was established as a defense against the Soviet Union and its satellite countries the US regarded as the main threat after WW II. The vast carnage of two world wars drained any hostility or suspicion between the European countries causing all those petty wars in your century. In fact, they cooperate very well these days.

JEFFERSON: Please give me a short version of why we fought in WW II.

PAUL: The ultimate reason was an attack on our naval base in Hawaii by the Japanese. Soon after the attack, Germany, allied with Japan, declared war on us.

JEFFERSON: But I am unfamiliar with the country Germany. Are you talking about the German Confederation?

PAUL: Germany became a nation when Prussia united all the German states under its rule in the late 19th century. Prior to World War II, Germany's leader, Adolf Hitler, had a vision to conquer Europe. At the time the Japanese attacked, he had conquered or occupied most of Eastern Europe including Poland and the Balkan countries. He also occupied Austria, Norway, Denmark, France, and the Low countries. His ally, Mussolini, was the leader of Italy, also united about the same time as Germany.

JEFFERSON: So, it appears we have a Napoleon appear every century.

PAUL: Hitler was a little more frightening than Napoleon. He espoused National Socialism, calling for a total militarization of society and the complete submission of the individual to the State, that is, Hitler. Additionally, he was ruthlessly anti-Jewish and established camps where he asphyxiated them with chemical gases and burned their bodies in large ovens. He murdered over 6 million Jews during the war.

JEFFERSON: 6 Million?

PAUL: Yes, unbelievable. However, Hitler, like Napoleon, invaded Russia, at the time called the Soviet Union, and like Napoleon, failed. The US along with Great Britain and the Soviet Union defeated both Germany and Japan. After the war, the Soviet Union kept what it had conquered from the Germans, such as Poland, the Balkans and what you know as Bohemia and established Soviet governments there.

JEFFERSON: I want to hear about this Soviet system, but continue with what you were saying.

PAUL: As we discussed earlier, after the war, the Congress changed the Department of War to the Department of the Army and subordinated it to the Department of Defense. During the Cold War, military Intelligence became overly important but some attempts at protecting the nation led some overzealous commanders to spy on Americans exercising First Amendment rights in protesting the Vietnam War.

JEFFERSON: I told you there was a problem with having a standing army. But, where is Vietnam?

PAUL: In your day, it was known as Cochin China. During the Cold War, the northern part was a Communist State aligned with the Soviet Union while the southern part was our ally. We attempted to keep the South from being overrun by the north but we lost. After the defeat, the Army went into decline. Most combat since Vietnam has been like Operation Desert Storm where our tanks rolled across Iraq.

JEFFERSON: Where is Iraq and why did we fight there?

PAUL: In your day, Iraq was Mesopotamia under the Ottoman sultans. In our day, it had a dictator, Saddam Hussein, who invaded one of our allies. We went in and forced the Iraqis back into their own country. Since that war, we have been embroiled in Afghanistan, the home of the group protecting Al Qaeda, a terrorist organization that attacked us in New York City. That gets us up to my present day.

JEFFERSON: Tell me about this terrorist group.

PAUL: Al Qaeda is a radical group based in the Middle East, which believes in a strict interpretation of Islam. It blames Western society for corrupting Islam and wants to eliminate Western influence in the Middle East.

JEFFERSON: Why are we in the Middle East?

PAUL: It contains the largest petroleum reserve in the world, and therefore a national security issue for the US.

JEFFERSON: Thank you.

PAUL: Unless you have more questions, we can proceed with the Army organization.

JEFFERSON: Proceed.

PAUL: You may be familiar with the tools of warfare but some may be new. The army has aircraft, artillery, air defense, armor, nuclear, biological, and chemical defenses, and a variety of wheeled and tracked vehicles.

JEFFERSON: No cavalry?

PAUL: Funny you ask. The Army has what is called Air Cavalry. Instead of horses, they ride helicopters, a type of aircraft. (Shows photo of Apache attack helicopter)

JEFFERSON: How can you call them ground forces when they are in the air?

PAUL: Very funny. It may become clearer as I discuss their missions. For example, the Army has geographical commands such as US Army Central to cover the Middle East, Northeast Africa and Southwest Asia, Iraq and Afghanistan, US Army North to cover North America, US Army South to cover Central and South America...

JEFFERSON: Wait a minute. The US controls these areas?

PAUL: No, I do not want to give that impression. The US has interests all over the world. The Army commands I mentioned are responsible for military action in their geographical areas if needed. For example, the US Army Central Command has their headquarters in South Carolina, far from the areas of its responsibility. However, some commands are actually in other countries.

JEFFERSON: Where?

PAUL: Well, US Army Europe, covering Western and Central Europe, is located in Germany.

JEFFERSON: We have an occupation army in Germany?

PAUL: No. We have bases there as part of NATO.

JEFFERSON: Earlier you said NATO was a treaty against the Soviet Union, but the Soviet Union is no more. Why do we still have NATO?

PAUL: I have no answer for that good question. To continue, we have US Army Pacific covering Asia and the Pacific except for Korea. The Eighth Army is in Korea.

JEFFERSON: Where is Korea and why are we there?

PAUL: Korea is a peninsula that, in your day, was under the Chinese Empire. Similar to Vietnam, it has a Communist North and a democratic south allied with us. The North attempted to conquer the south and we stepped in to stop it.

JEFFERSON: So, we took sides in a civil war.

29

PAUL: It was more than that. It was part of the Cold War.

JEFFERSON: Which the US apparently won. Why do we have an army still there?
PAUL: Although the Soviet Union no longer provides aid to the North Koreans, they still pose a threat to the South.

JEFFERSON: So, since that war, the South has not built itself up enough to defend itself against the North. Is the North powerful or the South so weak?

PAUL: The North has a large army with a population starving because of their policies. The South is very prosperous and exports its products all over the world.

JEFFERSON: Withdraw the troops we have there and let the two countries fight over their differences.

PAUL: Moving on... Special Operations Command – Airborne, Rangers and Night Stalkers. These special units are designed to conduct unconventional warfare, like the guerilla warfare we talked about earlier. The Surface Deployment and Distribution Command transports Army units and supplies everywhere. The Forces Command oversees deployments of Army units. The Training and Doctrine Command educates and trains officers and enlisted personnel. The Materiel Command procures and develops Weapons and Materials. The Space and Missile Defense Command/Strategic Command controls radar systems and anti-missile defenses.

JEFFERSON: What is radar?

PAUL: The system uses radio waves, which we discussed earlier, to detect distant objects such as aircraft, vehicles, or even weather.

JEFFERSON: Really, you can use this to see an approaching horse and carriage?

PAUL: Theoretically, but the use is mostly for military, air travel or weather related purposes.... The Intelligence and Security Command conducts intelligence, security and information operations for Army commanders. The Medical Command operates eight Army medical centers. The Corps of Engineers constructs buildings and other structures for the Army as well as water projects in the US. The Network Enterprise Technology Command/9th Signal Command maintains communications for all Army units.

JEFFERSON: Why does the Army have eight medical centers? Are these wars in your time so bloody?

PAUL: They do not just care for the wounded. They also provide routine medical exams and inoculations for active duty soldiers and their families.

JEFFERSON: Families? We provide medical care for a soldier's family?
PAUL: Congress established the practice in the late 19th century for families of the soldiers, space being available. Currently, the Army uses it as part of the recruitment package. Continuing...The medical centers are located geographically near the largest Army bases. The Criminal Investigation Command investigates crime where Army personnel are involved. In addition, the Test and Evaluation Command conducts test of weapons and systems.

JEFFERSON: How much does all this cost?

PAUL: $140 Billion in a recent year.

JEFFERSON: I am not used to these amounts. They are staggering.

PAUL: Well, defense contractors or Army arsenals provide all weapons, equipment, and supplies used by the army. Continuing...The Army also provides funds to various organizations for two big programs. One if for Military Medical Research and Development, $ 2 Billion and the other is for National Guard Military Operations and Maintenance, $ 1 Billion.

JEFFERSON: What is the National Guard?

PAUL: The National Guard descends from the state militias. Supposedly, it was named such because the Marquis de Lafayette, popular in the US, was head of the National Guard in France.

JEFFERSON: I knew that but what does that have to do with the militia?

PAUL: Evidently, the Marquis visited the US, met some former militia members, and proclaimed them the National Guard of America.

JEFFERSON: The Marquis, to my knowledge, has never revisited the US after the Revolution.

PAUL: Take my word for it. You will meet him again...So, Mr. President, that is lot to absorb, but what do you think of this organization?

JEFFERSON: The limiting clause in the Constitution allows the federal government "To raise and support Armies, but no Appropriation of Money to that Use shall be for a longer Term than two Years." Therefore, it is constitutional to support an army, so using federal money for these purposes is fine. However, the Constitution demands each Congress appropriate funds for these expenses every two years. Therefore, no contract can extend beyond two years without violating the Constitution. I do not know much about aircraft or tanks but it appears Congress must reauthorize some of these items including construction every two years.

PAUL: So, you suggest the next steps to be?

JEFFERSON: All federal contracts required to support the Army (not the Navy), must be terminated for the convenience of the government if the contract term exceeds two years.

PAUL: Don't you think this is inefficient and even hampers national security?

JEFFERSON: The Constitution is what the federal government lives by. If modifications are needed, the Congress must submit an amendment for State ratification. To do otherwise makes the Constitution meaningless.

PAUL: Thank you, Mr. President. We will stop here for a word from our sponsor.

Commercial Break

Segment 8 - Department of Defense: Department of the Navy

Paul Jefko: Proceeding on with our discussion of the current American government, you are familiar with the establishment of the US Navy and its experiences through the War of 1812, so we will not dwell on its origins. I will give you some history to bring your understanding up to our present time. Until the Civil War, the Navy was unemployed, except for its blockade of the Mexican coast during the Mexican-American War.

President Jefferson: What caused the war with Mexico?

PAUL: In essence, the war began over the Mexican province of Texas. Texas had a sizable population of US settlers. Resisting the rule of autocratic Mexican Presidents, they won their independence as a separate Republic of Texas. Southern slaveholders in Congress, led by President Polk, wanted to expand slavery further west. When the US annexed Texas, Mexico declared war.

JEFFERSON: Thank you. Please go on.

PAUL: Continuing on to the Civil War...In 1861, the US commander of the Norfolk, Virginia Navy Yard ordered all the ships there destroyed to prevent them falling into Southern hands but one ship, the Merrimack was not completely scuttled. Its hull and steam engine were intact and were used by the rebels to construct the ironclad ship renamed Virginia, ending the wooden ship era.

JEFFERSON: So, ships are not made of wood anymore?

PAUL: That is correct. Ships today are made of steel armor, and are propelled by petroleum-based fuels.

JEFFERSON: No steam engines?

PAUL: Well, yes, technically some navy ships are powered with nuclear fuel to heat water for steam, so technically, they are steam engines, but most ships use an internal combustion engine powered by petroleum.

JEFFERSON: Interesting, but please continue.

PAUL: When tensions arose between the US and Spain in the late 19th century, the US Battleship Maine went to Havana, Cuba where it mysteriously exploded and led to war with Spain.

JEFFERSON: Do you mean a line-of-battle ship?

PAUL: The name 'battleship' comes from your term. Battleships are armored, and armed with huge cannon and are definitely a threat.

JEFFERSON: Why did we send a battleship to Cuba?

PAUL: The Cuban people rebelled against their Spanish rulers and the US sent the ship to protect US interests on the island.

JEFFERSON: Why did the ship explode?

PAUL: No one really knows. The latest speculation is a fire spread to the powder magazine and blew up the ship. Moving to the 20th century, the Navy had to deal with submarine warfare initiated by Germany during WW I, a policy testing the US ability to remain neutral in the conflict.

JEFFERSON: Submarine warfare?

PAUL: Yes, you recall the Turtle, the underwater vessel used during the American Revolution to sink a British ship in New York harbor?

JEFFERSON: I heard rumors. It failed, didn't it?

PAUL: Yes, but technological advances have made it a dangerous weapon. Since it cannot be visibly detected, it can approach enemy naval vessels and destroy them with self-propelled torpedoes.

JEFFERSON: How long can this submarine remain under water?
PAUL: Well, in my time, indefinitely because, they are nuclear powered and do not need refueling for 25 years.

JEFFERSON: What?

PAUL: Well, I am exaggerating but not about the fuel. They dock for food and other supplies, but absent this, they never have to return to port and can stay underwater indefinitely. In fact, submarines routinely go under the North Polar Ice Cap.

JEFFERSON: I do not understand.

PAUL: Floating ice covers the North Pole year-round varying in thickness from three to 60 yards deep. The subs easily go under the ice a surface ship could not navigate. But...as I said, the Germans used unrestricted submarine warfare during WW I causing us to declare war against them.

JEFFERSON: Define the term unrestricted submarine warfare.

PAUL: The rules of war allow a submarine to destroy a military vessel without warning. However, a sub must warn a merchant ship and its crew must be placed in a lifeboat or other safe place before sinking the ship. Germany in 1917 declared all merchant ships would be destroyed without warning and the crew left to fend for themselves. Since we supplied the British and French, our ships became targets.

JEFFERSON: That, to me, is an act of war.

PAUL: And so it was. After WW I, in the 1920's, the US launched aircraft carriers, a new vessel designed to project air power. In effect, the ship carried aircraft and launched them to attack by air.

JEFFERSON: I assume, like birds, they can jump off, fly, and return.

PAUL: Exactly, but they need a running start. (Shows a picture of a modern aircraft carrier) An aircraft carrier has a flat surface to allow an aircraft a running start before it gets airborne. The same thing happens on the return landing, as the airplane needs room to stop. The carrier's importance showed during the WW II Battle of Midway when no vessels actually sighted or fired on each other but the aircraft on the opposing carriers attacked the others carriers and vessels.

JEFFERSON: How big are these carriers?

PAUL: They are approximately 1,000 feet long.

JEFFERSON: You don't say. Please continue.

PAUL: The US also engaged in submarine warfare in the Pacific by destroying Japanese naval vessels and merchant shipping, while the regular Atlantic fleet protected convoys of merchant ships from German submarines. The Navy also played a critical role in protecting the troops invading Normandy on D-Day.

JEFFERSON: D-Day?

PAUL: The day the US and its allies invaded Nazi occupied Europe. About 156,000 troops stormed the beaches at Normandy, France and began to push forward to Germany.

JEFFERSON: Thank you.

PAUL: After WW II, the Navy expanded the range of its fleets by launching nuclear powered submarines, carrying nuclear missiles, which stay underwater for long periods without detection. We also deployed attack submarines to sink Soviet submarines if a nuclear war were to occur. Under President Reagan, the Navy was tasked to build a 600-ship fleet to include new carriers and subs.

JEFFERSON: How many carriers does the Navy have now?

PAUL: Currently, the Navy has 12 carriers and supporting fleets as the basis of American sea power. That is the history of the Navy up to now. Do you have any questions?

JEFFERSON: Not at this time.

PAUL: To give you an idea of the Navy organization, let me discuss their basic structure. Naval aircraft form into squadrons and wings. Ships and subs are grouped into task units, task groups, task forces, and fleets. The main Navy organizations are as follows: Naval Forces Central Command has the Fifth Fleet with an area of responsibility from Northeastern Africa to Southwestern Asia. Pacific Fleet is the largest fleet of 178 ships with responsibility from the US West Coast to the East Coast of Africa.

JEFFERSON: All these ships are at sea somewhere in the areas you describe?

PAUL: Portions of the fleet are at Navy yards or bases for resupply or repair, but yes, the majority of the ships in a fleet are at sea at any given moment. Moving on...The Atlantic Fleet includes the Atlantic Ocean from the North to the South Pole, the Caribbean Sea, and the Gulf of Mexico. The Military Sealift Command delivers supplies and conducts special missions to bases worldwide. The Naval Network Warfare Command maintains communication networks linking all Navy commands and ships.

JEFFERSON: How does it do that?

PAUL: That is secret and not available to the public. Nevertheless, every ship in the Navy worldwide can receive a message almost instantaneously from Navy headquarters. Continuing...The Naval Special Warfare Command manages maritime special operations forces including SEALS.

JEFFERSON: Seals?

PAUL: Navy Seals are a special Navy operations force, not the water-loving animal...The Space and Naval Warfare Systems Command develops and acquires all the systems the Navy requires for its operations other than for ships, aircraft, and their associated weapons. The Strategic Systems Programs Office manages the Ballistic Missile program. The Office of Naval Intelligence gathers information on threats to the Navy. The Naval Air Systems Command develops and acquires airborne weapon systems.

JEFFERSON: The organization you describe seems to be a jumble of organizations all developing weapons. Why isn't there just one organization developing weapons?

PAUL: I believe it has to do with specialized knowledge. The weapons aboard an aircraft are quite different from those on a ship for example. Continuing...the Naval Security Group Command provides cryptology services. The Naval Sea Systems Command develops, builds and maintains ships, subs and their combat systems and handles foreign military sales of naval hardware and services. Are there any other questions?

JEFFERSON: No. Please continue.

PAUL: Now that we have reviewed the Navy, what is your view on the constitutionality of these programs, Mr. President?

JEFFERSON: Since the Constitution allows the federal government to provide and maintain a Navy, all the functions mentioned are constitutional. However, there seems to be a concern I have as to whether a flying machine is part of a navy. To me, a navy, a word derived from the Latin 'naves', means ship. However, as long as it leaves from a floating ship, like your aircraft carrier, it is just another cannon, a movable one but still a cannon. Congress, under the Constitution, can make Rules for the Government and regulate the land and naval forces. If Congress agrees flying machines are part of the Navy, I would not question its judgment.

PAUL: Thank you, Mr. President. Let us proceed to the next major component of the Department of Defense, the Air Force.

Segment 9 - Department of Defense: Department of the Air Force

Paul Jefko: We briefly touched on the Air Force earlier, so you do have some background on its inception. At the risk of repeating myself, I will review the information. In 1907, the Army Signal Corps took responsibility for air machines, military balloons, and related subjects. In 1914, Congress created an Aviation Section in the Signal Corps to train personnel in military aviation.

President Jefferson: Since we have discussed these briefly before, I am curious how these air machines work?

PAUL: (Shows a photo of a B-29 bomber) Well, the fixed wing aircraft look like birds in flight in having a body called a fuselage where the pilot sits along with passengers and cargo. The fuselage has wings attached to it just as a bird has. An engine attached to the fuselage turns a propeller pushing the air backward thereby pulling the aircraft forward. When the aircraft reaches a certain velocity, the wings provide lift raising the machine into the air similar to a kite, but more controlled.

JEFFERSON: I seem to understand. Please continue.

PAUL: During WW I, aviation had become so important, President Wilson created an Air Service as part of the US Army separate from the Signal Corps, but like the rest of the Armed Forces, it was downsized after the war. The time after WW I was spent in setting up aviation training. As WW II approached, President Roosevelt directed the Air Corps to expand to a 7,000-aircraft force.

JEFFERSON: 7,000 aircraft to do what?

PAUL: Well, the military uses three types of aircraft. One is cargo aircraft to transport food, weapons, clothing, and equipment and soldiers quickly to wherever they are needed.

JEFFERSON: How quickly?

PAUL: Well, modern aircraft can fly up to 360 miles per hour.

JEFFERSON: Extraordinary. Please go on.

PAUL: The second type is the Bomber, dropping explosives on the enemy from above. The third type is the Fighter, a small, maneuverable aircraft used to defend the other two from hostile aircraft and to shoot at enemy bombers and cargo craft.

JEFFERSON: What kind of hostile aircraft?

PAUL: Well, the enemy will not let you drop explosives on their country. They will send up their aircraft to shoot your bombers and cargo craft.

JEFFERSON: What happens if a fighter shoots your aircraft?

PAUL: It depends. A regular stream of bullets from a machine gun can kill the pilot and then the uncontrolled aircraft will just eventually drop to the ground and crash. Other weapons such as rockets or missiles can be used to destroy the aircraft itself, either exploding them or damaging them so much they hit the ground.

JEFFERSON: How many aircraft crashed during WW II?

PAUL: Almost 23,000 US aircraft. Despite these losses, by the end of WW II, the Air Corps had over 63,000 aircraft available. During the war's early stages, the US aircraft were outperformed by the Japanese and German fighters, but US aircraft gradually became superior, getting to the point where American bombers destroyed German cities, factories, and military centers.

JEFFERSON: How much destruction occurred?

PAUL: For example, aerial bombing destroyed 80% of Mainz, 75% of Hamburg and 61% of Cologne, Germany during the war.

JEFFERSON: I have been to Cologne and Mainz. I assume the old sections from medieval times are no longer there.

PAUL: The same thing happened in Japan as incendiary bombers destroyed huge sections of Japanese cities. The atomic age also started in 1945 when atomic bombs were dropped on Hiroshima and Nagasaki to force the Japanese to surrender and avoid a costly invasion of Japan. When the war ended, the importance of air power led Congress to authorize a force separate from the Army to focus strictly on air power.

JEFFERSON: So, the Army has no aircraft now?

PAUL: No, the Army probably still has more aircraft than the Air Force, but its mission differs. So... the US Air Force was born in 1947, with its first big mission to supply West Berlin, Germany with food and other necessities after the Soviet Union cut off surface access to the city. The Air Force also became paramount in the nuclear standoff with the Soviet Union, as the US targeted the Soviet Union with Intercontinental Ballistic Missiles and long-range aircraft carrying nuclear warheads.

JEFFERSON: Part of the Cold War as you discussed earlier, I take it. Why did we have to supply West Berlin?

PAUL: After the war ended, there was no government capable of ruling Germany. Each major combatant, the US, Great Britain, and the Soviet Union assumed control of the area they occupied. The capital city of Berlin was divided likewise. Unfortunately, Berlin was in the middle of the Soviet Union occupation zone. Although the postwar treaties guaranteed us a roadway to transport supplies from the US zone in Germany through the Soviet Zone to the US Zone in Berlin, the Soviet Union decided to close the road.

JEFFERSON: The US Forces did not try to force travel on the road?

PAUL: No, it might have embroiled us in a war with the Soviet Union President Truman did not want. He decided to put cargo into aircraft and transport it by air. The craft flew 24 hours a day in all-weather transporting about 5,000 tons of supplies each day. It lasted almost a year.

JEFFERSON: Why did the Soviet Union do such a thing?

PAUL: They thought we would back down and let them have all of Berlin for themselves. It did not work. During the Korean War, the Air Force used jet fighters, a new technology, in combat for the first time. Air Force pilots also flew highly secret high altitude reconnaissance missions over the Soviet Union. Moreover, during the Vietnam War, the Air Force conducted massive bombing of enemy targets exceeding the amount dropped on Germany and Japan in WW

II.

JEFFERSON: Well, I can see why airpower is so important.

PAUL: Also in Vietnam, Air Force planes dropped Agent Orange, an herbicide, to destroy the jungles where Viet Cong forces hid. Later, the stealth B-1 and B-2 bombers were developed along with MX missiles. President Reagan called for the development of a defensive shield against Soviet missile attack giving birth to the Star Wars program.

JEFFERSON: What is a stealth bomber?

PAUL: We talked earlier about radar, the technology showing incoming aircraft, balloons, even birds. Some radar tracks storms. Well, if you can see an aircraft on radar, you can shoot it down. The stealth aircraft cannot be detected by radar, so it can fly over an enemy territory without fear of detection.

JEFFERSON: Your time differs from mine. Please continue.

PAUL: The Air Force also became involved in the First Gulf War engaging Iraqi air and ground forces. After the 9/11 attack, the US Air Force took the lead in ensuring unidentified aircraft did not enter US air space. Do you have any other questions before I proceed to look at the organization of the Air Force?

JEFFERSON: No. Do go on.

PAUL: The Air Force has nine major commands to handle its missions. The Air Combat Command is in charge of fighters, bombers, reconnaissance and battle management. The Air Education and Training Command trains all Air Force personnel and manages Air Force recruiting. Air Force Materiel Command conducts research and acquires systems and logistics needed for the entire Air Force.

JEFFERSON: I take it these three commands as you call them are the most important as they deal strictly with the warriors, the training of the warriors and the equipment of the warriors. Correct?

PAUL: You are right on the money, Mr. President. Air Combat has 78,000 personnel, Air Education and Training has 73,000 and the Air Force Materiel has 82,000, the three largest commands in the Air Force. Other major commands include the Air Force Reserve Command, managing the aircraft used by the Air Force Reserve. Air Force Space Command defends the US through its space and intercontinental ballistic missile programs.

JEFFERSON: What does the Space Command do specifically?

PAUL: They launch satellites into orbit around the earth, as we discussed earlier, used for spying, communications, or weather tracking. Moving on... the Air Force Special Operations Command manages the Air Force Special Operations Forces. The Air Mobility Command provides aerial refueling for all US armed forces and the Pacific Air Forces provide air power for US interests in the Asia-Pacific.

JEFFERSON: Where are these commands located?

PAUL: They are located in Japan, Korea, Alaska, and Hawaii and they provide ready air power as needed to support our national interest in the Pacific and the Indian Ocean. Similarly, US Air Forces in Europe is part of the US European Command designed for combat operations as part of NATO. Now that you are familiar with this Department, Mr. President, what is your opinion?

JEFFERSON: First, the Constitution does not provide authority to establish an Air Force independent of an Army or Navy. Therefore, this entire program is unconstitutional. Provide no funding for this as long as it is separate.

PAUL: How would you remedy this?

JEFFERSON: Place control of the US Air Force under the Department of the Army. If Congress so wishes, have it pass a Constitutional Amendment to allow establishment of an Air Force and submit to the States for approval.

PAUL: Thank you, Mr. President. We will now be discussing an agency of the Agriculture Department.

Segment 10 – Department of Agriculture: Food and Nutrition Service

Paul Jefko: Mr. President, we already discussed the US Department of Agriculture. Now we will discuss the largest part of that department, the Food and Nutrition Service. Historically, the big program of the Food and Nutrition Service, the Supplemental Nutrition Assistance Program, began during the Great Depression as the Food Stamp Plan to feed hungry families. Later, Congress created the National School Lunch Program in 1946 reacting to the large number of men who were rejected for military service in WW II because of nutritional deficiencies, such as rickets and pellagra.

President Jefferson: You mean people were starving?

41

PAUL: No. People were eating diets high in corn and low in dairy products, resulting in vitamin deficiency that led to deformed legs and arms, general weakness, and lack of vigor.

JEFFERSON: What are vitamins?

PAUL: Vitamins are compounds in the foods we eat necessary for good health. You are familiar with scurvy, prevalent in sailors who spent long times at sea. The Scottish surgeon James Lind found citrus fruits prevented scurvy but did not know why. British ships carried a load of limes for the sailors to eat to prevent the disease. By the way, that is why British sailors are called limeys. Scientists solved the mystery in the early 20th century when they discovered the active ingredient in the citrus was Vitamin C. Without it, scurvy resulted.

JEFFERSON: Although limes will not grow in Virginia's climate, I do not recall people exhibiting the symptoms of scurvy.

PAUL: Other plants provide Vitamin C, such as parsley, broccoli, and melons. Continuing with the history...The Agricultural Act of 1949 allowed the government to buy surplus farm commodities and give them to school lunch programs and public charities. Additional programs were created in the 1960's such as the School Breakfast Program, the Nutrition Program for the Elderly, and the Food Distribution Program on Indian Reservations.

JEFFERSON: The government designed all these programs to ensure we do not contract nutritional diseases?

PAUL: Research indicated proper nutrition enhanced productivity and health. For example, many poor students did not have a proper breakfast before going to school. Their hunger caused loss of attention and discouraged learning. Expanding to meet the needs of a homeless population, the Soup Kitchen/Food Banks program was created in 1988. That concludes the brief history of this agency. We will now look specifically at the agency's programs.

JEFFERSON: Since we provide food and housing to everyone, why do we have a homeless population?

PAUL: All homeless people got in that state for one reason, a lack of money. Most of the homeless remain in that condition for a short time until they can get back on their feet. Some homeless are mentally ill and cannot hold employment or manage the wages they receive. Until they receive treatment for their illness, they will stay on the streets.

JEFFERSON: If they are mentally ill, why are they not in asylums?

PAUL: The Supreme Court decided authorities could not institutionalize a person without his or her consent unless they were a danger to themselves or others. That decision released many people from asylums and mental hospitals. Medicines can alleviate their problems, but doctors cannot force a patient to take them.

JEFFERSON: The court is right, since commitment to a lunatic asylum is akin to prison.

PAUL: Continuing...The biggest program, as I alluded to before, the Supplemental Nutrition Assistance Program enables a poor family to purchase food at approved stores. The Child and Adult Care Food Program provides meals to those who are in child and adult day care, after school programs, and emergency shelters.

JEFFERSON: Child and adult care?

PAUL: Yes. In many cases, both parents need to work outside the home to earn enough money to raise a family. There may not be a family member left in the home to care for young children, so various organizations or homes provide care for a child during work hours for a fee. Similar organizations provide care for adults who cannot care for themselves because of disability or age. Continuing...The Commodity Supplemental Food Program provides surplus food to States for distribution to poor, pregnant, post-partum and breastfeeding women, and infants, children and the elderly.

JEFFERSON: No private charities can provide these services?

PAUL: The largest charity in the US has a $34 Billion endowment. If they spent it all, it would provide one third of Food Assistance this agency pays out in one year. Not enough private funding is available...The Food Assistance for Disaster Relief Program distributes surplus food to community shelters and authorizes the issuance of EBT cards during disasters. The Food Distribution Program on Indian Reservations also provides surplus food to eligible individuals living on reservations.

JEFFERSON: American Indians are proud people who live off the land but now cannot feed themselves?

PAUL: Well, we have taken them from their traditional lives of hunting and gathering and kept them tied to a particular portion of land. However, some tribes have prospered by establishing gambling houses making tribe members quite wealthy.

JEFFERSON: So, not only do we take their land and sequester them to a particular place but also, we provide them a means of corruption. Go on, please.

PAUL: The Special Supplemental Nutrition Program for Women, Infants, and Children, known as WIC, provides food supplements to pregnant, post-partum and breastfeeding women and their children younger than age 5. The WIC Farmers' Market Nutrition Program provides WIC participants coupons to purchase fresh produce at farmer markets. The Senior Farmers Market Nutrition Program does the same for the elderly.

JEFFERSON: What is a Farmers' Market?

PAUL: A farmers' market is an area set aside in cities usually where farmers can set up stands to sell their produce directly to the customer rather than to stores and groceries. Moving on...The National School Lunch Program provides surplus food and cash to States to pay for meals for children in school.

JEFFERSON: What is next? A school dinner program?

PAUL: Perhaps. Another program is the Nutrition Assistance Block Grants Program, providing funds to territories for their nutrition assistance programs...Unless you have any other questions, Mr. President, that sums it up. What are your thoughts?

JEFFERSON: I took notes. The following programs are unconstitutional: The Supplemental Nutrition Assistance Program; The Child and Adult Care Food Program; The Commodity Supplemental Food Program; The Food Assistance for Disaster Relief Program; The Special Supplemental Nutrition Program for Women, Infants, and Children; The WIC Farmers' Market Nutrition Program, The Senior Farmers Market Nutrition Program and the National School Lunch Program. None can be justified under the enumerated powers of the Congress stated in the Constitution, nor do they contribute to the general welfare, just the poor, children, women, or the elderly. The Food Distribution Program on Indian Reservations is constitutional if part of a treaty with the Indian Tribe. Federal taxes can pay for this program. Nutrition Assistance Block Grants and Nutrition Assistance to Puerto Rico provide funds to territories for their nutrition assistance programs. Since Congress has power to make all needful rules and regulations over territories, it is constitutional. Federal taxes may be used to fund this also.

PAUL: How do we implement your plan?

JEFFERSON: First, the Food and Nutrition Service will cease providing funds to the States for all the unconstitutional programs I mentioned on a specific date to be set by Congress. Prior to that date, the States will decide

44

whether to assume the financial responsibility for the abolished programs if within their constitutions. The Food and Nutrition Service will support the States in initiating the programs if they choose but the federal government must not fund the program after the date set by Congress. The Food and Nutrition Service will continue to provide food to Indian Reservations only under existing treaties. The Food and Nutrition Service will continue to provide Nutrition Assistance Block Grants to territories under existing law. Moreover…with the reduced mission of the Food and Nutrition Service, the Congress may wish to consider merging it with another Department or agency for efficiency.

PAUL: Thank you, Mr. President. Your comments will certainly raise some hackles in the political establishment. That sums up our program for this week. We will see you next week on another session of 'They Are Here!'. On behalf of President Jefferson, I bid you good evening.

Program # 3

Paul Jefko: Good Evening, Americans, I welcome you to the third installment of our program: 'They Are Here'. This program continues our discussions with President Thomas Jefferson. Let me reintroduce the Third President of the United States, Thomas Jefferson…

President Jefferson: Thank you. I am enjoying our discussion.

Segment 11 – Government National Mortgage Association

Paul Jefko: Mr. President, although we have not discussed education yet, I know that education is an abiding interest of yours. You attempted to pass an education law as a delegate to the Virginia Legislature.

President Jefferson: Yes, I did. It was called the Bill for the More General Diffusion of Knowledge. I believed that a populace with a good education would be more likely to perceive the tyrannical ambitions of unscrupulous persons and thereby withstand and defeat them. However, my colleagues did not see fit to pass the bill.

PAUL: But a version was passed eventually.

JEFFERSON: Yes, it was finally passed as 'An Act to Establish Public Schools.'

Paul Jefko: Well, all good things take time. Getting back to our current program…Mr. President, the next agency requires some explanation. Congress passed the National Housing Act in 1934 creating the Federal Housing Administration. Congress set up the agency to increase homeownership by guaranteeing payment of home loans to protect lenders from default, and thereby encouraging them to lend to more borrowers. Congress amended the act in 1938 to create the Federal National Mortgage Association, known popularly as Fannie Mae, to provide the capital for any defaulting loans.

President Jefferson: Why did the federal government think it wise to enter the private housing market?

PAUL: During the Great Depression, large numbers of people became

46

unemployed and were unable to pay their mortgages and faced foreclosure. This led to a situation where the high number of foreclosures caused a surplus of vacant housing that banks could not sell at any price or only at large losses. Add to that the low value of the foreclosed housing on the bank's books which left the banks with little funds to lend even to credit worthy borrowers.

JEFFERSON: Let me rephrase my question. Why did the federal government care about the private banking system?

PAUL: When President Roosevelt took office in 1932, every state governor had closed the banks in his state because of the bank panic. You could not access your savings.

JEFFERSON: I am familiar with bank panics. They occur because of an excess of speculation. It occurred most recently last year.

PAUL: You refer to 1819 I take it?

JEFFERSON: Yes.

PAUL: Speculation was not the main cause of the Panic of 1819. Historians cite three main causes of the panic. First, the Second Bank of the US called in loans ahead of time thus removing money from the economy when it was needed most. Second, the Bank suspended specie payments because of the huge borrowings to fund the War of 1812. This act encouraged private banks to issue unsecured banknotes and create inflation. The final cause that broke the camel's back was the reduced demand for agricultural goods from Europe after its recovery from the Napoleonic Wars.

JEFFERSON: As I said, speculators saw an unending economic expansion spurring the issuance of bank notes, which could not be redeemed in specie. The Bank of the United States tried to control the speculation and collapsed the economy. This happens every so often and people do not seem to learn. However, you still have not answered my question.

PAUL: In short, the newly elected President could not stand by and watch the US financial system collapse. Consequently, one law he sponsored guaranteed the mortgage payment if the owner did not pay. This law provided capital to the banks so they could lend to more homeowners.

JEFFERSON: We had a financial panic in 1792 and Secretary Hamilton bailed out the banks. In 1796, we had another panic that ruined Robert Morris and James Wilson, both signers of the Declaration of Independence but the federal government did nothing. Businesses went bankrupt and persons went to prison. Congress under the Adams administration passed a Bankruptcy Act applying only to merchants and repealed it under my administration because it led to corruption. So, over a century later, the federal government performed a Hamiltonian bail out of the banks despite their folly in lending to persons who could not meet their mortgage responsibilities. Then we encourage them to continue this folly by giving them more money to lend and provide home ownership to persons who should be renting month to month. Excuse my rant. Please continue.

PAUL: Yes, well...In 1968, Congress created the Government National Mortgage Association, known as Ginny Mae, as a government owned corporation under the Department of Housing and Urban Development to also guarantee mortgages. Ginnie Mae guarantees principal and interest repayment on bonds backed by mortgages issued by the Federal Housing Administration, the Veterans Administration, HUD's Public and Indian Housing and Agriculture's Rural Housing service.

JEFFERSON: That is a mouthful. How does this work?

PAUL: All these federal agencies guarantee the payment and interest of mortgages provided by private lenders to qualified buyers. At times, however, a lender may want to sell the mortgage for various reasons. He can sell the mortgage to another lender or a broker who will place a number of mortgages into a bond he will sell to another lender. The bond buyer will receive a fixed amount of money periodically based on the amount of the mortgage payments. To make the bond easier to sell, Ginnie Mae guarantees the mortgage payments backing the bond.

JEFFERSON: What happens if there is another great depression and Ginnie Mae has to cover all these mortgage payments?

PAUL: Funny you ask as this recently happened. We had a major housing collapse but Ginnie Mae did not suffer much since the quality of the mortgages in the bonds they insure is higher than the regular market. On the other hand, Fannie Mae had major problems since it guaranteed bonds based on private mortgages. The problem is the private mortgages were given to persons who were subprime, that is, they were not credit worthy.

JEFFERSON: Why would someone lend money to a person who was not credit worthy?

PAUL: As I just told you, the lender who provided the loan sold it to a broker who bundled it along with others into a bond and sold it to an investor. Each person along the path of the sale pockets a fee. The more loans made, the more bonds sold, the more fees collected.

JEFFERSON: That is criminal.

PAUL: On the other hand, Ginnie Mae deals only with mortgages funded by federal agencies, so the borrower had to meet more stringent qualifications.
JEFFERSON: How many mortgages are included in a bond?

PAUL: A Ginnie Mae insured bond might contain more than a thousand mortgages. The minimum bond issue is $1 Million. However, a new program, Ginnie Mae MBS II guarantees bonds with a minimum size of $250,000. The risk is minimal. In fact, Ginnie Mae spent $11 Million in a recent year to insure $100 Billion in mortgage backed bonds. So, Mr. President, what is your opinion on this?

JEFFERSON: The program is patently unconstitutional. No authority exists to guarantee a bond backed by mortgages. Nowhere does the Constitution allow public funds to insure mortgages of its citizens because it certainly does not contribute to the general welfare but only the welfare of bankers and speculators.

PAUL: What are the next steps to take?

JEFFERSON: Ginnie Mae must no longer insure new bonds. Those securities insured will remain so until liquidated. When all guarantees are liquidated, Ginnie Mae will be abolished.

PAUL: Thank you, Mr. President.

Segment 12 – Department of Veterans Affairs

Paul Jefko: As you recall, Mr. President, the Continental Congress promised pensions during the American Revolutionary War as an inducement to enlistments. On the other hand, the States or local communities provided medical and hospital care to the wounded. After the war, the federal government provided certain benefits to disabled Revolutionary war soldiers unable to work. In 1808, Congress established the Bureau of Pensions under the War Department and then transferred it to the Navy Department when the criteria for a pension changed from disability to need.

President Jefferson: If I recall, the criteria only applied to Revolutionary War veterans, not all veterans.

PAUL: That is correct. After the Civil War, 1.9 million veterans were on the federal rolls and many State veteran homes were established to assist disabled veterans. To help meet this need, Congress established the National

Home for Disabled Volunteer Soldiers.

JEFFERSON: The States normally provided this assistance in my time.

PAUL: That is true, but the number of disabled veterans overwhelmed State facilities. The Home for Soldiers provided room and board to disabled veterans and medical care whether service related or not. During the war, Congress passed laws creating a national military cemetery system to bury the Civil War dead and later created a reburial program to locate and rebury over 300,000 soldiers into national cemeteries.

JEFFERSON: Why? Weren't they already buried?

PAUL: The Civil War took place mostly in the Southern States. Since they buried dead soldiers where they fell, they were interred in places all over the South on private land. Congress decided to build these National Cemeteries near the battlefields and relocate all the dead soldiers for reinterment. After WW I, Congress created a new program of disability compensation and vocational rehabilitation and insurance for active duty personnel and veterans.

JEFFERSON: Room and board, medical care, a burial plot, a pension, insurance, and rehabilitation. Sounds like the federal government instituted a dole.

PAUL: Well, these veterans did put themselves in harm's way.

JEFFERSON: If a miner, a carpenter or smith injures himself in his work, does the government provide them a lifelong pension? No.

PAUL: If I may interrupt, if a person does become disabled these days, they are entitled to Social Security.

JEFFERSON: So, now the government has responsibility to take care of all the veteran's needs, even if he did not come within 100 miles of a battle?

PAUL: At some point in time, Congress thought it appropriate...As I said, after World War I, the number of veterans' hospitals expanded from 64 to 91. By the 1920's, three federal agencies handled veteran benefits: The Veterans Bureau, the Bureau of Pensions in the Interior Department and the National Home for Disabled Volunteer Soldiers. In 1930, Congress consolidated these functions under the Veterans Administration.

JEFFERSON: Well at least, some efficiency was put into the system but it also created one agency for all veterans to lobby for more largesse.

PAUL: That may be true. However, it did highlight certain issues affecting veterans. For example, the rise of tuberculosis in veterans during the Depression created more demand for medical care.

JEFFERSON: I thought you cured tuberculosis.

PAUL: That occurred later. The lack of proper nutrition during the Depression caused many people to develop diseases healthy individuals warded off. Nevertheless, after WW II, Congress created the GI Bill of Rights, adding an educational and housing benefit to veterans of that war. The bill was later extended to veterans of the Korean and Vietnam wars and even to those who served in peacetime. In 1973, the Veterans Administration assumed control of all the national cemeteries, except Arlington National Cemetery.

JEFFERSON: Didn't I say you create a place for persons to obtain favors when you create a government program?

PAUL: The nation was so grateful to its soldiers and sailors for winning the war, they decided to provide them these benefits. Anyway, after the Vietnam War, new medical conditions such as Post Traumatic Stress Disorder appeared in veterans.

JEFFERSON: What is posttraumatic stress disorder?

PAUL: You probably know it as shell shock. Homelessness plagued many veterans of that war who were diagnosed with PTSD, as it is known. In 1988, President Reagan signed a law elevating the Veterans Administration to the Department of Veteran Affairs. It contained three branches: Veterans Health, Veterans Benefits, and the National Cemetery Administration.

JEFFERSON: You say if I serve in the military, I get free medical care for life.

PAUL: Yes, with some exceptions. Finishing up on this topic…outpatient clinics have expanded to 850 by 2004.

JEFFERSON: What is an outpatient clinic?

PAUL: A veterans' clinic is a small hospital for a veteran with a minor ailment. If it is a major problem, the veteran will need to go to a full-fledged hospital. Let us now look at the organization of the Department. The department has three main divisions: The Veterans Benefits Administration provides veterans and their families' education and vocational rehabilitation, pensions, home loans and life insurance.

JEFFERSON: I suppose Congress justified this as an inducement to recruitment.

PAUL: The recruitment package does include many benefits. Veterans receive disability payments if they have service connected disabilities and non-service related disabilities if the veteran served during wartime and became permanently and totally disabled outside of military duty.

JEFFERSON: Let me get this straight. If a veteran became disabled outside of his military duties, even after he leaves the military, he can collect a disability payment.

PAUL: Yes, if he served during wartime. Survivors of wartime veterans can also receive pensions. In addition, 36 months of funding for veterans to study at a college, technical or vocational school is also provided. Spouses and children of veterans can also receive 45 months of education assistance. Rehabilitation and counseling services are also available to help veterans gain and keep employment. The housing program provides veterans with loans to purchase homes and life insurance for those who cannot purchase it at a reasonable cost on the private market.

JEFFERSON: With all these benefits, do we need to pay the military a monthly salary?

PAUL: I take that question as rhetorical...The second branch, the Veterans Health Administration provides medical services to 5.5 million veterans through a network of health care facilities and through private and public hospitals. They also conduct research, rehabilitate blind veterans, assist homeless veterans, and care for veterans with multiple war related injuries. The National Cemetery Administration maintains the national cemeteries across the US for the burial of veterans and family.

JEFFERSON: What happened to the State veteran cemeteries?

PAUL: They still exist for those who wish interment near their hometowns. In fact, the National Cemetery Administration provides funds to establish state veteran cemeteries as well as maintaining soldier's monuments, and providing headstones for veterans.

JEFFERSON: How many national cemeteries are there?

PAUL: This department maintains 130 of the 146 national cemeteries in the US. The Army maintains two, and 14 are maintained by the Interior Department as part of an historical monument. The American Battle Monuments Commission manages twenty-four overseas cemeteries.

JEFFERSON: That is a lot of room to bury people.

PAUL: Approximately 1,100 World War II veterans die each day. That is our largest war, but Korea and Vietnam also had many veterans participating. We will look at each of these Department's branches later. But now, we will now turn to the Department of Transportation.

Segment 13 - Department of Transportation

Paul Jefko: Mr. President, Congress created this Department in 1965 after a Presidential task force recommended a Department to include the Federal Aviation Agency, the Bureau of Public Roads, the Coast Guard, the Saint Lawrence Seaway Development Corporation, the Great Lakes Pilotage Association, the Car Service Division of the Interstate Commerce Commission, the subsidy function of the Civil Aeronautics Board and the Panama Canal.

President Jefferson: Hold on. You overwhelm me. Let us take them one at a time. Did you say "Coast Guard"?

PAUL: Yes, the Coast Guard is a federal agency for enforcement of water navigation laws. The Saint Lawrence Seaway Development Corporation works with Canada to maintain and encourage navigation on the St Lawrence River. The Great Lakes Pilotage Association regulates commercial boating on the Great Lakes. What did I miss? Oh, yes, the Car Service Division regulates haulage rates for trucks used in interstate commerce, the Civil Aeronautics Board makes aircraft rules and regulations, and investigates aircraft accidents and the Panama Canal is a canal we dug across the Isthmus of Panama to connect the Atlantic and Pacific oceans.

JEFFERSON: Where is the Isthmus of Panama?

PAUL: You know it better as the Isthmus of Darien.
Continuing…Congress passed the organization legislation in 1966 creating the fourth largest cabinet department. Subsequent to this reorganization, the President transferred the urban mass transit functions from the Department of Housing and Urban Development to this Department.

JEFFERSON: Urban mass transit?

PAUL: Major cities have public transportation systems enabling persons to get to and from their place of work, usually via vehicles powered by internal combustion engines following a prearranged route throughout the day.

JEFFERSON: Why is the federal government involved in city

53

transportation?

PAUL: The federal government has become involved in many programs lying within the provenance of a State, as you have seen already. Moving on…in 1970, Congress created the National Highway Traffic Safety Administration to develop safety rules for highway travel and the Federal Highway Administration to manage highway design, construction, and maintenance.

JEFFERSON: Explain to me why these two were needed.
PAUL: We have not discussed the automobile, the personal travel vehicle everyone around the world uses.

JEFFERSON: No, we have not. What is it?

PAUL: People referred to early automobiles as 'horseless carriages' because that is what they looked like. (Shows a picture of a Model T) It is a four-wheeled carriage with a mechanical engine to power the wheels instead of horses.

JEFFERSON: What powers this carriage, steam?

PAUL: Some early automobiles were powered by steam engines but they went out of fashion quickly. Today most automobiles, we call them cars, use a petroleum distillate called gasoline, which is burned in an internal combustion engine. The car eliminated the need for horse transportation and made a personal vehicle available to almost everyone. Consequently, the industry grew spectacularly. Cities began to have traffic congestion and accidents as the number and speed of these cars increased.

JEFFERSON: How many accidents happen a year?

PAUL: Almost 34,000 people died last year in traffic accidents, but the number was much higher forty years earlier when over 54,000 people died…The federal government responded to popular cries for action. Later, in 1975, Congress made the National Transportation Safety Board into an independent federal agency.

JEFFERSON: How does it differ from the Highway Traffic Safety Administration?

PAUL: The Board investigates all transportation accidents, primarily aviation, but also certain crashes on railways, highways, and even watercraft. Expanding the Department, President Carter established what became the Research and Special Programs Administration, wherein he placed the Transportation Systems Center, and the hazardous materials and pipeline safety programs.

JEFFERSON: What are pipelines?

PAUL: (Shows a photo of the Alaska Oil Pipeline) Pipelines are hollow cylinders similar to pipes that transport water, but are hundreds of miles long and transport oil from the well area to a refinery. Continuing...President Reagan transferred the Maritime Administration from the Department of Commerce into this department. After the 9/11 Disaster, Congress set up the Transportation Security Administration, or TSA to increase security at airports and other terminals. Later TSA as well as the Coast Guard were transferred to the new Department of Homeland Security. The Department enforces federal laws on use of roads, highways, airports, railways and seaports. It also provides funds to States and local communities to improve transportation systems. Major offices include the Federal Highway Administration that funds interstate highway maintenance.

JEFFERSON: It provides funds to local communities? How can the federal government provide support to a local community for transportation unless engaged in interstate commerce?

PAUL: The Supreme Court has defined interstate commerce thusly. First, Congress may regulate the channels of interstate commerce; second, Congress can regulate and protect the instrumentalities of interstate commerce, or persons or things in Interstate Commerce, even though the issue may come only from intrastate activities; and, finally, Congress's commerce authority includes the power to regulate those activities substantially related to interstate commerce.

JEFFERSON: That opens the barn door wide.

PAUL: Yes, it does. The National Highway Traffic Safety Administration regulates safety standards in the automobile industry and transportation industry. It also enforces manufacturer compliance with safety standards.

JEFFERSON: Let me pose a question: Why are there so many accidents?

PAUL: The top reason is a distracted driver who talks on a telephone or eats while driving.

JEFFERSON: What is a telephone?

PAUL: We will get into this technology later, but to answer it quickly, it is a device transmitting and receiving sounds, particularly the human voice. (Shows a picture of a person making a call on a desktop telephone) If you had one right now, you could call your friend John Adams and converse with him, if he also had one and there was the necessary system in place to transmit your voice.

JEFFERSON: That is extraordinary. I would never have to leave Monticello.

PAUL: To finish the answer to your question…the other four causes of accidents are speeding, driving while drunk, reckless driving, and rain.

JEFFERSON: You know, the same causes except for the first one can occur when one rides in a horse and buggy.

PAUL: Times have not changed. Moving on…The Federal Motor Carrier Safety Administration regulates the safety of commercial vehicles.

JEFFERSON: Is it too much to ask one agency handle the safety of all vehicles?

PAUL: Good point. The Federal Aviation Administration oversees the US commercial aviation industry. It sets rules for airport operations and pilots and operates the air traffic control system.

JEFFERSON: Air Traffic Control? Are there that many aircraft flying about at any one time?

PAUL: I believe an airport can become so crowded as aircraft land and take off, the chances of a craft hitting another are enhanced. At some airports, an aircraft lands or takes off every two minutes around the clock.

JEFFERSON: Really. Where do all these people go?

PAUL: Businessmen who go to meetings or make sales have to get from one place to another quickly. For example, if you wanted to go to New York from Washington, you can get there by air in less than an hour. Traveling by automobile will take you about 4 hours.

JEFFERSON: That is not much of an advantage. In my time, it would take 7 days.

PAUL: Yes…Well…The Federal Railroad Administration enforces rail safety regulations and is charged with rehabilitating Northeast Corridor passenger rail service.

JEFFERSON: What is that?

PAUL: You are familiar with rail travel?

JEFFERSON: I have read England uses steam engines for travel over iron rails. But I have not seen one.

PAUL: Until the advent of air travel, rail passenger travel was the main mode of intercity travel in the US. (Shows a picture of an Amtrak train) However, air travel has reduced the demand for rail travel except in certain areas like the Northeast Corridor from Washington to Boston. The federal government has taken over responsibilities for maintaining the rails to ensure safe passenger rail travel.

JEFFERSON: This does not make sense. Why does the federal government transport people?

PAUL: That question will be answered in a later program. But... continuing...The Surface Transportation Board regulates the rail industry.

JEFFERSON: For God's sake, how many agencies do we need to regulate transportation?

PAUL: Just a few more. The Maritime Administration regulates waterborne transportation in the US. It also is responsible for the US Merchant Marine program and maintains a cargo fleet for use during national emergencies.

JEFFERSON: What is the merchant marine?

PAUL: Ships engaged in commerce. The reason it is controlled by the federal government is to serve as an adjunct to the Navy during war to ensure we can obtain all the supplies we need. Moving on...The Saint Lawrence Seaway Development Corporation manages and promotes navigation on the St Lawrence River in conjunction with Canada. They inspect all ocean vessels entering the seaway.

JEFFERSON: You refer to the St Lawrence River separating us from Canada?

PAUL: Yes, the US and Canada improved the waterway so ocean going ships could use it to travel to our ports on the Great Lakes.

JEFFERSON: Very good.

PAUL: The Federal Transit Administration funds mass transit systems in the US. We discussed that previously. The Pipeline and Hazardous Materials Safety Administration regulates safety for pipelines and hazardous material transport.

JEFFERSON: What is in the pipelines besides petroleum?

PAUL: Generally, it is liquid petroleum or natural gas, a fuel you know more as methane, or swamp gas.

JEFFERSON: I seem to recall a scientist named Volta determined swamp gas to be methane. So, it is used as a fuel?

PAUL: Huge gas deposits lie buried deep in the earth...Anyway, that is the basic organization of the Department. We will now take a break before looking at another Department: Education.

Commercial Break

Segment 14 – Department of Education

Paul Jefko: To give you some background on this Department, it all started in 1867 when Congress set up a Department of Education as a non-Cabinet level agency to collect information on schools and teaching as an assist to the States. The Department eventually became the Office of Education in 1890 to provide support to land grant colleges under the Second Morrill Act passed by Congress.

President Jefferson: Why did the federal government become involved with a program normally handled by the States?

PAUL: Congressman Morrill helped found the Republican Party and wanted to modernize American society. He got the 1867 Act passed because he wanted to know the state of education in the US. The Department head had to provide an annual report on his work to Congress. So, originally it was done to collect information. Earlier in 1862, Morrill convinced Congress to pass the Land-Grant Colleges Act wherein the federal government provided property to each state to establish a college for agricultural and mechanical study.

JEFFERSON: Was there a federal land surplus in the States?

PAUL: The States that were original colonies did not have much public land but the States formed from Federal Territories had plenty. For those states not having enough federal land, they were given scrip to allow them to claim federal land in other states and sell it to fund a land purchase in their own state.

JEFFERSON: That is an ingenious idea.

PAUL: The second Morrill Act in 1890 provided cash to the former

58

Confederate States to establish colleges in the same manner as the other States.

JEFFERSON: Why was there a separate act for Confederates?

PAUL: The first time the Morrill Act was passed by Congress in 1858, President Buchanan vetoed it. Buchanan believed it trespassed on State authority. When Lincoln was President, Congress passed the bill again in 1862, adding a requirement that the colleges teach military skills. Lincoln signed it into law. However, by that time, 11 states had seceded from the Union and did not participate in the Land Grants.

JEFFERSON: They did have the right to secede. Which states were they?

PAUL: South Carolina, Mississippi, Florida, Alabama, Georgia, Louisiana, Texas, Virginia, Arkansas, Tennessee, and North Carolina.

JEFFERSON: What caused Virginia to secede?

PAUL: The original States that seceded included South Carolina, which bombarded Fort Sumter, a US military post. President Lincoln called for volunteers to suppress the rebellion and based on that, Virginia seceded.

JEFFERSON: A current discussion in the Congress concerns the admission of Missouri. I am not sure what will happen but it foretells the dissolution of the Union. Of course, you already told me it resulted in Civil War.

PAUL: Yes, and the Civil War ended any discussion on a state's right to secede.

JEFFERSON: In what way?

PAUL: The Supreme Court has said that since the Constitution established the Union as indivisible, no right to secede exists. To get back to our discussion, the Second Morrill Act stipulated the colleges established in the Confederate states had either to accept all races or establish a separate college for blacks.

JEFFERSON: What schools were established in my home state?

PAUL: Virginia Polytechnic Institute and State University is in Blacksburg and what is now known as Virginia State University is near Petersburg. Virginia State was the college set up for black students. Later, another law affecting education was the GI Bill to fund postsecondary education for WW II veterans. The Lanham Act and Impact Aid Laws of 1950 provided payments to school districts having military and other federal institutions within their jurisdiction.

59

JEFFERSON: Why did we pay school districts?

PAUL: The children of the military stationed there attended the local schools. But since there was no way the school district can tax the federal government on its property, a method had to be found to recompense them for providing the education.

JEFFERSON: More problems stemming from having a standing army. Please continue.

PAUL: In 1953, President Eisenhower created the Department of Health, Education and Welfare in his cabinet to consolidate the federal education programs. In response to the launch of Sputnik, Congress passed the National Defense Education Act to fund loans to college students, improve science, math and language instruction in elementary and secondary schools, and fund graduate education, and vocational/technical training.

JEFFERSON: What was Sputnik?

PAUL: During the Cold War, we had with the Soviet Union I mentioned earlier, the US and the Communist countries competed not only militarily and diplomatically but also over our way of life. The Soviet Union took the US by surprise by launching a rocket into the air carrying an artificial satellite called Sputnik that orbited the earth for a considerable length of time. That provoked a crisis in Congress questioning how we had slipped so far technologically behind the Soviets.

JEFFERSON: How did the act solve this problem?

PAUL: Congress passed the Act to emphasize math and science in our secondary schools and provide loans so students could attend college.

JEFFERSON: I can see that, for defense purposes, the Congress had to do something.

PAUL: Later, as part of the 1964 Civil Rights Act, the Department became responsible for ensuring equal access to education for all. In 1965, Congress passed the Elementary and Secondary Education Act to provide aid to disadvantaged children. The Rehabilitation Act of 1973 extended protections to those discriminated based on sex and disability. The Higher Education Act provided financial aid to needy college students.

JEFFERSON: What was the essence of the Civil Rights Act?

PAUL: There were several parts. Part 1 required voting rules to be applied to all races equally. Part 2 prohibited discrimination based on race, color, religion, or national origin in all public accommodations. Part 3 prohibited States from denying access to public facilities on basis of race, color, creed, or national origin. Part 4 required integration of public schools. Part 5 provided enforcement powers to a Civil Rights Commission.

JEFFERSON: Wait a minute. What do you mean by school integration?

PAUL: Prior to this act, a Supreme Court case known as Plessy vs. Ferguson declared separate facilities could be maintained for blacks as long as the facilities were equal. So, there were white public schools and black public schools. The Civil Rights Act prohibited segregated public schools.

JEFFERSON: Does that apply to private schools and colleges?

PAUL: No, it only applies where taxpayer funds are used to operate the school.

JEFFERSON: So, my Alma Mater, William and Mary, is still not integrated?

PAUL: Not true. William and Mary is now a state supported institution as is your University of Virginia by the way. The Civil War closed William and Mary for a while, but not the University of Virginia. Both had financial problems requiring state funding to resolve...Continuing with the Civil Rights Act...Part 6 prevented discrimination by any organization receiving federal funds. Part 7 prohibited discrimination by employers based on race, color, creed, or national origin.

JEFFERSON: Are you saying a private employer must hire a Negro?

PAUL: If he qualifies, yes...Part 8 required voting data to be collected as determined by the Civil Rights Commission. Part 9 allowed transfer of civil rights cases from state courts to federal courts. Part 10 established a Community Relations Service to assist in local disputes. Part 11 provided criminal penalties for violating the Act.

JEFFERSON: Nothing in the Constitution gives Congress the right to interfere in private affairs or State affairs except as enumerated.

PAUL: The 14th Amendment to the Constitution, passed after the Civil War, provided that authority. It said, "No State shall make or enforce any law which shall abridge the privileges or immunities of citizens of the United States; nor shall any State deprive any person of life, liberty, or property, without due process of law; nor deny to any person within its jurisdiction the equal protection of the laws."

JEFFERSON: That only talks about State Law. How does that relate to the Federal Civil Rights Law?

PAUL: Wait just a second...It also said in another part: "The Congress shall have power to enforce, by appropriate legislation, the provisions of this article." The problem was Congress did not pass a Civil Rights Act until 1957 because the Southern States continued to filibuster any such bill brought before the Senate.

JEFFERSON: You use a term I am unfamiliar with in this context. I know a filibuster as a pirate or freebooter who attempts to seize property illegally via military action.

PAUL: The term has been used after your time to describe a parliamentary tactic. According to Senate rules, there is unlimited debate on any question. Therefore, when debating any topic, one can simply talk until the bill's sponsors agree to table the measure to free up the Senate's time.

JEFFERSON: I understand the purpose of the rule, but debate should not obscure an issue but clarify it. So, Negroes have equal access to all businesses?

PAUL: All businesses, professions, colleges, public offices, housing...any business open to the public.

JEFFERSON: I cannot imagine sharing my dining room with a Negro, or sharing accommodations.

PAUL: Well, your private dining room is not a public accommodation. But believe me, Mr. President, your attitude would be considered low class in my time.

JEFFERSON: It would be low class to refuse to be associated with Negroes?

PAUL: Of course. Your Declaration of Independence statement that all men are created equal has achieved reality in modern America.

JEFFERSON: That statement did not apply to Negroes. They are property.

PAUL: Not anymore. If you voiced those opinions in public, you would find several lower-class persons agreeing with you, but most upper class people would shun you.

JEFFERSON: Continue please.

PAUL: Yes, finally, President Carter, through Congress, established a separate cabinet level Department of Education. President Bush and Congress passed the No Child Left Behind Act removing federal funding from schools failing to educate students to a level based on standardized tests.

JEFFERSON: The federal government tests American students?

PAUL: No. Under the law, the States are required to set up standardized tests for Reading and Math, but the content of the test is designed by them. If a school fails to meet the State standard, then it will not receive federal funding. The law encourages marginal schools to improve and closes failing schools.

JEFFERSON: Please continue.

PAUL: We have concluded the discussion of the Department's history. Here it is how it is organized. The Office of Elementary and Secondary Education provides grants to the States to improve teaching quality, equal access, and equal opportunity in elementary and secondary schools. The Office of Postsecondary Education administers the Federal Student Aid program, provides funds to institutions serving low income and minority students, and administers the Fulbright-Hays scholarship program.

JEFFERSON: What is the Fulbright-Hays scholarship program?

PAUL: It provides grants to students, scholars, teachers, and organizations, for work-study abroad in languages and foreign studies. It was established by Senator J William Fulbright to increase mutual understanding between the US and other countries.

JEFFERSON: Funded by the taxpayer?

PAUL: Yes. The Office of Vocational and Adult Education provides funds for adult literacy programs, technical schools, rural schools, and community colleges. The Office of English Language Acquisition provides funds to integrate non-English speaking students into the school system. The Office of Indian Education provides grants to evaluate the quality of Indian Education.

JEFFERSON: We have a federal program to teach English to non-English speaking students?

PAUL: Yes, to help assimilate immigrants more quickly into our culture...The Office of Special Education and Rehabilitative Services provides grants to States and local communities to educate children with disabilities. The

Institute of Education Sciences produces and disseminates scientific research on education. The Office of Innovation and Improvement manages the No Child Left Behind Act, discussed earlier.

JEFFERSON: What disabilities are you talking about?

PAUL: Both physical and mental, such as inability to walk, or even use their hands. On the other hand, they could be mentally retarded or have emotional issues.

JEFFERSON: If education's best use is to better mankind, I do not see how in some cases, a crippled person who does not have use of his hands or is so retarded that he could not perform useful work can benefit from education.

PAUL: One of the world's most prominent physicists, Stephen Hawking, is completely paralyzed and communicates through a special speech device. In addition, many mentally challenged persons are able to perform certain jobs others find boring. Continuing...Federal Student Aid provides loans and grants to students in postsecondary schools.
JEFFERSON: So, anyone wishing to attend college can obtain a loan?

PAUL: Yes. Continuing...The Office of Safe and Drug-Free Schools provides funds for drug and violence prevention programs.

JEFFERSON: Violence and drugs in what schools?

PAUL: In our elementary and secondary schools.

JEFFERSON: Children take opium?

PAUL: Unfortunately, yes and other drugs besides opiates...That sums up the organization. Of course, we will be looking at more detail of this department in later programs.

Segment 15 – Department of Veterans Affairs: Veterans Benefits Administration

Paul Jefko: As you may recall, Mr. President, the Continental Congress authorized half pay for officers and an $80 bonus to enlisted men if they served until the end of the Revolution against Great Britain. Disabled soldiers received land and pensions. The first Congress under the Constitution assumed these burdens and continued the pensions. In 1812, Congress established the Naval Home for Veterans and the Bureau of Pensions in 1833 to assist veterans.

President Jefferson: Actually, the Pensions Bureau was established in 1815, if my memory serves me. Prior to that time, the War Department called it the Military Bounty Lands and Pension Branch.

PAUL: I will take your word on that. The Mexican-American War in 1848 generated hundreds of thousands more veterans. Moreover, after the Civil War, there were 1.9 million Union Army veterans, and the same number for the rebels but the rebels were not granted benefits. As I mentioned before, Congress in 1865 created the National Home for Disabled Volunteer Soldiers, providing room and board and incidental medical care.

JEFFERSON: Where was this Home?

PAUL: There were a number of Homes. The first one opened in Maine in 1866 and later in Wisconsin and Ohio. Later, one was based in Hampton, Virginia to serve African-American Civil War veterans. Congress created them as needed later throughout the country.

JEFFERSON: Things have changed considerably from my day when even freed Negroes were not citizens, let alone allowed to serve in the Army. I cannot imagine it would be taken very well in my home state to see a Negro carrying a firearm.

PAUL: Yes, things have changed markedly. As I said, World War I created 5 million new veterans and 200,000 wounded. For these veterans, Congress created disability compensation benefits and vocational rehabilitation plus insurance. In 1930, Congress merged the Veterans Bureau, the Bureau of Pensions in the Interior Department and the National Home for Disabled Volunteer Soldiers into the new Veterans Administration.

JEFFERSON: So, we do not need the National Homes anymore, since we compensate veterans.

PAUL: Well, only two federal homes remain now, but a number of state veterans' homes exist to provide nursing care for those who cannot care for themselves. However, you are correct. The trend has been to give veterans cash benefits. That is what the Veterans Benefits Administration does. As I started saying earlier, a major political issue occurred during the Depression revolving around veteran benefits.

JEFFERSON: Let me guess. A number of veterans could not find work and petitioned the government for help.

PAUL: You're close. After WWI, Congress promised veterans a $1,000 bonus to be paid in 1945. In the Great Depression, 15,000 veterans came to Washington DC to demand immediate payment, earlier than authorized. They camped out in shantytowns near the Capitol. The House passed legislation authorizing immediate payment, but the Senate and President Hoover balked at the $2 Billion cost.

JEFFERSON: Interesting. In 1933, the Congress balks at paying out $2 Billion but doles that out each month, thirty years later.

PAUL: Well, in response, the veterans protested in the streets of Washington until Hoover called out the Army to clear out the shantytowns.

JEFFERSON: Seriously, the President called out the Army to drive out veterans?

PAUL: Yes. At the time, the veterans did not have the influence they have now. In fact, the incident may have stimulated the veterans to organize. WW II raised the number of veterans to 16 million. For them, Congress passed the GI Bill of Rights. The law authorized money for tuition, books and living expenses for four years of college or vocational school, low interest home, farm and business loans, $20 a week allowance for vets looking for work and funds to establish veterans' hospitals and rehabilitate disabled veterans.

JEFFERSON: It seems the veterans found their voice. Did they eventually get their bonus?

PAUL: Ironically, the next President was faced with a law allowing the bonus in 1936, but he also vetoed it. However, Congress passed it over his veto and the veterans got their bonus. Congress extended the GI Bill of Rights I referred to earlier to the Korean and Vietnam War veterans and even to those who served in peacetime. Later, the new Montgomery GI Bill updated the benefits available to handle specific medical problems stemming from the Vietnam War, such as Agent Orange, an herbicide causing cancer.

JEFFERSON: Isn't it interesting the federal coffers become prey for any organized group?

PAUL: Later, President Reagan elevated the Veterans Administration to Cabinet Status in 1988 with three divisions: Health, Benefits, and the National Cemetery Administration. That is the history until my time.

JEFFERSON: So now, we have a new Department serving as a conduit for federal funds.

PAUL: A pattern does exist here. Anyway, here is how the VBA is organized. It operates 57 regional offices and 9 delivery networks. The VBA provides monthly pension, disability, or survivor benefit checks to 2.7 million veterans and their survivors. The VBA also provides funds to veterans for college, technical or vocational school tuition.

JEFFERSON: Is this part of the recruiting contract they sign if they enlist?

PAUL: Yes. The benefits can be used up to 10 years after the discharge date. Spouses and children of veterans can also receive education through the Dependents' Educational Assistance program. The VBA also provides disabled veterans with assistance in finding a job, medical and dental care, financial counseling, and training in job skills. The program also helps disabled veterans who are unemployable to achieve independent living.

JEFFERSON: Why do we provide benefits to spouses and children?

PAUL: Again, it is an incentive to recruitment. VBA also provides veterans with loans to purchase homes and veterans with disabilities up to $43,000 to purchase or remodel a home to meet accessibility standards. In addition, VBA provides life insurance to those who cannot purchase it because of active duty military service or disability.

JEFFERSON: Again, do we need to pay these soldiers? They seem to have a lifetime sinecure.
PAUL: Well, these benefits are in laws passed by Congress. That concludes my discussion. How do you see these programs, Mr. President?

JEFFERSON: First, all these programs are unconstitutional for any armed force other than the Army or Navy, and for an Army veteran to receive these benefits for more than 2 years without the funds being reappropriated. However, Navy veterans can receive these benefits as Congress determines.

PAUL: What do you think the next steps to resolve these issues should be?

JEFFERSON: First, I would maintain for fairness that all current obligations made to veterans remain in place for two more years as they were part of the recruitment contract. Second, do not extend current benefits to veterans except for Navy veterans unless Congress renews the law every two years for Army veterans. Third, no new benefits will be provided to any armed service veteran unless they were in the Navy or Army.

PAUL: Thank you. Mr. President. That ends our program for this week. I thank our guest, President Thomas Jefferson for his stimulating opinions and hope we continue in that vein. Until next week, so long.

Program # 4

Paul Jefko: Good Evening, fellow Americans and welcome to the fourth installment of our program: 'They Are Here'. We will continue our discussions with President Thomas Jefferson. Let me reintroduce President Thomas Jefferson...

President Jefferson: Thank you. I hope your audience is enjoying this as much as I am.

Segment 16 – Department of Labor

Paul Jefko: Based on our ratings, they are. Mr. President, besides serving as our third Chief Executive, you also were our first Secretary of State. You were criticized by your opponents for being pro-French during that period.

President Jefferson: Well, that may have been because, prior to President Washington asking me to be Secretary of State, I was an ambassador to France. I also was attempting to persuade Britain to admit that they were violating the terms of the Treaty of Paris which gave us our independence. I was most concerned that those around President Washington were less Republican and more Monarchists. I believed France, even during its Revolution, was more in sympathy with our Republic than the British monarchy was.

PAUL: That is very enlightening. But, to continue with our conversation...Congress created a Bureau of Labor in 1888 under the Department of the Interior. It moved to the Department of Commerce and Labor when that department was established in 1903. In 1913, President Taft signed a bill establishing it as a separate cabinet level department. The new Department consisted of a newly established US Conciliation Service, mediating labor disputes plus four bureaus from the old department: The Bureau of Labor Statistics, the Bureau of Immigration, the Bureau of Naturalization, and the Children's Bureau.

JEFFERSON: Tell me why we have immigration, naturalization, and children in a department called 'Labor".

PAUL: At the time, we had a labor shortage in the US. Immigrants from Europe were recruited to meet the needs of our growing industrial sector. The Department almost became an employment agency for immigrants. Of course, immigrants require naturalization services. In addition, children performed many jobs in factories.

JEFFERSON: Children worked in factories?

PAUL: Yes. It was a natural extension of children working on the family farm. In your time, part of the textile manufacturing process was done by women who did the work at home. Their children assisted them. When it became more efficient to work at a central place, such as a factory, the women took their children with them. Eventually, children as young as 5 years old worked 12 hours a day in dangerous jobs around machinery. (Shows photo of children working at a machine loom in a textile factory)

JEFFERSON: That is insidious.

PAUL: Do you not have your slaves as young as five years working on your plantation?

JEFFERSON: Young servants are not placed in dangerous occupations.

PAUL: To continue…During WW I, the Department enforced a worker's right to bargain collectively, to submit grievances to management and established an 8-hour workday. However, that changed in the 1920's when Republican administrations favored business and were anti-labor union.

JEFFERSON: What is a labor union?

PAUL: A union is a group of workers in a single profession who unite to demand conditions of their labor from their employer.

JEFFERSON: What conditions of labor?

PAUL: The length of the workday, wages, etc.

JEFFERSON: I understand a good worker can demand better pay or other perquisites. Why would a good worker band with other workers to obtain benefits he can receive on this own?

PAUL: Because in a factory situation, a good worker's skills are not as important. Most workers are treated almost like a piece of equipment or a tool. The job is designed to require minimal training. A warm body will serve. A worker does not ask for a higher wage, because there will always be another worker willing to work for the wage provided.

JEFFERSON: That is as it should be. Why should an employer pay any more wages than he believes the worker is worth?

PAUL: That attitude begot labor unions. Once workers understood they had no bargaining power individually, they banded together and staged a strike.

JEFFERSON: You mentioned this earlier. Workers walk off the job and surround the area to prevent any other worker from entering the workplace to replace them. That is illegal.

PAUL: Originally, it was deemed illegal as a restraint of trade.

JEFFERSON: As it should be.

PAUL: Understand, Mr. President, just as not every master treats his slaves properly, not everyone is an enlightened employer. Women worked as weavers in textile mills for 16 hours a day to earn maybe $1.25 a week. They had to buy their own needles and thread and paid a fine if they were late. Often, they did not receive their entire pay and if they protested, they were dismissed. They worked in unheated shops, often open to the weather.

JEFFERSON: Our servants are treated much better than this.

PAUL: Your servants, as you refer to them have no freedom to leave your plantation. Some slave-owners beat and mutilate them and rape the women. (Shows photo of the back of a former slave with whip scars) They work without pay or hope of advancement until they die. How do you see their condition as better?

JEFFERSON: I am only making a point that the conditions in a textile factory as you described for 'free' labor as it is referred to are worse than the Southern system the North derides. The factory owners do not have to provide housing for their workers, or food or medical care. If one worker dies, another one takes his place at minimal cost. If one of my servants dies, I must purchase his or her replacement, so it is in my best interest to keep them healthy.

PAUL: Let me put it to you this way. No one wished to be either a black slave in your day or a worker in a textile factory in the 19th century. However, the textile worker could leave his job and move elsewhere. He could also join a labor union to ameliorate some of these abuses.

JEFFERSON: Let us put our disagreements aside. Tell me more of these labor strikes.

PAUL: Here is one example. In the latter part of the 19th century, the Pullman Company cut its workers' wages due to an economic depression. The workers joined the American Railway Union and went on strike. Within a few days, 129,000 workers walked off the job on 18 railroads. A railroad lawyer went to court to get an injunction ordering the strikers back to work. However, the strike continued and the President sent in 2000 army troops and US Marshals to end the strike during which 13 strikers were killed.

JEFFERSON: So, these workers were forced back to work? Sounds like slavery.

PAUL: That is one example. Many such strikes occurred where the government sided with the company owners to suppress labor rights. But labor unions have other ways to put pressure on owners. For example, they can parade around the work site with picket signs protesting the company. They can also boycott company goods.

JEFFERSON: What is a boycott?

PAUL: The union members refuse to buy company products and encourage others to do the same. In any case, eventually, laws were passed stating human labor was not a commodity like materials or equipment used in commerce. Since then unions have organized for wages and better working conditions. In effect, an entire body of law, labor law, has arisen to meet the needs of this sector.

JEFFERSON: I've heard of international law, constitutional law, criminal law, contract law, tort law and property law but not labor law.

PAUL: Law disciplines have expanded from your day, including civil rights law, immigration law, social security law, family law, intellectual property law, tax law, banking law, environmental law and consumer law among others. Anyway, back to the history of this department…during the Roosevelt administration, to relieve unemployment during the Great Depression, Congress established the Civilian Conservation Corps to employ unemployed young men to work at rural projects.

JEFFERSON: What were the States doing?

PAUL: Not much. Their budgets had been overwhelmed with relief payments. A number of laws were passed affecting labor. The Walsh-Healey Public Contracts Act of 1936 established an 8-hour day and safe working conditions for contractors manufacturing goods for the US. The Taft-Hartley Act of 1947 reduced the ability of unions to strike. The US Conciliation Service moved from the department and renamed The Federal Mediation and Conciliation Service.

JEFFERSON: What do they do?

PAUL: It mediates between companies and unions in disputes involving interstate commerce. Continuing...President Nixon created the Occupational Safety and Health Administration to develop and enforce safety standards across the country. In 1978, Congress transferred the Mine Safety and Health Administration from Interior to the Labor Department. Under President Reagan, safety and health standards were weakened to make them less costly to business.

JEFFERSON: Miners have a separate agency?

PAUL: Yes, Congress set up the agency early in the 20th century to help reduce the fatalities in the mining industry. Moving on...President Clinton provided funds to establish one-stop career centers to handle unemployment insurance, job counseling, and job training.

JEFFERSON: Unemployment Insurance?

PAUL: Yes, if an employee loses his job through no fault of his or her own, the government will pay them a weekly wage for a period until the employee can get another job. The program is funded by companies, who pay a fee to the federal or state government based on the wages the employer pays.

JEFFERSON: The company pays the premium for the insurance but the employee benefits. Interesting. How much is the benefit and how long is the employee able to collect it?

PAUL: They collect 36% of their average weekly income for 26 weeks. So, in summary, the Department is responsible for enforcing federal laws on worker's rights to safe and healthful working conditions, minimum wage and overtime pay, freedom from discrimination, unemployment insurance and other income support. For example, the Fair Labor Standards Act prescribes standards for wages and overtime pay.

JEFFERSON: With all these restrictions, it is a wonder anyone wants to open a business.

PAUL: Yes, well, obviously, businesses are still making money even with the restrictions. Continuing…the Employee Retirement Income Security Act regulates employers who offer pension benefits. The Migrant and Seasonal Agricultural Worker Protection Act regulates their hiring and employment practices. The Department's key offices include the Employment and Training Administration, distributing funds for employment training for first time workers or those displaced by factors beyond their control.

JEFFERSON: Wait. The federal government trains workers to do their jobs?

PAUL: In a manner of speaking. The federal government provides grants to the States to set up training programs for their citizens... The Job Corps helps young disadvantaged people complete their education and obtain job training, including room and board for two years. The Office of Disability Employment Policy provides employers with tools and assistance to encourage employment of the disabled.

JEFFERSON: How is a disabled person able to work?

PAUL: It depends on the extent of the disability. But there is a job for almost any disability. Obviously, a paralyzed person or amputee may have some limitations in a manual labor job, but he or she can do other jobs.

JEFFERSON: I understand a deaf person can still perform as well as a hearing person. But how about a blind person.

PAUL: Some actual jobs have been done by the blind to include piano repairs, barbering, and even a lawyer, depending on whether the impairment can be accommodated. Continuing... The Veterans' Employment and Training Service provides financing and policies to help veterans obtain grants, training, and employment after completing military service.

JEFFERSON: It sounds like the federal government has taken responsibility for ensuring employment of American citizens. The taxpayer funds the costs for this?

PAUL: Yes... The Employment Standards Administration enforces nondiscrimination, affirmative action, workers' compensation, labor union, minimum wage, overtime, and child labor laws. The Occupational Safety and Health Administration develops and enforces standards on worker protection for all workers except for miners, transportation workers, public employees and the self-employed.

JEFFERSON: Hold on. What do the terms affirmative action, workers compensation, minimum wage, and overtime mean?

PAUL: Affirmative action is a program designed to compensate a group of people to counter the effects of a history of discrimination. In other words, blacks, Hispanics, and other groups were discriminated in the past because of their race, national origin, or color.

JEFFERSON: And what do they get under this program?

PAUL: They may get preference for jobs or places in college for example.

JEFFERSON: So, these people cannot attend college not because of their academic ability, but because they are black?

PAUL: Not these people directly. They may have had ancestors who were discriminated against and they suffer for it generations later.

JEFFERSON: I do not quite understand this. Does the person getting the benefits of this affirmative action program lack academic credentials to enter the college?

PAUL: Let me lay out the reasons for this program. 1. For several centuries, the US enslaved African Americans and oppressed Native Americans and other minorities. African Americans provided uncompensated labor, Native Americans had land stolen from them and did not receive the protections of our Constitution. Look at it as recompense to their descendants. 2. Until affirmative action was implemented, African Americans were considered less capable.

JEFFERSON: I know from my own experience the Negro is racially inferior and is as incapable as a child.

PAUL: You are mistaken. When African Americans have the opportunity to succeed or fail, the results proved the stereotypes were not justified. 3. Affirmative action allowed people to work in occupations, such as men as nurses or women as engineers and lawyers. 4. Minority students usually come from lower income families and thus have less opportunity for early education that prepares them for college.

JEFFERSON: Aha. Negroes have lower incomes because they are incapable of work providing higher incomes.

PAUL: How do you explain billionaire Robert Johnson owning a large communications business or Oprah Winfrey, another billionaire woman owning a large publishing and communications business? Let me continue. 5. Since the world has become more global, our work forces us to interact with cultures and people much different from us. Affirmative action ensures we will interact with people different from us early in life to prepare us.

JEFFERSON: From what you have told me of the Negroes' progress, it does appear the process has some advantages. However, it does seem unfair to white people who lose out to Negroes but have done nothing to merit the unfavorable treatment. But…please continue.

PAUL: The Mine Safety and Health Administration enforces safety regulations designed to eliminate accidents and health hazards in the mining business. The Pensions Benefit Guaranty Corporation protects private sector pensions even though the companies may no longer be in business. The Employee Benefits Security Administration protects pension participants and beneficiaries from abuse or theft of their pension assets.

JEFFERSON: What is all this about pensions? Normally they are given only to disabled soldiers for past service.

PAUL: They became popular during World War II when the government froze wages to prevent inflation. To compensate, owners promised workers pensions when they reached a certain age. Later they became part of the wage and benefit package given to a person when they worked for a company. Of course, if a company goes bankrupt, the person lost the promised pension.

JEFFERSON: Do you mean the company promised these pensions but did not set money aside to pay for them?

PAUL: They are required by law to provide a financial statement of the pension assets each year, but there is no requirement to maintain a certain level of investment assets. Consequently, the federal government stepped in to protect the pensions of those persons.

JEFFERSON: I am amazed at what companies will do to avoid their obligations and place further burdens on the taxpayer.

PAUL: Yes…Finally…The Bureau of Labor Statistics collects and disseminates data on employment, prices, compensation, productivity, and health. That sums things up. We will look at the organizations under this Department later. For now, let's review the United States' newest Cabinet Department.

Segment 17 – Department of Homeland Security

Paul Jefko: Next we look at the Department of Homeland Security, the newest cabinet department set up after the terrorist attacks of September 11, 2001. The department devises systems to prevent future terrorist attacks. Although President Bush initially rejected the idea, Congress pushed the idea of a separate department eventually accepted by the President.

President Jefferson: I am confused. You informed me we have a Department of Defense that by its very name protects us from attack. Why another one?

PAUL: I do not have an answer for that very good question. Perhaps the

75

military cannot defend our country by itself, but other aspects of the federal government have to participate.

JEFFERSON: I understand diplomatic and economic measures can be used for our defense in situations outside our military control. But if this Department provides our national defense, let us call it that, eliminate the current Department of Defense and split it into the Department of War and the Department of the Navy as it used to be.

PAUL: The military arms should be under the Department of Homeland Security?

JEFFERSON: No. The idea of permanent ground forces was not in the minds of the founders of this country. The only time we have a national Army would be during war. It appears in your time, the US has gotten away from the idea of a permanent Navy along with State militias being the backbone of our national defense. Create a national Army only when a national emergency exists.

PAUL: Well, the US has been engaged in warfare since World War II.

JEFFERSON: That is my point. If your entire existence is one long national emergency, there are really no emergencies. Therefore, the Army is permanent with a temptation to use it even in instances with no need. Let me ask you a question. Since World War II, how many times has the Army been involved in a seemingly unnecessary war?

PAUL: Well, let me see. Nine occasions have occurred since World War II where the Army has participated in combat. Whether one thinks they were necessary is in the eye of the beholder. Let me list them: Korean War, Vietnam Conflict, Persian Gulf War, Lebanon Peacekeeping, Grenada, Panama, Somalia, Iraq, and Afghanistan. One could make the case against US involvement in these affairs.

JEFFERSON: How many resulted from an invasion or attack on our country?

PAUL: Well...the only one meeting those criteria is Afghanistan where the terrorists who orchestrated the attack on us on 9/11 were hiding.

JEFFERSON: Exactly. We have this wonderful Army. Let us use it. That is not what the founders intended. But to get back to our discussion, let me hear what is in this wonderful Department.

PAUL: Most staff was taken from other departments. For example, the Department has an agency called US Customs and Border Protection combining the US Customs Service from the Treasury Department and the Immigration and Naturalization Service from the Justice Department. The remainder merged into what is now known as Immigration and Customs Enforcement within Homeland Security.

JEFFERSON: What has collecting customs duties to do with Homeland Security?

PAUL: I guess the two functions are inseparable, that is, while you inspect incoming shipments for substances harming the public, you might as well collect the duties. Moving on...a color-coded chart was publicized by the Department showing terrorist threat levels. Green was low risk of attack, Blue was general risk of attack, Yellow was significant risk, Orange was high risk, and red was severe risk. (Shows the chart)

JEFFERSON: What were you supposed to do under these levels?

PAUL: That was the problem. No one knew what to do.

JEFFERSON: So, the chart was ineffective.

PAUL: Let us say it confused and frustrated those who were to respond in an attack.

JEFFERSON: Yes, let us say that.

PAUL: Now, let us look at the agencies under the department. The Federal Emergency Management Agency provides aid to state and local governments to prepare and recover from disasters. The Directorate for Science and Technology develops Surveillance and Cybersecurity devices for securing US borders and waterways. The Domestic Nuclear Detection Office develops nuclear detection devices for use at seaports, airports, and border crossings. The Federal Law Enforcement Training Center trains officers and agents from federal, state, and local governments.

JEFFERSON: Wait, the Training Center trains State and Local Governments?

PAUL: Yes, the defense of this nation against terrorism depends on every law enforcement organization being aware of terrorist threats. The Office of Infrastructure Protection identifies critical locations and assesses their vulnerability to attack. The Office of Intelligence and Analysis gathers information and analyzes it for potential threats. The Transportation Security Administration safeguards airports, airplanes, mass transit, highways, seaports, railroads, and buses. Immigration and Customs Enforcement enforces immigration and customs laws and prevents terrorists from obtaining US weapons and technology.

JEFFERSON: What are buses?

PAUL: Buses are commercial vehicles designed to transport up to 40 persons on the highways. (Shows a photo of a city bus)

JEFFERSON: We have a separate agency guarding airplanes, railroads, and buses? If these are commercial vehicles, why isn't the private company providing such security?

PAUL: The original attacks on September 11 used aircraft of American Airlines, a corporation having responsibility for the security of its passengers and aircraft. It obviously was ineffective.

JEFFERSON: Therefore, the federal government decided to take over their security. I hope they pay the costs.

PAUL: Actually, taxpayers fund this.

JEFFERSON: Really! And the people stand for that?

PAUL: Apparently. Continuing...The US Citizenship and Immigration Service decides a person's eligibility for lawful residence in the US. US Customs and Border Protection guards the national borders to prevent terrorists, drugs, illegal immigrants, traffickers, and contraband from entering our territory. The US Coast Guard guards the navigable water borders, enforces marine licenses, maintains waterways, conducts water rescues, and inspects vessels for safety. The US Secret Service investigates counterfeiting, computer fraud, identity theft, financial fraud and protects the President and other politicians.

JEFFERSON: What is identity theft?

PAUL: Pretending to be someone else to obtain money or benefits. You are most familiar with it in espionage situations. However, it occurs more in my time because most financial transactions are electronic. If you can obtain a person's credentials, you can access their bank accounts, their investments etc.

JEFFERSON: So, someone could impersonate me and take my money.

PAUL: Yes, because you do not have to appear in person. Even in your day, if someone came to your banker and said you had authorized the bank to give them a sum of money, what would happen?

JEFFERSON: My banker would not give my money to just anyone and he would have to have written authorization signed by me.

PAUL: Today, almost anyone can duplicate your signature and develop an authorization even a banker in your day would accept.

JEFFERSON: I will take you at your word on that. So how does one protect oneself from 'identity theft?'

PAUL: In a non-face-to-face situation, you need a user identification number and a secret password allowing you to access your funds. You may also have to answer some personal questions no one else knows to establish your identity. In a face-to-face situation, you need an identification card with your picture on it issued by the government. Moving on…The Federal Emergency Management Agency or FEMA assists after disasters.

JEFFERSON: What assistance?

PAUL: Most money goes to States and local governments as grants to plan for disasters and to repair State and local public structures damaged in disasters. They also provide emergency shelters for persons rendered homeless by a disaster and low cost loans to repair or replace damaged private property. Flood insurance is offered to those in areas subject to flooding.

JEFFERSON: Not to seem unfeeling, but we had the 1804 snow hurricane that devastated New York and New England. The States involved handled their own damages. We had earthquakes in 1811 and 1812 in the Midwest causing severe damages. No State asked for federal relief. If I recall, Louisiana did request disaster relief from the federal government, but that was a territory not a State.

PAUL: Now, Congress has tasked FEMA to provide such relief to disaster victims...Money is given to the States after Natural Disasters to fix up any public hazards resulting from the disaster.

JEFFERSON: The Federal Government has assumed responsibility for this?

PAUL: Yes, as a key FEMA mission. But we will look into FEMA and other agencies later. Let us turn to another component of the Department of Defense. But before that, here is a word from our sponsor.

Commercial Break

Segment 18 - Department of Defense: Defense Logistics Agency

Paul Jefko: Mr. President, during WW II, the huge military buildup required quick procurement of large amounts of supplies and munitions. Although the military services coordinated during the war on petroleum, medical supplies, and clothing, Congress called for more efficient coordination in the whole supplies and services area. After the war, Congress created The Munitions Board to organize procurement of common items.

President Jefferson: I assumed the Army Quartermaster General handled this. Am I missing something?

PAUL: Sir, the problem was that the Army and the Navy procured the same items from the same source. One organization procuring common items for both branches was more efficient. That is why in 1952 all the military services were required to apply a common nomenclature to items they procured and in 1961, the Defense Supply Agency was established to provide common supplies and services to all Department of Defense agencies.

JEFFERSON: Were there many items a soldier and a sailor had in common? I guess they use the same firearms, but their uniforms are different, their heavy weaponry must be different and even the food may be different.

PAUL: I believe initially the agency only supplied replacement parts for weapons and consumable items. I'll provide a better rundown when we get to the agency organization. DSA eventually became responsible for administering defense contracts through a sub-organization called Defense Contract Administration Services (DCAS). In 1973, it became responsible for disposing of defense property overseas as well as worldwide procurement, management and distribution of coal and petroleum.

JEFFERSON: So, the Army Quartermaster submitted any requests for these common supplies through the Defense Supply Agency.

PAUL: Yes, sir. However, it became more than a supply and contracting group when in 1977, its name changed to the Defense Logistics Agency, and it assumed control over DOD Food Services. In 1988, it assumed control of strategic materials from the General Services Administration. Today, DLA procures, manages, stores, and distributes over 5 million items to the US military.

JEFFERSON: What are strategic materials?

PAUL: Rare elements that must be imported and are necessary to national security. For example, Bauxite, Manganese, Rare Earth Metals, and Thallium. The DLA organization consists of: The Defense Energy Support Center managing fuels, gas, and electric power; The Defense Supply Center, Columbus OH, providing maritime and land based weapon systems' spare parts and end items; The Defense Supply Center, Richmond VA, providing aircraft weapon systems' spare parts and end items; and, The Defense Supply Center, Philadelphia PA that purchases food, clothing, textiles, drugs, medical supplies, and industrial items.

JEFFERSON: It appears to be very efficient.

PAUL: In addition, Service Centers meet special needs: The Defense Logistics Information Service Center provides logistics and IT services; The Defense National Stock Pile Service Center stores, secures, and sells raw materials; The Defense Reutilization and Marketing Service Center disposes of defense property; The DLA Document Automation and Production Service Center provides offset printing to online document services; and, DLA Enterprise Support provides administrative support to Defense agencies.

JEFFERSON: I did not question the use of this term earlier, but Logistics is another word for supply operations?

PAUL: It encompasses the entire gamut of identifying the need, the best method to satisfy the need and delivering a solution at a fair cost in a timely manner and disposing of the item at the end of its useful life. In performing this function, DLA uses many contractors. Mr. President, what do you say?

JEFFERSON: The problem is the language in two clauses in the Constitution. The Army can be funded for only two years at a time, the Navy has no funding limit, and the Air Force and other military organizations are not addressed. Here is how I resolve the conflict, very simply:
Navy – No restriction.
Army – Restricted to those items usable over a two-year span
Other military services – No procurement allowed.

PAUL: What steps do we need to take to address the issues you highlighted?

JEFFERSON: Any contract exceeding these limits will be modified or terminated as appropriate. Any equipment, supplies, or materiel possessed by the United States that are unauthorized must be disposed of, if possible, through sale or auction. If such disposal is not feasible because of lack of interest or national security, then the items shall be destroyed.

PAUL: Thank you, Mr. President. Let us turn now to the Federal Highway Administration.

Segment 19 – Department of Transportation: Federal Highway Administration

Paul Jefko: Mr. President, we will delve into the largest agency in a Department we had some difficulty with early on. Let me describe how the federal government became involved in highway construction. In 1892, a group in Chicago formed the National League for Good Roads to promote highway legislation. In 1893, the Office of Road Inquiry was established in the Department of Agriculture, becoming the Office of Public Roads in 1905. It conducted demonstration projects in several states, inventoried the road system, and pushed passage of a Federal Aid Road Act providing for road construction with a 50/50 federal/state contribution.

President Jefferson: What was the state of the road system?

PAUL: The only paved roads in 1892 were those within cities and towns. Outside the city limits were dirt roads, muddy in winter and spring.

JEFFERSON: Why did Congress not use its Constitutional authority to build post roads between cities?

PAUL: When the railroad came into existence, it carried much of the intercity mail making intercity roads superfluous. Within a city or town, a postal worker delivered mail but outside the city limits, a person trudged to the nearest post office on a secondary road to pick up his or her mail.

JEFFERSON: I send a servant to Charlottesville to pick up my mail.

PAUL: Since that was the expected method, Congress saw no need to do anything about it. Even States did not sponsor any road construction. It was left to the cities or the counties to maintain or construct what roads were needed. In 1912, an Indiana man promoted the idea of an East-West national highway. Congress established the Lincoln Highway in 1913. In 1919, Major Dwight D Eisenhower traveled from Washington DC to San Francisco in a military convoy to test the ability of military vehicles to make the trip, following the Lincoln highway for most of the trip.

JEFFERSON: Is San Francisco the same as the Presidio of San Francisco?

PAUL: Yes, the same city is in the state of California, which we took from Mexico during the Mexican-American War. In your time, it was a Spanish fort known as the Presidio of San Francisco. Anyway, on Eisenhower's trip, most roads were unpaved and it took them 53 days to arrive in California, convincing the future President better roads were needed for national defense. His experience in WW II traveling on Germany's superhighways convinced him of the need for them in the US.

JEFFERSON: What was notable about the German highways?

PAUL: They were multilane wide roads with smooth paving, designed for high speed and high capacity autos. (Shows a photo of an autobahn) Currently, no speed limit exists on them. After WW II, many intercity roads in the US had 60 miles per hour speed limits, but they only had two lanes and slower traffic kept the speed much below that. The idea for high-speed intercity highways in the US started in 1938. President Roosevelt received a proposal for Direct Route Highways across the country by the head of the Bureau of Public Roads.

JEFFERSON: 60 miles per hour seems fast enough. I am not sure how fast a horse can run in miles per hour.

PAUL: The fastest racehorse in my time, Secretariat, ran one ¼ miles in 2 minutes, about 37.5 miles per hour.

JEFFERSON: That is a fast horse. Unbelievably fast.

PAUL: For comparison, a railroad train in 1945 went about 60 miles per hour. In fact, Mr. President, until the railroad was constructed, you could not move any faster than Julius Caesar could. In any case, on most intercity roads, a car going 40 miles per hour in front of you forced you to go the same speed unless you had the opportunity to pass. Additional traffic lanes to allow an auto to pass without running into an oncoming auto became necessary. To meet this need, the Federal Aid Highway Act of 1938 required the Bureau of Public roads to prepare a plan for a toll network of three east-west and three north-south superhighways.

JEFFERSON: What highways went through Virginia?

PAUL: (Lays out current map of Virginia) The original plan linked Washington with Richmond, Norfolk, Lexington, and Staunton. Since then, the agency has built numerous interstate highways crisscrossing your State with one segment going from Staunton to Richmond through Charlottesville. The current Interstate Highway System was begun when Eisenhower asked Congress for $27 billion via bonds to be paid by a gasoline tax to build and maintain the Interstate highway system. Congress passed the Federal Aid Highway Act of 1956 for that purpose.

JEFFERSON: So, I can travel from Charlottesville to Richmond at 60 miles per hour today?

PAUL: Yes, you can, as it certainly saves time. In addition, the Act set standards for construction, speed, and access. During construction, cost estimates rose due to land acquisition costs, and unexpected higher construction costs in urban areas. President Kennedy got Congress to pass the Federal Aid Highway Act of 1961 making an additional four cents per gallon tax on gasoline permanent to complete the system. The Bureau of Public Roads was transferred to the Department of Transportation created in 1967 and renamed what it is today.

JEFFERSON: How much would those 4 cents per gallon of fuel yield in dollars?

PAUL: Last year the US used 134 billion gallons of gasoline, yielding $5.4 billion at 4 cents a gallon. With that money, the Federal Aid Highway program must maintain 160,000 miles of highways and 1 million more miles of urban and rural roads. Here is its organization. First, the Resource Center provides assistance to state and local agencies on transportation disciplines.

JEFFERSON: What does that mean?

PAUL: The States turn to this organization to get answers on any highway construction problem. The Office of Planning, Environment and Realty handles planning, environmental control and real property acquisition and management. The Office of Infrastructure develops innovative techniques in highway design. The Office of Operations deploys Intelligent Transportation Systems. The Office of Safety develops safety initiatives.

JEFFERSON: What is an Intelligent Transportation System?

PAUL: Envision a transportation system without constraints. For example, you entered a vehicle and said, "Take me to Monticello' and it took you there while you took a nap. Alternatively, how about a system detecting high traffic in an area and automatically rerouting you around it? Continuing…The Office of Research Development and Technology operates a facility in Virginia. The agency gives money to state, local, and tribal governments for Bridge Technology, Ferry Boats, and Scenic Byways.

JEFFERSON: A Scenic Byway?

PAUL: Yes, while traveling, people like to view the scenery. Some roads are designed to run along the Blue Ridge Mountains or along a seashore. What are your thoughts on this agency, Mr. President?

JEFFERSON: The agency can maintain all the offices described dealing with highways connecting post offices, defense facilities and federal institutions. Any other offices are unconstitutional. Specifically, The Resource Center providing assistance to state and local agencies on transportation disciplines is unconstitutional as it a State responsibility. On the other hand, The Federal Lands Highway Office is constitutional as it deals specifically with federally owned lands.

PAUL: What should be the next steps taken to act on your recommendations?

JEFFERSON: Identify all highways connecting federal facilities. Most of this information is probably already available. The federal government shall maintain all the highways on the list. States and local governments must maintain the others. All the offices you mentioned can provide the needed services only for those highways designated as Federal. Besides this, abolish the Resource Center.

PAUL: Thank you, Mr. President. We'll proceed to another Department.

Segment 20 – Department of Housing and Urban Development

Paul Jefko: Mr. President, in 1934, the National Housing Act created the Federal Housing Administration (FHA) to insure mortgage loans made by approved lenders. Three years later, the Housing Act of 1937 created the US Housing Authority to tear down slums and construct low rent housing for the poor. A year later, The National Housing Act Amendments of 1938 created the Federal National Mortgage Association, now called Fannie Mae to buy loans from lenders and thus furnish more capital to lend. In 1947, Congress created the Housing and Home Finance Agency to help people buy homes after the War.

President Jefferson: We discussed this earlier.

PAUL: Yes. The Housing Act of 1959 provided funds for elderly housing. The Housing Act of 1964 provided rehabilitation loans for homeowners. In 1965, HUD was created as a cabinet agency to include FHA. The Fair Housing Act of 1968 eliminated discrimination in housing.

JEFFERSON: A classic example of how a program expands to meet a political need.

PAUL: Or a constituent need.... The Housing and Urban Development Act of 1968 created the Government National Mortgage Association we already discussed to expand mortgage funds for moderate-income families. In 1969, the Brooke Amendment mandated that low-income families only pay 25% of their income for rent. In 1974, the Housing and Community Development Act provided community development block grants to States and local communities. In that decade, mortgage interest rates hit historic highs as inflation rose.

JEFFERSON: What caused the inflation? Printing paper money again?

PAUL: The problem analyzing economic events is that almost every economist has an opinion disagreeing with others. Let me explain it thus. When demand for an item increases, the price increases. When the supply of an item decreases, the price increases, both natural economic laws. For example, during and after a war, there is inflation. The war fighting nations buy a lot of stuff, raising demand and prices.

JEFFERSON: That is natural in wartime. What about normal times.

PAUL: In the 1970's, a number of things happened. We fought a war in Vietnam that increased demand for resources. The Organization of Petroleum Exporting Countries or OPEC flexed its muscle and limited the world oil supply. Since oil is a major part of everything we produce, that caused the price of almost everything to rise. Inflation then began to feed on itself. People started buying things before the price rose, increasing demand and further stimulating price increases. It led to a spiral difficult to stop. At one time, FHA insured mortgages were 15% per annum.

JEFFERSON: Mortgages were 15%? How did it end?

PAUL: The Federal Reserve took actions to end it. The Federal Reserve Bank is a national bank of sorts that controls the prime lending rate. Let me explain. The Federal Reserve determines the percentage of money a bank can lend based on the amount the bank has in its vault. The banks have to maintain that amount by law. Every night the banks compute the amount they have in reserve and how much they need to have. They then borrow money from each other as needed to maintain that reserve. The Federal Reserve sets the interest rate they charge each other known as the Federal Funds Rate.

JEFFERSON: It seems to me this Federal Reserve has the power to limit the amount of money available.

PAUL: You are correct, sir. If the Federal Reserve raises the Federal Funds Rate, it discourages interbank borrowing and thus bank lending to its customers and reduces demand. Doing this can cause an economic downturn, which did occur. That ended the inflation spiral.

JEFFERSON: Will we discuss this Federal Reserve?

PAUL: Yes, the Fed is one of the smallest agencies but one of the most important ones. To continue on Housing legislation, the Financial Institutions Reform Recovery and Enforcement Act bailed out bankrupt thrifts. The Federal Housing Enterprises Financial Safety and Soundness Act provided HUD oversight of Fannie Mae and Freddie Mac. The Housing Opportunity Program of 1996 gave public housing authorities the power to evict dangerous residents. In 1998, HUD opened its first enforcement center to enforce laws and regulations.

JEFFERSON: What are thrifts?

PAUL: Thrifts are Savings and Loan Institutions. They began to form early in the 19th century to allow investors to band together, establish a bank-like institution to provide mortgages. They were originally given licenses only to issue mortgages, but in the 1980's they were given authority to make commercial loans. They overreached and some went bankrupt. In response, the Federal Government established the Office of Thrift Supervision to regulate the industry.

JEFFERSON: We allow financial institutions to go hog-wild with other people's money and then we set up a government agency to regulate them. Why didn't Congress let them all go bankrupt?

PAUL: Because no one would put their money into banks or any other financial institution. Without money to lend, the economy would collapse. When we review the Federal Deposit Insurance Corporation later, you will find Congress passed earlier laws protecting depositors' money. In this case, however, so many thrifts faced bankruptcy, the protections were not adequate...That covers the Department's history. The department organization begins with the Federal Housing Administration providing mortgage insurance and setting interest rates for lenders under its programs. The Office of Public and Indian Housing provides grants to help low income and American Indian families pay for housing. The Office of Community Planning and Development provides grants to help develop low-income communities and alleviate homelessness.

JEFFERSON: The government setting interest rates for mortgages bothers me. Why is that done?

PAUL: Well, the FHA will only insure a mortgage if the person qualifies, provides a minimal down payment and pays FHA a fee. But other than that, the lender is protected from default. Therefore, in all fairness, the insurer can set the interest rate.

JEFFERSON: Well, I agree, but can a person obtain a mortgage without FHA?

PAUL: Of course, conventional mortgages are available.

JEFFERSON: Then isn't the FHA competing with the private lenders and artificially keeping interest rates low?

PAUL: Yes, but that was Congress' intent. They believed home ownership, especially for returning veterans was a good thing that stimulated the general economy and raised the general welfare.

JEFFERSON: Please continue.

PAUL: The Office of Healthy Homes and Lead Hazard Control regulates, provides grants, and conducts research in eliminating lead based paint in private and low-income housing.

JEFFERSON: Why was lead put in paint?

PAUL: Lead in paint makes it durable and washable. The problem is that as paint ages, the lead escapes into the air. It causes nervous system damage for children under 6 years old. The Office of Federal Housing Enterprise Oversight manages Fannie Mae and Freddie Mac to ensure stability, liquidity, and affordability in the US mortgage market. The Office of Policy Development and Research works with universities and communities to address urban problems.

JEFFERSON: What kind of urban problems?

PAUL: For example, the lack of available affordable housing, building code enforcement, environmental problems and hazards, housing financing, people with special needs, and the homeless.

JEFFERSON: All these problems seem to be local or state based. However, please continue.

PAUL: The Office of Fair Housing and Equal Opportunity enforces federal law on civil rights in housing. The Government National Mortgage Association or Ginnie Mae buys mortgages from lenders and packages them into securities it then sells to investors while guaranteeing principal and interest payments, thus providing fresh capital to the mortgage market.

JEFFERSON: We discussed Ginnie Mae earlier didn't we?

PAUL: Yes. Other agencies like the Enforcement Center fine, suspend and refer to the Department of Justice those housing projects not meeting standards. Faith Based and Community Initiatives implement policies for the religious community to become involved in housing issues. Well…that is how the department is organized.

JEFFERSON: Wait a minute. The religious community is involved with the federal government?

PAUL: Yes. It was an initiative of President George Bush. We will discuss the major parts of this Department in a later session. Well, ladies and gentlemen, that is our program for the week. Tune in next week for another session of 'They Are Here!' On behalf of President Jefferson and myself, I bid you good night.

Program # 5

Paul Jefko: Good Evening, tonight is the fifth installment of our program: 'They Are Here', a series of discussions with President Thomas Jefferson on the contemporary US government. Let me reintroduce the author of the Declaration of Independence, President Thomas Jefferson...

President Jefferson: I look forward to more of this discussion.

Segment 21 - Department of Defense: National Guard Bureau

Paul Jefko: Mr. President, when you initiated the Louisiana Purchase that doubled the size of the United States, did you have any qualms?

President Jefferson: Not at all. I was mostly concerned with New Orleans, which we did not control but had rights to use as a port for our agricultural goods. First France had it, then Spain, and then France again under Napoleon. I believed that in order to protect our agricultural economy, we needed to control it. I sent James Monroe and Robert Livingston to Paris to negotiate an outright purchase of New Orleans. At the time, there were real concerns among our citizens that Napoleon would use Louisiana as a base to conquer the United States. However, Napoleon's futile attempt to subdue the rebellion in Haiti led him to believe that the entire New World was useless to him. He was also at the time, I believe, preparing to invade England. Surprisingly, he offered the entire territory to us. I had authorized Livingston to offer $10 million for New Orleans. Napoleon offered to sell the entire Louisiana Territory for $15 Million. Livingston agreed.

PAUL: Some have said that your action was unconstitutional.

JEFFERSON: Some of my enemies at the time did. The Constitution gives the President the right to negotiate foreign treaties with the consent of the Senate. A nation acquires territory in only two ways: conquest or acquisition through a treaty. The purchase was approved by the Senate and the $15 million was appropriated in the House and Senate. All done according to the Constitution.

PAUL: Thank you for informing us on that historical issue. I am sure that the current residents of that area are grateful to be Americans...Mr. President, the National Guard succeeded the original State militia that required all males between 16 and 60 to own arms and defend the community. The Marquis de Lafayette coined the term National Guard and applied it to all the organized militia units in the US when he visited in 1824. The Militia Act of 1903 established procedures for the federal government to train and equip the National Guard in line with Army standards. To implement the act, the War Department created the Division of Militia Affairs to manage National Guard organization and training, although Governors retained control over Guard mobilization.

President Jefferson: This concurs with the Constitution wherein the Congress sets the rules for the militia, but the States appoint its officers.

PAUL: Yes, sir. After World War I, the National Defense Act of 1920 determined the US Army to be the regular Army, the Organized Reserve and the National Guard when in federal service. After World War II, in 1947, Congress established the Air National Guard along with the Air Force. Since then, Presidents have used the National Guard to quell domestic disturbances. For example, in 1956, President Eisenhower federalized the National Guard to oversee integration of Little Rock High School.

JEFFERSON: We discussed this earlier. Negroes and Whites were forced to attend the same schools. Refresh my memory on why this happened and why the National Guard had to be summoned to oversee the process.

PAUL: After slaves were freed by the 13th Amendment to the Constitution, southern states segregated the blacks from whites in all public areas, including public schools. The blacks had their own schools and the whites had theirs. The Supreme Court blessed school segregation in the late 19th century as long as the schools were equal. However, in the mid-1950's the Supreme Court decided segregated schools violated the Constitution.

JEFFERSON: What clause in the Constitution did they use to justify overturning the State law?

PAUL: The 14th amendment's equal protection clause states: "All persons born or naturalized in the United States, and subject to the jurisdiction thereof, are citizens of the United States and of the State wherein they reside. No State shall make or enforce any law which shall abridge the privileges or immunities of citizens of the United States; nor shall any State deprive any person of life, liberty, or property, without due process of law; nor deny to any person within its jurisdiction the equal protection of the laws."

JEFFERSON: But if the Negro had a school separate but equal to the school for whites, how did the State law violate the Constitution?

91

PAUL: The Court held that "separate educational facilities are inherently unequal." In response to the court's decision, the Little Rock Arkansas School Board determined to integrate its schools in 1957. However, several citizen councils supporting segregation planned to protest the black student admission to the previous all white Little Rock High school. To prevent public unrest, the Arkansas Governor called out the State National Guard to prevent the black students from entering the high school.

JEFFERSON: Interesting. The Governor ignored a Supreme Court ruling.

PAUL: The School Board condemned the Governor's actions and the Little Rock Mayor asked President Eisenhower to send federal troops to enforce integration and protect the students. The President federalized the National Guard, taking it from the Governor's hands and protected the black students.

JEFFERSON: The Constitution was supposed to ensure controversial decisions like this were to be handled by Congress, not the courts.

PAUL: Unfortunately, our Civil War illustrated that sometimes Congress could not agree and the only solution would be violence. Moving on...organizationally, the Bureau consists of the Army and Air National Guard and jointly reports to the Army and Air Force. It has 54 entities, one for each state, and one each for Guam, the US Virgin Islands, Puerto Rico, and the District of Columbia. During peacetime, it trains and maintains its equipment and performs humanitarian and contingency operations. The Air Guard is responsible for the entire US air defense.

JEFFERSON: Does it seem strange to you the Air Guard, a state militia organization defends the entire US?

PAUL: Yes, it does. What is your opinion?

JEFFERSON: Parts of this bureau are unconstitutional. Under the Constitution, the States may have militias to defend themselves from invasion and control domestic disturbances. Only the federal government is constitutionally tasked with the common defense of the US. The President can call forth the militia into federal service under emergency conditions. However, if the Air Guard provides air defense of the entire US, even in non-emergency situations, it is by definition not a state agency but a federal one and cannot be under control of the State Governor. If it is under federal control then it must be under either the Army or the Navy, since a separate Air Force is unconstitutional. If it is not under either, it is unconstitutional.

PAUL: What are the next steps?

JEFFERSON: Change the Air National Guard mission to provide defense to a State, not for US defense, or it must be placed under the Army or Navy.

PAUL: Thank you, Mr. President. Let us move on to another agency.

Segment 22 - Department of Veteran Affairs: Veterans Health Administration

Paul Jefko: Mr. President, let's resume our look at the programs for military veterans. The first effort to provide medical care to disabled veterans was, as you know, the founding of the Naval Home in Philadelphia in 1812. Later, Congress created the Soldier's Home in 1853 and St Elizabeth's Hospital in 1855. The Civil War created so many disabled veterans, Congress created the National Home for Disabled Volunteer Soldiers in 1873, providing room and board to former soldiers and medical care to poor disabled veterans.

President Jefferson: Like all the programs you have mentioned, this is another indication of federal expansion. Having a permanent Navy as the Constitution specifies is fine as is a home for disabled sailors. However, when you create a National Army apart from the State militia, the federal government must assume the costs of that decision afterwards. If State militia fought the wars you mentioned, the costs of the care of veterans would have been a State responsibility. The only federal medical responsibility would have been on the battlefield to care for the wounded. After mustering out, the States would have had the responsibility for veteran care.

PAUL: Unfortunately, as you surely know, the War of 1812 proved the State militias were incapable of defending the country against a professional army. The British army burned the White House for heaven's sake. Knowing this, President Lincoln did not bother to activate the militia during the Civil War. He called for volunteers. In the 20th century, Military hospitals were overwhelmed with the sheer number of disabled veterans from World War I. Congress in 1917 authorized rehabilitation and training for veterans with permanent disabilities to add to the workload. The States could not possibly have handled this.

JEFFERSON: All right, if there were no alternatives, then establishing hospitals to handle wounded veterans would be necessary. However vocational training?

PAUL: Congress believed it to be part of a benefit a returning veteran would need. Following that, in 1921, Congress created the Veterans Bureau to manage these health programs. In 1929, the Veterans Bureau was merged with the Bureau of Pensions and the National Home for Disabled Volunteer Soldiers to form the Veterans Administration. The number of veterans' hospitals built increased to 91 in the next few years. Tuberculosis among indigent veterans during the Depression along with shell shock created a large number of patients.

JEFFERSON: Would it not have been cheaper for the federal government to pay private hospitals for the care of the disabled?

PAUL: According to medical experts, the average doctor or hospital has neither the facilities, equipment nor knowledge to handle the damage and trauma soldiers experience on the battlefield. After World War II, the 97 hospitals available were not sufficient and Congress authorized construction of more hospitals to make 151. After the Korean War, the number increased to 541. In 1996, the Veterans Health Care Eligibility Reform Act opened up VA health care to all veterans, not just those with service-connected illnesses.

JEFFERSON: Wait. A veteran is entitled to health care even if he did not suffer a battle wound?

PAUL: Yes. Congress probably considered it as an inducement to recruitment. In addition, over 850 Outpatient clinics were established throughout the country to service veterans. To summarize the entire organization, VHA operates clinics, hospitals, medical centers, and nursing homes, including Vietnam Veterans Outreach Centers. The VHA also provides veterans' health care in non-VA hospitals and funds graduate medical education. Blind Rehabilitation services include counseling, patient and family education, benefits determination, residential inpatient training, outpatient rehabilitation, and research.

JEFFERSON: This agency funds medical education also?

PAUL: Yes, as it helps train doctors who may choose to treat veterans and their health issues. The Center for Women Veterans assures women veterans receive the same benefits as a male veteran. The Homeless First program provides outreach to those veterans living on streets and shelters, assesses their health problems, and refers them for treatment. Polytrauma care is for veterans with wounds to more than one organ system resulting in physical, cognitive, psychological, or psychosocial impairments.

JEFFERSON: I do not understand. The US has women in the military?

PAUL: Yes, women have been in the military since early in the 20th century.

JEFFERSON: You mean as nurses.

PAUL: No, much more than that. Women serve in all aspects of the military except for those occupations involved in direct combat. You may not know this, but the first American woman soldier was Deborah Sampson of Massachusetts, who enlisted under a man's name during the American Revolution. She served three years.

JEFFERSON: Her fellow soldiers were obviously not very perceptive. But that was an exception. What can they do now?

PAUL: In our recent wars in Iraq and Afghanistan, over 200,000 women served, 84 killed in action with the enemy.

JEFFERSON: Did we run out of men?

PAUL: No. These women volunteered and went through the same basic training a man goes through.

JEFFERSON: Why would we want women to be engaged in combat? That would destroy all their femininity.

PAUL: Mr. President, our nation is at the stage where the individual has the right to pursue his or her own happiness, in your own words, even though it might not look right to others. What is your judgment on this agency, Mr. President?

JEFFERSON: This is similar to the Veterans Benefits Administration we previously discussed. For Navy veterans, the program is constitutional if Congress declares it necessary to maintain the Navy. For Army Veterans, the program is constitutional only if reauthorized every two years. For all other military veterans, the program is unconstitutional.

PAUL: How would you handle these problems?

JEFFERSON: I would treat them similarly. Maintain all current health benefits for all veterans for two years. After that two-year period, Navy veterans will continue to have the health benefits described under current law. However, Congress will need to approve the benefits for Army veterans after that two-year period and every two years thereafter. Other military veterans, however, cannot receive an extension beyond the two years, unless Congress places them under either the Army or Navy or a constitutional amendment is passed to allow the existence of military organizations other than the Army or Navy.

PAUL: Thank you, Mr. President.

95

Segment 23 – Department of Health and Human Services: The National Institutes of Health

Paul Jefko: Mr. President, as we discussed before, Congress established the Marine Hospital Service in the 1790's to care for merchant seamen. By 1870, the Secretary of the Treasury administered a network of these hospitals. In the late 1870's, Congress provided funds to research the cause of the recurring cholera and yellow fever epidemics in the nation and required the Marine Hospital Service to examine passengers on inbound ships for such diseases.

President Jefferson: In my time, the States handled immigration.

PAUL: That was true until Congress took over immigration in 1890. Continuing, in 1887, Congress created the Laboratory of Hygiene at the New York Marine Hospital. In 1891, it was relocated to Washington DC and in 1930, renamed the National Institute of Health. The National Cancer Institute was established in 1937 and became part of the National Institute of Health in 1944. Two additional divisions, Industrial Hygiene and Pathology and Pharmacology studied industries in WW II to protect defense workers.

JEFFERSON: What is Pharmacology?

PAUL: Pharmacology is the study of drugs. The pharmacologist studies the effect of drugs on the human body. To add to this, after WW II, Congress created divisions for Mental Health, Dental Disease, and Heart Disease. In 1948, the National Microbiological Institute and the Experimental Biology and Medicine Institute were established. By 1998, the NIH had 27 Institutes and Centers. I would like to describe these various organizations and their missions.

JEFFERSON: Proceed.

PAUL: The National Cancer Institute conducts and supports research to prevent and cure cancer. The Center for Scientific Review reviews all applications submitted to the NIH for research funds. Many other Institutes are self-explanatory: The National Heart, Lung, and Blood Institute; The National Institute of Allergy and Infectious Diseases; The National Institute of Dental and Craniofacial Research; The National Institute of Diabetes and Digestive and Kidney Diseases; The National Institute of Mental Health; The National Institute of Neurological Disorders and Stroke.

JEFFERSON: It amazes me how the medical profession has advanced. Can one physician absorb all the knowledge in these areas?

PAUL: Although some doctors in our time are generalists, most have specialties. If you go to your own physician, for example, and he detects a heart problem, he will normally refer you to a specialist in heart disease, a cardiologist.

JEFFERSON: Really!

PAUL: Yes, and in some specialties, even more defined. Some cardiologists specialize only in heart surgery. Moving on...Other Institutes require some explanation. The NIH Clinical Center provides support for training in clinical research. The National Library of Medicine collects, organizes, and makes available biomedical science information to scientists, health professionals and the public. And, The Eunice Kennedy Shriver National Institute of Child Health and Human Development is self-explanatory.

JEFFERSON: Who is Eunice Kennedy Shriver?

PAUL: President Kennedy's sister who was involved with handicapped children...Another laboratory, The National Institute of General Medical Sciences funds studies on genes, proteins, and cells.

JEFFERSON: You mentioned proteins earlier. What are they and what are genes and cells?

PAUL: The gene is the molecular basis for inherited characteristics. As you know, offspring inherit certain characteristics from their parents. The mechanism for inheritance is the gene. A cell is the building block of all animal and plant structures. You have cells in your body delineated by the organ system involved. For example, you have skin cells, blood cells, muscle cells, nerve cells etc., all having a complete copy of your genes or genetic makeup.

JEFFERSON: If each cell has a complete copy of my genes, how does the cell know what to become?

PAUL: At a certain point, a cell becomes differentiated, that is, in a muscle cell, the gene making it a skin cell turns off. How that process works remains a mystery. As you asked, a protein is a biological collection of atoms called molecules providing the basis of animal and plant structure. Proteins make up much of the non-bone structure of your body. You consume proteins when you eat meat, fish, and eggs. That is about all I know about them.

JEFFERSON: Thank you. Please continue.

PAUL: The National Center for Research Resources develops tools needed to understand, detect, treat, and prevent a wide range of diseases. The Center for Information Technology combines computational biosciences research, computer systems, and computer facilities. The John E. Fogarty International Center for Advanced Study in the Health Sciences promotes research and training internationally to reduce disparities in global health.

JEFFERSON: Who is John E Fogarty?

PAUL: A congressman who increased the National Institute of Health budget.

JEFFERSON: What a surprise!
PAUL: Still continuing with the institutes. We have The National Eye Institute, The National Institute of Environmental Health Sciences, The National Institute on Alcohol Abuse and Alcoholism, The National Institute on Drug Abuse, The National Institute on Aging, The National Institute of Arthritis and Musculoskeletal and Skin Diseases, The National Institute of Nursing Research and The National Institute on Deafness and Other Communication Disorders.

JEFFERSON: Did we leave anything out?

PAUL: A few more. The National Human Genome Research Institute supports worldwide research effort designed to analyze the human DNA structure.

JEFFERSON: Genome? DNA?

PAUL: As I said earlier, the basis for our heredity is the gene. Each gene is made up of DNA, or Deoxyribonucleic acid. (Shows a model of the DNA helix) The genome is the unique collection of genes each person has that determines his or her makeup. Still continuing...The National Center on Minority Health and Health Disparities. The National Center for Complementary and Alternative Medicine explores complementary and alternative medical (CAM) practices.

JEFFERSON: What is Minority Health?

PAUL: Minorities in the US, that is, blacks, Asians, Native Americans have different health issues than whites. The Institute studies them to ascertain their causes so cures can be developed...Finally, The National Institute of Biomedical Imaging and Bioengineering. That is all of the institutes. Most of the money spent is on contracts with private companies and universities for basic medical research and computer aided design and manufacturing.

JEFFERSON: Computer aided...

PAUL: We talked about using computers to process data. We have computers that show an architectural design and allow you to change it instantaneously.

JEFFERSON: What about issues such as stress, soil conditions, and materials?

PAUL: From what I know of the process, it can automatically compute those issues as you change the design. What do you think of this agency, Mr. President?

JEFFERSON: The agency meets the condition of general welfare since the health of all is important and is constitutional if Congress deems it important. It might be more efficient if the commercially viable products produced provide a royalty to the government. I suggest Congress establish a system to patent ideas produced and obtain royalties to reimburse the research cost.

PAUL: That is a very good idea, Mr. President. We will now proceed to look at Federal Student Aid.

Segment 24 – Department of Education: Federal Student Aid

Paul Jefko: Mr. President, the federal government role in education was almost non-existent until Congress passed the GI Bill in 1944, but that law was limited to post-secondary education for veterans. However, the federal role expanded when the Higher Education Act of 1965 provided financial assistance for college to large numbers of students. In 1972, Congress expanded this aid for vocational education, community colleges, and trade schools.

President Jefferson: You have mentioned this Bill several times before. Can you provide some details on this?

PAUL: The letters GI referred to the American soldier in World War II. A law passed after the war, the Servicemen's Readjustment Act, provided benefits including tuition for college, high school or vocational school plus living expenses.

JEFFERSON: Since this was a program exclusively for military veterans, how did it become a program for everyone?

PAUL: The Higher Education Act was part of President Johnson's Great Society program hoping to eliminate poverty and racial injustice. Although the

99

original law provided for direct grants to students, most money now goes for student loans. The Department of Health, Education and Welfare managed the program until the department of Education was formed in 1980, followed by The Office of Federal Student Aid in 1998 to consolidate the grant and loan programs under one agency.

JEFFERSON: How does the program work?

PAUL: The process is simple. The agency receives applications from prospective students via FAFSA, the Free Application for Federal Student Aid. For those with financial need, grants are available if funds are available. Others are eligible for subsidized or unsubsidized loans. Private lenders provide the actual money but the agency guarantees loan repayment. If the loan defaults, the agency pays the lender the loan amount.

JEFFERSON: Instead of guaranteeing a private loan, why not just loan the student the money?

PAUL: They do. The agency also provides direct loans to students and collects repayments but the money for this purpose is limited. Because of this program, the federal government is the largest single funding source for higher education in the US. The program cost was $17.3 Billion in a recent year.

JEFFERSON: I was just joking about loaning a student the money. I am shocked to know my joke was real. I know what my opinion on this is: Unconstitutional, as it is not an enumerated power of Congress and is not for the general welfare or common defense.

PAUL: What should be done?

JEFFERSON: Do not issue new loans or guarantees. However, current loan obligations should be honored until matured.

PAUL: Thank you, Mr. President. Now we will look at Rural Development after this important message.

Commercial Break

Segment 25 – Department of Agriculture: Rural Development

Paul Jefko: Mr. President, Congress created Rural Development in 1994 during a reorganization of the Department of Agriculture. It manages the financing for rural housing, rural business and community facilities, and rural electrification. These programs began in 1935 when the Resettlement Administration was formed to relocate families affected by the Depression. Its mission expanded in 1946 to include funding for housing, community projects and business development.

President Jefferson: Why did families have to be relocated?

PAUL: An environmental disaster occurred in the Great Plains in the early 1930's, called the Dust Bowl.

JEFFERSON: Where are the Great Plains?

PAUL: The Great Plains describe most of the land between the Mississippi River and the Rocky Mountains. Because of its low rainfall, it was typically suitable only for grazing. There were some wet years prior to the Great Depression encouraging farmers to plow up the virgin soil and plant. During the draught of the next decade, the upturned soil dried up, turned to dust, and blew away, creating great dust storms that blackened the skies and stretched to the US East Coast.

JEFFERSON: That is hard to imagine.

PAUL: Yes, it affected 100 million acres. In some storms, you could not see a yard in front of you. The farmers who were there had to move somewhere. The Resettlement Administration provided relief camps for them in California.

JEFFERSON: The federal government set up camps for them to live? Where did they work?

PAUL: They moved as hired labor from farm to farm during harvest and planting season in California. Besides these camps, the Resettlement Administration also developed planned communities throughout the US for the impoverished farmers. Much of what they did failed and the agency moved into the Department of Agriculture.

JEFFERSON: A waste of taxpayer money.

PAUL: Well, when Roosevelt became President, he vowed to act to mitigate the effects of the Depression. He said he would experiment with various schemes and some would work and some wouldn't. One, the Rural Electrification Administration brought electricity and telephone service to rural areas. The agency became part of the Rural Development Agency with three main sub-offices: Rural Business-Cooperative Service, Rural Housing Service, and Rural Utilities Service.

JEFFERSON: We discussed this before. Supposedly, providing this electricity was too costly for a private investor. Why didn't the States do this for their citizens?

PAUL: I believe the States having the greatest rural population are also the poorest. The Rural Utilities Service serves 11 % of the population spread over 75% of the nation's land area. A rural utility company helped by the Service normally serves only 10,000 customers making it a costly investment for a private company. Similarly, access to broadband telecommunication coverage is only 51% in the rural areas.

JEFFERSON: Broadband...?

PAUL: A new technology allows communication throughout the world. You can sit in your home and via a simple device access almost all the information the world has available. If this process had been available in your time, a person in London or Jerusalem could watch you direct the planting of your crops at Monticello and talk with you at the same time. (Shows on a laptop computer the Monticello website)

JEFFERSON: (Speechless.)

PAUL: Besides electricity and communication, water costs more for rural residents especially for environmental compliance and maintenance. Besides helping with utilities, another office, the Rural Housing Service, provides low-income rural Americans loans to buy or rent homes. What is your opinion on this agency, Mr. President?

JEFFERSON: In my judgment, all functions of this agency are unconstitutional except for those involving Indian Tribes under a treaty to provide such services. No specific authority appears in the Constitution to invest in business, utilities, or housing and this is not a general welfare issue but only for the welfare of rural communities.

PAUL: What should the next steps be?

JEFFERSON: Authorize no new loans or grants. Current loans will be maintained until liquidated.

PAUL: Thank you, Mr. President. We'll turn to the Office of the Attorney General.

Segment 26 - Department of Justice

Paul Jefko: Mr. President, the Attorney General was initially one person to advise the President and Cabinet on legal matters and represent the government before the Supreme Court. However, as the government expanded, legal issues arose beyond the knowledge or capability of one person. Instead of giving the Attorney General his own staff, Congress chose to create attorney positions in other cabinet departments. For example, in 1829, the Congress created the Solicitor of the Treasury to handle Departmental lawsuits and manage the US Attorneys throughout the country.

President Jefferson: The President appoints the US Attorneys, but with the other demands of his job, does not have the time to supervise their affairs adequately. Setting up a position to do so whether under the Attorney General or the Secretary of the Treasury was a good move.

PAUL: When the proliferation of attorneys proved inefficient, Congress, in 1879, established the Department of Justice, headed by the Attorney General, and created the Solicitor General under him, to litigate before the Supreme Court. In 1887, the Department began to assume federal law enforcement responsibilities when Congress passed the Interstate Commerce Act. Earlier, in 1884, the Interior Department transferred federal prisons to the Department of Justice. Since then, the Department has assumed the role of chief law enforcement officer for the federal government.

JEFFERSON: What of the US Attorneys?

PAUL: The same act creating the Department of Justice placed the US Attorneys under the Attorney General although the President still appoints them. Currently, the Department has a number of subsidiary agencies. The Federal Bureau of Investigation is the main federal law enforcement agency. The US Marshals Service arrests federal fugitives, protects the federal judiciary, operates the Witness Protection Program, transports federal prisoners, and seizes illegally obtained federal property.

JEFFERSON: I am familiar with the US Marshals, but what is the Federal Bureau of Investigation?

PAUL: The FBI, as it is better known, is the primary federal criminal investigative service. It also has the counterintelligence mission within the US. Moving on…The Bureau of Alcohol, Tobacco and Firearms investigates unlawful use of firearms and explosives and illegal trafficking in alcohol and tobacco. The Drug Enforcement Administration combats the sale of narcotics and other illegal drugs. The Office of Justice Programs manages crime prevention programs. The Office of Community Oriented Policing Services promotes community based policing.

JEFFERSON: What is community based policing?

PAUL: A law enforcement technique promoting police involvement with the community and problem solving. Instead of reacting to each crime as it occurs in isolation, the program supports planning to analyze criminal situations to prevent future crime. Continuing…The Federal Bureau of Prisons administers the federal prison system. The Office of the Federal Detention Trustee oversees detention activities. The US Parole Commission decides on parole for federal and District of Columbia prisoners.

JEFFERSON: I understand the term 'parole' granting military prisoners of war release after giving their word they will not become combatants again, but what is its meaning with federal prisoners?

PAUL: If a convicted prisoner meets certain conditions, he can be released from prison earlier than his sentence allows.

JEFFERSON: Really! What conditions?

PAUL: He usually has to have had good conduct while in custody and he must have served at least half his sentence. The Parole Commission reviews his case and can grant or withhold parole. He must periodically report to a parole officer who monitors his situation. The parolee also cannot own a gun or abuse alcohol or drugs and can be re-arrested if he violates these provisions. Moving on…as stated earlier, the US Solicitor General represents the government before the Supreme Court.

JEFFERSON: How many times does the Solicitor General appear before the Supreme Court?

PAUL: The Solicitor General argues 15-20 cases per year…Continuing…The Office of Professional Responsibility investigates ethical violations of departmental attorneys. The Foreign Intelligence Surveillance Court approves requests for Wiretapping of those deemed a threat to national security. The National Security Division handles national security functions of the Department. The US Bureau of Interpol works with INTERPOL, the international police organization. The Foreign Claims Settlement Commission settles claims by US nationals in foreign countries.

JEFFERSON: Wiretapping?

PAUL: Remember when we discussed the technology allowing you to talk to someone anywhere in the world via a simple device, the telephone? Well, the Constitution prohibits listening in on any conversation over the telephone based on unreasonable search and seizure rules. However, law enforcement personnel, with a warrant, can tap or listen in if they can convince a judge a crime is planned or was committed. The technique is also used to ensure national security by tapping the phones of foreign agents or traitors.

JEFFERSON: Why was this considered an unreasonable search according to the Fourth Amendment?

PAUL: A Supreme Court case, Katz vs. the United States determined if a person expects privacy, and the expectation is reasonable then government activity to observe or listen in constitutes a search and requires a warrant. Congress established the special court as a measure to ensure oversight. The final agency in the Department, the Radiation Exposure Compensation Program, pays claims for persons injured in nuclear programs during the Cold War. That covers the organization. We will look at their main branches in a later session.

JEFFERSON: I look forward to it. What's next?

Segment 27 – Department of Energy

Paul Jefko: Mr. President, the Department of Energy is one of the newest Cabinet offices. The Department can trace its origins to The Office of Fossil Energy established in the early 1900's to ensure oil availability for the US Navy, which had switched its fleet from coal power to oil. The Office's main purpose was to remove oil-bearing lands from the public domain as a reserve for national defense.

President Jefferson: I think you mentioned this before. Modern ships use steam engines aboard their crafts to power them. Are they similar to the side-wheel steamboats running along the coasts in my time?

PAUL: Modern ships are different from the steamboats you are familiar with. First, they are made of steel rather than wood, second, they do not burn wood to create steam and third, they do not have paddles, but an underwater propeller, similar to an Archimedes screw. (Shows several photos of ships)

JEFFERSON: Ah, now I understand. The screw rotates and propels the ship through the water. But why switch to oil from coal?

PAUL: During the War with Spain, we experienced serious problems in maintaining coal supplies to our ships. A large ship burns 10 tons an hour, requiring coal ships and coaling stations. You also needed sailors to shovel coal into large boilers to keep steam pressure up. Liquid petroleum has greater energy per pound and simpler refueling, without the need for coal shovelers.

These days, most of our fleet is nuclear powered and does not require refueling at all, leading to another Energy Department function having its origins in 1942, when the Army set up the Manhattan Project to develop an atomic bomb.

JEFFERSON: You mentioned this project earlier. Tell me more about this atomic bomb.

PAUL: A natural element called uranium comes from various ores, one you know as pitchblende.

JEFFERSON: Yes, I am familiar with pitchblende.

PAUL: Well, uranium has a unique property called radioactivity, where the uranium atom spontaneously emits radiation. As long as the uranium is combined with other elements in an ore, the particles emitted are absorbed by the other elements. As uranium becomes refined, the radioactivity can be high enough to create heat. If enough pure material is packed together into what is called a critical mass, it can explode. In a bomb, half the critical mass remains separate from the other half within a bomb casing. To cause the explosion, you thrust both halves together to create the critical mass.
JEFFERSON: Very understandable.

PAUL: After the war, the Congress transferred the bomb to civilian control and established the Atomic Energy Commission or AEC to control the entire atomic weapon complex. The AEC concentrated on further developing nuclear weapons and nuclear reactors for the Navy. In 1954, the Atomic Energy Act gave the technology to the private sector but gave the AEC the authority to regulate it. The Energy Reorganization Act of 1974 split the AEC into the Nuclear Regulatory commission to regulate the nuclear power industry and the Energy Research and Development Administration to manage nuclear weapons, naval reactors, and energy development.

JEFFERSON: What is a nuclear reactor?

PAUL: As I said earlier, if you have a pure level of uranium, it can generate heat. As long as you do not achieve a critical mass, that heat can be used to boil water, create steam, and drive a propeller. (Shows diagram of a nuclear reactor in a submarine)

JEFFERSON: Quite so.

PAUL: The Department of Energy Organization Act consolidated all the Energy programs into a single Department in 1977. Its mission was to develop high-risk energy technology, sell federal power, develop and promote energy conservation programs, develop and manage nuclear weapons, regulate national energy facilities and collect and analyze energy data. The Reagan Administration emphasized nuclear weapons research to help win the Cold War while a few nuclear accidents turned the public against nuclear power as a future energy source.

JEFFERSON: What nuclear accidents?

PAUL: The one best known is Chernobyl in Russia, where a design flaw caused a reactor explosion releasing radioactive particles over a vast area even to Western Europe. The US had its own disaster at Three Mile Island, Pennsylvania when a reactor had a partial meltdown releasing radioactive gases into the atmosphere.

JEFFERSON: Are these reactors similar to the ones on ships?

PAUL: Yes, but instead of a turbine turning a propeller, the turbines generate electricity. (Shows photos of a power plant and its turbines) We have power plants throughout the world producing electricity powering almost everything we do. Some plants use coal or oil to generate electricity, but nuclear plants produce electricity cleanly, without resulting ash or fumes. Therefore, they are the preferred method of producing electricity, except for the nuclear waste byproducts.

JEFFERSON: You mentioned these radioactive particles or gases were released into the air. What happens after the release?

PAUL: Well, contact with pure uranium can kill you within hours as the radioactive particles destroy cells and animal tissue. Over time, even uranium ores or particles from small amounts of uranium can cause cancer. Well...that is the Department history. It has a number of offices. The Office of Nuclear Energy promotes and develops nuclear power.

JEFFERSON: Promotes nuclear power?

PAUL: Well, the agency develops the technologies to improve the reliability, affordability and safety of nuclear reactors. Moving on...The National Nuclear Security Administration oversees the nation's nuclear weapons complex. The Office of Environmental Management oversees the cleanup of the nation's nuclear weapons complex.

JEFFERSON: Cleanup?

PAUL: Development of the atomic bomb during WW II created large amounts of waste products. It contaminated ground water, land surface and some waste was even dumped into the Columbia River. The site is literally radioactive.

JEFFERSON: Who allowed that to happen?

PAUL: You must realize during WW II, speed in developing the bomb was critical. The US thought Germany was close to developing a bomb and we needed to get one first. We were not concerned with maintaining a tidy area. A related agency, The Office of Legacy Management, manages the areas the previous office has cleaned up. The Office of Civilian Radioactive Waste Management disposes of the nation's nuclear waste and spent fuel. The Office of Health, Safety and Security oversees worker safety and security at nuclear weapon facilities. The Office of Energy Efficiency and Renewable Energy develops and promotes alternative fuels.

JEFFERSON: What are these alternative fuels?

PAUL: Biomass takes organic material and converts it into liquid fuel. Geothermal uses the heat from deep within the earth to generate steam. Hydrogen fuel cells produce electricity from a chemical reaction. Solar energy produces electricity from the reaction of the sun with a substance such as silicon. Even the wind can generate electricity similar to the windmills of Holland. The National Renewable Energy Laboratory develops these renewable energy technologies. Another set of agencies known as Power Marketing Administrations market hydropower produced by federal hydro projects.

JEFFERSON: Hydropower?

PAUL: Yes, you know it as waterpower, like a water mill used to grind corn in your day. The same principle can be used to generate electricity. (Shows photo of Hoover Dam) Continuing...The Federal Energy Regulatory Commission oversees the electrical, natural gas and oil industries. The Office of Electricity Delivery and Energy Reliability oversees electricity availability in the country. The Office of Fossil Energy oversees research projects in coal, natural gas, and oil exploration. The Office of Science distributes research funds for the Department. The Department spends about $20 Billion a year on contractors.

JEFFERSON: That is a lot of money. It seems the federal government has taken over the development of energy from the marketplace.

PAUL: Sometimes it can appear that way. However, the private market provides most energy used by Americans. That concludes my basic presentation on the Department. We will continue our review of the Department branches at a later session.

JEFFERSON: Thank you. This has been most interesting.

Segment 28 – Department of Housing and Urban Development: Office of Public and Indian Housing

Paul Jefko: Mr. President, during the Great Depression, Congress established relief programs to help struggling citizens. One, the Housing Act of 1937, created the Office of Public and Indian Housing. Its purpose was to provide federal money to State and local public housing agencies. Currently, its mission is to manage housing for 1.3 million families. It has five branches. 1. Native American Programs improve housing conditions for Native Americans. 2. Community Relations and Involvement provides subsidies to low income housing communities at the State and local levels. 3. Public and Assisted Housing Operations give vouchers to low income families to help pay for rent. 4. Public Housing Investments look for sites to develop and build low-income housing. 5. Policy, Program and Legislative Initiatives manage policy for the agency.

President Jefferson: How did the States become involved in providing housing?

PAUL: Originally, States and cities established building requirements to ensure safe and livable housing with proper ventilation. Since overcrowded urban areas fostered disease, cities provided public housing to replace substandard housing as a public health benefit. In a recent year, the largest recipient, the New York City Housing Authority, was given $700 million in assistance grants by the federal government. In that same year, the agency spent $2.8 billion on Public and Indian Housing while $900 million was provided for Indian Housing Block Grants.

JEFFERSON: What is the difference between Public and Indian Housing and Indian Housing Block Grants?

PAUL: The government manages the Public and Indian Housing directly by providing housing and money directly to persons for their housing needs. Whereas the Block Grants are given to Indian Tribes for them to manage their housing needs. Now that we have looked at this agency, what is your opinion?

JEFFERSON: The only constitutional function of this office is to provide Indian Housing, which the President must establish by treaty.

PAUL: What are the next steps for this agency?

109

JEFFERSON: Any help provided to an Indian tribe not under a treaty with the US must be terminated. Any subsidies provided to State and local governments for low-income housing must also be terminated as must rent vouchers to low-income families. Any property owned by the federal government for low-income housing must be sold and the proceeds returned to the Treasury. The Office should be able to do this in one year. The various States may, if their Constitution permits, take over these functions from the federal government.

PAUL: Thank you Mr. President.

Segment 29 – Independent Agencies: General Services Administration

Paul Jefko: President Jefferson, throughout most US history, no central organization handled the administrative functions of the federal government. Today we have the General Services Administration to do that job. When Congress established GSA, its original mission was to dispose of WW II surplus military supplies, manage and store government records, conduct emergency preparedness and manage wartime strategic supplies. In 1960, GSA established FTS, the Federal Telecommunications System for all agencies.

President Jefferson: What purpose does the FTS serve?

PAUL: At the time, telephone communication, we discussed earlier, had a government sanctioned monopoly dominated by one corporation, American Telephone and Telegraph. The monopoly provided telephone service to individuals, businesses, and government agencies in the US. Businesses with large usage received a better rate under rules set up by the government. Since the federal government was the largest telephone user in the nation, it obtained a special contract with AT&T negotiated and administered by GSA: FTS.

JEFFERSON: That is an intelligent decision.

PAUL: Impressed with its success, Congress set up GSA as the federal property owner in 1971 to centrally manage federal buildings and collect rent from the agencies occupying them. In 1973, GSA took over Procurement Policy, introduced credit cards in 1984, and set up and operated Child Care Centers in 1987.

JEFFERSON: Child Care Centers? What are those?

PAUL: Women are a vital part of the work force in the US today. If no one

110

can care for their children, they cannot work. GSA operates facilities to care for employees' children during work hours. (Shows photos of child care center in operation)

JEFFERSON: Why do women work outside the home?

PAUL: More and more families need two incomes to make ends meet. In addition, many single mothers have no means of support other than their own labor. Moving along...In the late 1990's GSA developed an online procurement service and set up a website for citizens to contact their government. In 2005, Emergency Response and Recovery was set up to prepare for national disasters. In 2007, GSA implemented the National Continuity Policy Implementation Plan to ensure recovery of the federal government in case of enemy attack.

JEFFERSON: I have heard enough to know this agency simply performs administrative functions to support the federal government. All functions are constitutional.

PAUL: Thank you, Mr. President. That concludes this program for the week. We hope you enjoyed it and hope you tune in next week for another discussion with President Jefferson. United States Marines should tune in.

Program # 6

Paul Jefko: Good Evening, welcome to the sixth part of our program: 'They Are Here'. We will continue our discussion with President Thomas Jefferson on the contemporary US government. At this time, I reintroduce our Third President, Thomas Jefferson...

Segment 30 - Department of Defense: United States Marine Corps

Paul Jefko: Mr. President, you sent Meriwether Lewis and William Clark on the expedition to explore Louisiana Territory. Can you tell us how that came about?

President Jefferson: With pleasure. When I was ambassador to France in the 1780's, I met John Ledyard, an American explorer who had the idea to explore the American northwest. I encouraged it and with the help of the Marquis de Lafayette, Ledyard attempted to cross Russia into Alaska and down the Pacific Coast to arrive in Virginia. However, he was stopped by the Russian Empress in Siberia and returned to Moscow. Another explorer, Alexander Mackenzie had written a book that I read around 1800 where he described his journey across Canada to the Pacific Ocean. As President, I asked Congress for money to fund a Corps of Discovery to explore the recently purchased Territory of Louisiana. Meriwether Lewis was my secretary and also an Army captain. I commissioned him the leader of this Corps to explore the new territory, establish relations with Indian tribes in the area and help lay claim to the Pacific Northwest which was not part of the Louisiana territory.

PAUL: Well, the expedition was a success and today the people of that area owe their prosperity to you, Mr. President. But, to return to our objective...I will recount some history with which you are already familiar. In 1775, the Second Continental Congress created two Marine battalions to serve as landing forces for the new Continental Navy. That was the beginning of the Marine Corps. In 1783 at the end of hostilities, the Continental Congress disbanded all the military units, including the Marines. The Marines were reestablished in 1798, seeing action in the quasi war with France, the war against the Barbary Pirates and the Battle of New Orleans during the War of 1812.

JEFFERSON: Yes, they were very effective in the war against the Barbary pirates. They marched from Alexandria, Egypt to Derne, in the Tripolitan State and captured it.

PAUL: The Marines also participated in three Seminole Indian wars in Florida and the Mexican-American war where they participated in the battles in Mexico City. The Marines saw little action in the Civil War, but they acquired some notoriety as part of US gunboat diplomacy in the late 19th century. They were also used to help quash the Boxer Rebellion in China and were heavily involved in the decisive battles of WW I.

JEFFERSON: The Boxer Rebellion? A revolt by fighters?

PAUL: The term arose from an anti-foreign movement in China named the Righteous Harmony Society mistranslated as Righteous Uniting Fists. The rebellion targeted foreigners, who were massacred. The US sent Marines as part of an international relief expedition to relieve a siege of foreign troops and diplomats. Moving on...In WWII, the island-hopping strategy used the Marines extensively against the Japanese.

JEFFERSON: Island hopping?

PAUL: Yes, after the Japanese attacked our naval base in the Hawaiian Islands to disable our fleet as we spoke of before, they also aggressively attacked all the islands lying between Hawaii and Japan, occupying them easily to deny their use to us as naval or air bases. They believed it would generate so many American casualties and time for us to reconquer all these islands we would give up. So, instead of attacking each separate island, we attacked only certain ones and left the others occupied.

JEFFERSON: Wouldn't this mean there were Japanese troops on islands threatening the rear of our forces?

PAUL: We only attacked the islands having naval or air bases. If the island did not have any ships or aircraft, the troops stationed there did not present a threat. After WW II, the Marines saw a reduced role. They were used in the Korean Conflict in the amphibious landing at Inchon and the liberation of Seoul. During the Cold war, they participated in invading the Dominican Republic to avert a Communist takeover.

JEFFERSON: Communists took over the Dominican Republic? It normally is under Spanish control.

PAUL: By that time, the Republic was independent, but a recent election had put a radical President in power. President Johnson did not want a second Communist nation in the Caribbean, so he sent the Marines to take control while

113

the US held an election three years later placing an American-friendly President in power. But the Marines' most crucial impact was in Vietnam. Later, Marines went to Lebanon to help avert a civil war, invaded Grenada to avert a Communist takeover and even ousted the President of Panama.

JEFFERSON: Although you said the war with the Communists was a Cold one, it appears there was some fighting, especially close to our home shores.

PAUL: Yes, and as in our hemisphere, we violated other nations' sovereignty. In Operation Desert Storm and Desert Shield, over 90,000 Marines saw combat. They also landed in Haiti to halt internal strife in its government and later participated in invading Iraq. Over the years, the Marine Corps has evolved into the leading expert in amphibious warfare and become larger than the British Army.

JEFFERSON: Really?

PAUL: The British Army today has 130,000 soldiers, compared with 195,000 US Marines. And, although it has ground units like the Army and aircraft like the Air Force, it remains under Navy authority.

JEFFERSON: When I authorized the Navy to protect our shipping in the Mediterranean, I believed the Marines as a fighting force, along with the Navy, provided enough defense for our country. During the War with Great Britain in 1812, that belief was shattered, as we obviously needed a trained Army to counter the British forces. But I never envisaged a standing Army as you have in your time. In fact, I question the need for a Marine Corps, if we also have a standing Army, one of them being superfluous.

PAUL: Some have questioned the need for a Marine Corps in my time also. Amphibious assaults as the Corps managed in WW II are outdated. Experts claim such a strategy will not work against a capable enemy in modern warfare.

JEFFERSON: Since the Marines are under the Navy and establishing a Navy is an enumerated power of Congress, this agency is constitutional. Whether the Corps continues lies with Congress.

PAUL: Thank you, Mr. President. Let's leave the earth now and explore outer space.

Segment 31 - Independent Agency: National Aeronautics and Space Administration

Paul Jefko: Mr. President, the US saw a national security threat in the Soviet Union Sputnik launch in 1957. In response, the US launched its own artificial satellite in 1958 under the Navy's Vanguard Project. To compete in the Space Race on a long-term basis, the Congress set up NASA. President Kennedy provided the goal of landing a man on the moon and returning him safely to earth. The agency tested launch vehicles and propulsion systems but its first big mission was Project Mercury to see whether humans could survive in space.

President Jefferson: We talked about this before: objects orbiting the Earth. So, we sent men into space. What is up there?

PAUL: Nothing: No air, No heat. NASA devised special suits to provide oxygen and heat to the occupant. The first astronauts, as we called them, traveled inside a capsule heated and filled with air. Later they had to venture outside the capsule. Despite our best efforts, the US lost the first part of the Space Race to the Soviet Union who put the first person into space and returned him alive. (Shows photo of astronaut floating in space)

JEFFERSON: Did the Soviet Union ever reach the moon?

PAUL: No. Curiously, their program never achieved its potential. The rockets they had developed for moon missions did not pan out. Moving on...the next Project Gemini was designed to see whether a trip to the Moon was possible. Project Apollo actually placed humans on the Moon and returned them. Later in the 1970's, NASA placed a space station in orbit around the Earth, called Skylab. A shuttlecraft resupplied the station.

JEFFERSON: Let me get this straight. The United States of America placed a man on the moon?

PAUL: Yes, 12 men have walked on the Moon in six different missions. (Shows photo of Neil Armstrong and American flag on the moon). In 1990, a large telescope was launched and placed in orbit to provide greater clarity because it would not have to deal with atmospheric distortion. Later NASA and other nations placed an International Space Station in orbit. In 2010, the President tabled a plan to place a permanent settlement on the Moon in lieu of developing new technologies and enticing private companies to participate in space flight.

JEFFERSON: So, we sent men to the Moon and brought them back, but we decided not to stay there permanently?

PAUL: The moon missions were specifically designed to get to the moon, stay a little bit of time and return to Earth. Putting a settlement on the Moon

115

required billions of dollars. Shuttles would need to transport everything, including air, water, food, housing, and whatever. It was too costly. NASA did send space probes to Saturn, Mercury, and Jupiter and mechanical landers to Mars.

JEFFERSON: Mars! What did they find there?

PAUL: A hostile environment to live in: -100 degrees Celsius, air about 1/250 of earth. (Shows photo of Mars Lander) In any case, that brings NASA up to the present time. NASA is organized into 10 centers and 4 directorates. The first directorate, Aeronautics, conducts research into traditional and emerging fields of flight. Exploration Systems manages the International Space Station, Commercial Space Transportation, Crew Vehicle and Launch Systems, Human Health and Safety, Analog Missions and Field Testing and Human Exploration Technology.

JEFFERSON: What is the international space station?

PAUL: Five national space agencies agreed to place an artificial satellite up in space for scientific experiments. It has been occupied for 12 years. The third Directorate, the Science Mission Directorate, develops satellites and probes. The Space Operations Directorate develops technologies to support launch, transportation, and communications.

JEFFERSON: You do not need to tell me more. The agency is constitutional as it contributes to the general welfare of the nation through its scientific discoveries, similar to my sending out Lewis and Clark to explore Louisiana.

PAUL: Thank you, Mr. President. Let us look at another department.

Segment 32 - Department of the Interior

Paul Jefko: The 1st Congress considered establishing a department to handle domestic affairs in 1789 but decided to put those functions within the Department of State instead. President Polk's Secretary of the Treasury said in 1849 that many federal functions were in departments unrelated to their basic missions, such as the Land Office in Treasury, the Indians Affairs Office in the War Department and the Patent Office in the Department of State.

President Jefferson: I know as Secretary of State, I had responsibility for the US Mint, which should have been given to the Secretary of the Treasury. I also was on the Patent Board, approving all new patents for inventions. These responsibilities detracted from my primary duty of foreign relations.

PAUL: In 1849, Congress agreed with both you and President Polk's Secretary of Treasury when it established the Department of the Interior to serve as a place for those functions not related to other departments. Originally, it was responsible for building the Federal District, its water system, and jail. Eventually some functions became the basis of other Departments, like the Department of Agriculture.

JEFFERSON: So, we return to the original idea of a Secretary of Domestic Affairs.

PAUL: Yes. The new Department helped colonize freed slaves to Haiti, promoted Western exploration, regulated Territories, managed federal hospitals, colleges and parks and managed issues related to Native Americans, public lands, pensions and patents. In addition, Congress in 1879 established the US Geological Survey under this Department to document the resources in federal territories and in 1902 created the Bureau of Reclamation to build dams and aqueducts to provide water to arid areas of the West.

JEFFERSON: These dams and aqueducts were built in US territories, I presume?

PAUL: Well, most of the west in 1902 was already divided into States. The agency built these dams in existing States.

JEFFERSON: What authority was there to build these structures in States?

PAUL: Congress believed Western development required water resources for farming and settlement.

JEFFERSON: Why didn't the States build them?

PAUL: I cannot answer that definitively. There may have been an interstate commerce issue where rivers crossed State boundaries. Any dams built by the States may have affected the water flow into other States.

JEFFERSON: That would occur whoever built the dam. Who funded these projects?

PAUL: Federal lands in the western states were sold and the proceeds were used for construction.

JEFFERSON: So, we sell the property belonging to the entire American people to benefit a portion of a State's population?

PAUL: That is so. Other additions included the National Park Service in 1916, the Bureau of Mines in 1910 and the Fish and Wildlife Service in the 1940's. Later, the Department assumed the management of US Territories, regulated strip mining and collected fees for minerals mined on federal land including the outer continental shelf.

JEFFERSON: The outer continental shelf?

PAUL: Yes, a geographical term describing the land surface from the shoreline to the underwater surface where it drops precipitously. (Shows a chart picturing the continental shelf off the Atlantic coast) A more rigorous definition is used in international law. US Law provides that area to be in the province of the federal government...That concludes the functions of the agency. We will look at its major agencies later. Thank you, Mr. President.

JEFFERSON: You are quite welcome.

Segment 33 - Department of Education: Office of Elementary and Secondary Education

Paul Jefko: Mr. President, the Office of Elementary and Secondary Education implements the 1965 Elementary and Secondary Education Act as part of President Johnson's Great Society Program to eliminate discrimination and poverty. A large reach of federal power into programs normally State controlled and managed, it has been attacked since it began, but the entire federal foray into education has been questioned since the late 19th century.

President Jefferson: With good reason.

PAUL: Federal authority into elementary and secondary education has been confirmed and strengthened by the No Child Left Behind Act of 2001.

JEFFERSON: What have the courts said about these programs?

PAUL: Although the Supreme Court has ruled on religious issues in schools, student issues and rights, teacher issues and rights and school district liability, no case has dealt directly with the constitutionality of federal aid to schools...Currently, the agency manages several programs. The Academic Improvement and Teacher Quality Program provides grants to set teacher standards. The Impact Aid Program provides funds to school districts having students who do not pay property taxes for school support, because they reside on federal property.

An Interview with Thomas Jefferson

JEFFERSON: What people reside on federal land besides Indians?

PAUL: A good example is the US Military Academy at West Point. The staff and teachers there have families and children. They live on the academy grounds, but their children attend local schools. Although property taxes fund public schools, the staff and teachers at the Academy are exempt because they live on federal land. In order to ensure their costs are covered, funds are provided to the school district.

JEFFERSON: Why aren't the staff and teachers paying for their children's schooling?

PAUL: Because other students do not have to pay for their education.

JEFFERSON: But they do. Their parents pay property taxes to support the school district as you said.

PAUL: Indirectly. Some families have several children and own a few acres. Some families have a large acreage and fewer children. Some families have no children and some property owners are not even married...Continuing, the Office of Indian Education helps local agencies and Tribes in providing equal education to American Indians and Alaskan Natives.

JEFFERSON: Wait a minute. Did you say earlier the federal government determines the standards for teachers? Isn't that a local issue?

PAUL: The No Child Left Behind Act, passed in 2001, required schools to meet certain standards. The States set the standards, but a school not meeting the standard would suffer drastic measures taken such as replacing the entire teaching staff.

JEFFERSON: What?

PAUL: Seriously. The requirements of the act have led some States to reduce the standards so schools will meet them.

JEFFERSON: This program does no good for the student, the teacher or the school, let alone society.

PAUL: Many people agree with you. Continuing...The Office of Migrant Education provides funds to ensure children of migrant workers have the opportunity to meet graduation requirements. The School Support and Technology Program funds technology installation in school facilities and assistance centers. Finally, The Student Achievement and School Accountability Program supports schools in low-income communities. What is your opinion on this agency?

JEFFERSON: Based on what you have told me, the following programs are unconstitutional: The Academic Improvement and Teacher Quality Program; the Office of Migrant Education; School Support and Technology Programs and Student Achievement and School Accountability Programs. No specific authority exists in the Constitution for these programs and they are not general welfare issues as they apply only to elementary and secondary schools. The Impact Aid Program is constitutional only if the consent agreement allowing the purchase of the federal property included such a payment as a stipulation. The Office of Indian Education is constitutional only if provided as part of a treaty with the Tribes.

PAUL: What should be done with this agency?

JEFFERSON: Eliminate the Academic Improvement and Teacher Quality Program, the Office of Migrant Education, School Support and Technology Programs and Student Achievement and School Accountability Programs. Review each project under the Impact Aid program to determine if current agreements allowed the payment. If not, make no payment. Enact laws to prevent such payments for future land acquisitions. Review each grant under the Office of Indian Education to ensure a treaty with a Tribe supports it. No treaty, no grant.

PAUL: Thank you, Mr. President. Right now, we look at more housing.

Segment 34 – Department of Housing and Urban Development: Office of Community Planning and Development

Paul Jefko: Mr. President, we will be looking at another agency located within the Department of Housing and Urban Development. We previously looked at the Office of Public and Indian Housing. The Office of Community Planning and Development provides funds to communities to assist them in planning and financing development and increasing their capacity to give shelter and services to the Homeless.

President Jefferson: More housing! I know we have gone through this before, but convince me the federal government has a role in this area.

PAUL: I cannot convince you unless you accept the fact the nation as a whole has a stake in providing opportunities for everyone.

JEFFERSON: Well, you will never convince me. The government should remove obstacles to opportunity for all, but to provide them is a different story.

PAUL: Aren't we talking about two sides of the same coin?

JEFFERSON: No, because building a road between postal stations to provide news to a farmer differs from providing him insurance if his crops fail. He has a responsibility to be a good husbandman of his acreage, and if he faces a poor market or lack of rainfall, that is something he personally must deal with. However, if poor mail delivery service causes him to miss information on a farmstead for sale, that is an obstacle the government must remove.

PAUL: Many Congresses have taken your second example to justify the first. In essence, the conflict between a strict interpretation of the Constitution and a looser one still goes on. Shall I continue?

JEFFERSON: Please.

PAUL: The agency has seven sub-offices: Economic Development assists communities in planning. Community Development helps regions recover from disasters. Affordable Housing gives funds to State and local communities for building affordable housing. In addition, another sub-office, Homeless Assistance, provides job skill training and counseling to the homeless. Environment and Energy pays for environment improvement and energy efficiency. Real Estate Acquisition and Relocation helps those displaced because of federal housing projects. HIV/AIDS provides funds to individuals with AIDS to pay the rent. Assistance is provided through grants to cities, communities, and persons. What do you think of this agency, Mr. President?

JEFFERSON: Every one of these functions is unconstitutional except for the Real Estate Acquisition and Relocation Program providing funds to those persons displaced by federal projects. I understand this may be necessary to avoid tort litigation by the persons displaced.

PAUL: What should the next steps be?

JEFFERSON: Abolish the entire agency and its programs except for transferring the Real Estate Acquisition and Relocation to another part of the Department.

PAUL: Thank you, Mr. President. Let us now look a small but critical part of the Department of Defense.

Segment 35 - Department of Defense: National Security Agency/Central Security Service

Paul Jefko: During World War I, the US Army created the Cipher Bureau in the Military Intelligence Division to provide cryptographic services. In 1924, the Navy developed a similar cryptanalytic bureau in the Office of Naval Communication. The knowledge in this area advanced to the point that the military broke Japan's codes prior to World War II. In 1943, a technological breakthrough helped discover that machines processing and transmitting information produced electronic signals that could be captured.

President Jefferson: Explain that to me.

PAUL: I must explain electricity first. If you recall Benjamin Franklin's experiment with lightning, he proved lightning was electricity. Lightning travels from the clouds to the ground. Therefore, electricity can travel between two objects. This concept led to using electricity as a power source. In my world, electricity, among its other uses, provides a communication system via copper wire or through the air via radio waves.

JEFFERSON: So, electricity can travel through the air?

PAUL: Not directly, but electricity can generate electronic waves, like a pebble thrown into a still pond. We can receive, interpret, and convert those waves into information. Therefore, if you have a transmitting device in one location and a receiving device in another, you can transmit messages, voice, or data. (Turns on a radio to a classical music station.) But, the message, either by wire or through the air, can be intercepted by another receiver designed for the purpose.

JEFFERSON: That is amazing.

PAUL: That probably was not a good explanation but I really only know its application, not its science.

JEFFERSON: Fine. I can grasp the process.

PAUL: After the end of the War, a State/Army/Navy Communications Intelligence Board was set up to coordinate all communication intelligence. Later, Congress, via the National Security Act of 1947, established the Central Intelligence Agency and the National Security Council. In 1949, the military consolidated its communication intelligence in the Armed Forces Security Agency, tasked with Communications Intelligence and Communications Security.

JEFFERSON: What is the difference between the Central Intelligence Agency and the National Security Council?

PAUL: The Central Intelligence Agency or CIA is, in short, the spy agency for the US. It works to collect intelligence from overseas to help identify national security threats. The National Security Council works directly for the President advising him on national security threats. The Armed Forces Security Agency was renamed the National Security Agency under the Secretary of Defense.

JEFFERSON: How does the mission of the CIA and the National Security Agency differ?

PAUL: The CIA collects intelligence via humans, and the NSA collects it via signals. The NSA deals strictly with gathering electronic intelligence from all over the world. They intercept electronic communications that they feed to the CIA and the National Security Council. Most projects and funding are secret. What do you think about this agency?

JEFFERSON: This agency is constitutional as it collects only foreign data for national defense.

PAUL: Thank you Mr. President. It is a good time to break here for a message from our sponsor.

Commercial Break

Segment 36 – Department of Transportation: Federal Aviation Administration

Paul Jefko: Mr. President, we have touched on aviation when discussing the Department of Transportation. We now look at a Department segment having a large impact on air transportation in the US, the Federal Aviation Administration. Congress passed the Air Commerce Act of 1926 establishing an Aeronautics Branch in the Department of Commerce to develop aircraft safety standards, license pilots and establish airways.

President Jefferson: Airways? I assume the pilot can fly anywhere he wants.

PAUL: The Post Office provided the original airways to assist pilots transporting mail via air. At night, when landmarks are not visible, flying is hazardous. Bonfires, and later, flashing lights were placed on the ground a pilot traversed to arrive at the intended destination. Moving on...after renaming itself the Bureau of Air Commerce, the agency persuaded the airlines to construct air traffic control centers, over which the Bureau later assumed control.

JEFFERSON: What are these air traffic control centers?

PAUL: To ensure planes do not crash into each other, originally, towns and cities set up airport traffic control centers to control the takeoffs and landings. (Shows a video of an airport tarmac with planes lining up to take off) The airlines set up air traffic control centers to monitor traffic between airports. Later, the Civil Aeronautic Act of 1937 gave the agency authority to set airline fares and establish routes for commercial travel. In 1940, that agency was divided into the Civil Aeronautics Administration to manage air traffic control centers, certify pilots and aircraft, enforce safety rules, and develop airways and the Civil Aeronautics Board to make safety rules, investigate accidents, and regulate the airlines.

JEFFERSON: How many aircraft accidents occur each year?

PAUL: About 20 worldwide may have injuries or deaths. Four years ago was the latest an accident occurred to an American-owned airline. A bird flew into an aircraft engine causing a malfunction, forcing the craft to land in the Hudson River in New York City.

JEFFERSON: Really! Did people drown in the river?

PAUL: No, there were no fatalities or injuries as the craft floated for a while until the passengers left the craft. (Shows photo of plane in the Hudson) Continuing...in 1966, the Congress created the Department of Transportation, moved the CAA there, and renamed it the Federal Aviation Administration. In 1970, Congress deregulated the industry and removed its authority to set fares. After 9/11, Congress federalized airport security and created the Transportation Safety Administration to implement new security rules.

JEFFERSON: Excuse me. I wanted to ask this question earlier. The FAA had authority to set fares for traveling on the aircraft?

PAUL: Yes, in fact not only did the FAA determine the fares to be charged for a particular route from city to city, it actually determined which airline served which cities.

JEFFERSON: That is not regulation. That is interference with commerce.

PAUL: Well, that all changed in 1970. Deregulation caused airline fares to drop because of competition and many airlines went out of business or merged. In operation, the FAA has many programs. Regulations and Policies develops standards for commercial carriers, pilots, ground instructors, and airport operations. Certification certifies commercial aircraft, pilots, companies, and airports in accordance with the above standards.

JEFFERSON: So, airlines can set their own fares?

PAUL: Yes, and decide when and where they fly. Airports and Air Traffic manages all commercial, private, and military aviation in the US. Safety gives advisories and alerts to pilots, runways, and airports.

JEFFERSON: What is a runway?

PAUL: As I described earlier, an aircraft starts from a standstill on a flat hard surface where it builds up speed while traveling along the ground. (Shows video of plane taking off) When the craft reaches sufficient speed, the craft rises into the sky and accelerates into the atmosphere. The same process occurs on landing as the aircraft approaches the ground. It slows and lands on the flat level surface, known as the runway.

JEFFERSON: I understand.

PAUL: Moving on...Data and Statistics collects and provides information on airline operations, airports and the airline industry. Airports and the Environment assists airports in complying with environmental laws. Finally, Technology manages the hardware, software, and infrastructure in airport operations. What is your opinion of this agency?

JEFFERSON: Overall, the federal government can only perform the functions of this agency as it relates to interstate or military aviation or mail delivery. I assume pilots, aircraft, and airports are all involved with interstate travel at one time or another. Because of that, it seems easier to focus on the individuals, equipment, and facilities to determine legal federal involvement. On that basis, all the functions described for pilots, aircraft, and traffic control are in the federal interest even if some functions occur solely within a State. Persons, equipment or buildings at airports are local even if they involve interstate travel.

PAUL: What should the Congress do?

JEFFERSON: How are these operations funded?

PAUL: Taxation and Congressional appropriation.

JEFFERSON: Well, Congress should look at providing these services through a fee. Moreover, all regulations dealing with ground personnel and airport operations, airport certifications, safety and environmental standards and technology at airports shall be eliminated after one year during which affected States and localities will develop substitute regulations and standards.

PAUL: Thank you, Mr. President. We will now look at another independent agency, the Tennessee Valley Authority.

Segment 37 – Independent Agencies: Tennessee Valley Authority

Paul Jefko: Mr. President, Congress established TVA during the Great Depression because of the dire poverty of the people in the Tennessee River Valley. President Roosevelt envisioned the agency as operating like a private corporation with federal government backing. It constructed a series of dams to provide low cost electricity, improved river navigation and flood control. The TVA also provided advice on new agricultural methods to those who used inefficient traditional methods.

President Jefferson: These dams produce electricity as you described earlier. How do the dams prevent flooding?
PAUL: The dam holds back the water of a creek or river to create a lake as the water backs up the valley. (Shows a picture of Hoover Dam) The dam has sluices or openings allowing water through the dam to maintain a proper lake level. When rainy conditions arise in the area above the dam, the dam holds back the floodwater, raising the lake level, allowing the water to be released downstream days later in a controlled manner.

JEFFERSON: Ingenious. I have seen the dams in the Netherlands used to hold back the North Sea, but to use a dam in this way is ingenious.

PAUL: The construction projects created jobs for the unemployed. The cheap electricity also attracted textile mills employing the residents of the valley. During WW II, it provided aluminum for the war effort. At the end of WW II, the TVA had a 650-mile long navigable waterway and was the largest electricity supplier in the US. In 1959, Congress made TVA self-supporting with no further tax dollars.

JEFFERSON: Why does the federal government still own it? Why not sell it?

PAUL: Because if it is sold to a private company, the rates will go up. Congressional representatives in the area say it will harm their constituents.

JEFFERSON: That is not the point. The federal government should not provide services to the people they can obtain elsewhere. This is what happens when government provides largesse. It creates its own constituency.

PAUL: Moving on...TVA expanded from its original hydropower programs by constructing nuclear power plants. However, the Three Mile Island accident in Pennsylvania ended new nuclear power plant construction and the Endangered Species Act halted dam construction. Since then, it has developed solar, wind and gas as energy sources for its power. That concludes its history.

JEFFERSON: What is the Endangered Species Act?

PAUL: It was a law passed to prevent species extinction due to economic growth and development.

JEFFERSON: How many species are extinct today?

PAUL: We know about hundreds of extinct species from fossil evidence. For example, you have heard of the Mastodon fossil discovered over a century before your time.

JEFFERSON: Of course. I had fossils shipped to the White House from the Ohio Valley. Let me rephrase my question. It appears species become extinct all the time. Why do we have a law to prevent it?

PAUL: In your time, these American animals existed: The California Golden Bear. The Cascade Mountains Wolf, The Eastern Cougar, the Eastern Elk, the Sea Mink, the Smith Island Cottontail, the Carolina Parakeet, the Great Auk, the Heath Hen, the Passenger Pigeon, and the Ivory Billed Woodpecker. None exists today.

JEFFERSON: What happened to them?

PAUL: It varies. Most succumbed to hunting and habitat destruction.

JEFFERSON: That is very sad. What does the law do?

PAUL: It authorized the Secretary of the Interior to compile a list of endangered species and provide funds to set aside habitats for them. It also bans interstate commerce in them, and establishes penalties for those who kill or harm them.

JEFFERSON: Has it worked?

PAUL: Yes, it has. Recently, some species were removed from the list because their population has recovered. These include the Virginia Northern Flying Squirrel, and the Gray Wolf. Other species protected and recovered include the Bald Eagle, the Brown Pelican and the Peregrine Falcon. Continuing...TVA is the largest public power company in the US and sells power to 158 local distributors, 58 industries and the federal government.

JEFFERSON: Who governs the TVA?

PAUL: A 9-member board of directors, nominated by the President and confirmed by the Senate for five-year terms runs the agency. What do you think of this agency, Mr. President?

JEFFERSON: No special authority to perform these functions exists in the Constitution and no general welfare issues or national defense areas appear for Congress to insert itself. Therefore, the agency is unconstitutional.

PAUL: What should be the next steps?

JEFFERSON: The US should take action to sell agency properties to a private owner or if that is not possible, to turn them over to the State where they are located. If neither action is feasible, the federal government should demolish the structures, restore the land to how it was prior to erection of the facilities, and abolish the TVA.

PAUL: Thank you, Mr. President. Let us turn to a program in the Office of the President.

Segment 38 - Executive Office of the President: Office of National Drug Control Policy

Paul Jefko: To continue with our program, Mr. President, here is an agency, created by the Anti-Drug Abuse Act of 1988, requiring all federal contractors to provide a drug free workplace. The Violent Crime Control and Law Enforcement Act of 1994 added to the agency's mission by requiring a drug control policy and a system to measure performance on that policy.

President Jefferson: I am not familiar with this. What drugs?

PAUL: Mr. President, in your time, traveling caravans promoted what we refer to today as patent medicines, designed to cure fever, tooth ache, rheumatism, and women's problems. They contained opium, a painkiller but also a euphoric on the human brain giving the imbiber a sense of wellbeing. It

128

was addictive. There was no federal or state regulation and some did not realize the addictive properties it had.

JEFFERSON: What is the result of this addiction?

PAUL: An addict needs a continuous supply of the drug and will do anything to get it, including theft and in some cases murder. Once addicted, a person without it can experience tremors, cramps, muscle pain, chills, perspiration, rapid heartbeat, cold symptoms, vomiting, diarrhea, dizziness, and even suicidal thoughts. Realizing the danger, our government tried to stem its production, trade, and use. The drugs are marijuana or cannabis, cocaine and heroin.

JEFFERSON: You realize President Washington grew the cannabis plant at Mt. Vernon as a treatment for toothache.

PAUL: No, I did not. Today, he would go to prison.

JEFFERSON: For growing a plant on your own land?

PAUL: Yes, that is part of the drug laws currently in place. In 1997, Congress passed the Drug Free Communities Act providing funds to communities to eliminate drug abuse. Adding to these measures, the Media Campaign Act of 1998 established a national campaign to reduce drug abuse among America's Youth. The Reauthorization Act of 2006 expanded the agency's mission even though evidence showed the program was ineffective.

JEFFERSON: Why was it ineffective?

PAUL: Because of the drugs' addictive properties and its availability. Although most opium, cocaine, and cannabis are produced outside the US, the porous borders and huge demand make it almost impossible to reduce their use. Criminal gangs have used it to make outrageous profits. These gangs corrupt politicians and law enforcement.

JEFFERSON: What does this agency do to combat these problems?

PAUL: Don't laugh. It produces an annual National Drug Control Strategy report. It promotes policies such as Random Student Drug Testing. It provides funds to combat high intensity drug trafficking. It also funds communities to prevent youth drug abuse. And, as stated before, it promotes a National Youth Anti-Drug Media Campaign. Mr. President, what do you think of this organization?

JEFFERSON: Despite the national nature of this problem, it seems to be a problem better addressed by state and local governments. The Anti-Drug Abuse Act of 1988 is constitutional in requiring federal contractors to provide a drug free workplace if explicit in the contract. The Violent Crime Control and Law Enforcement Act of 1994 is constitutional only as it applies to the federal government. However, the Drug Free Communities Act of 1997 is unconstitutional as it is not specifically a power of Congress nor does it provide for national defense or general welfare of the nation. The Media Campaign Act of 1998 is unconstitutional for the same reason.

PAUL: What should we do?

JEFFERSON: Current grants for those programs shall not be renewed. Eliminate the Media campaign. However, the Office may remain as a clearinghouse for information between the President and Congress.

PAUL: Thank you Mr. President. Let us now turn to an agency in the Department of Education, the Office of Special Education and Rehabilitative Services.

Segment 39 - Department of Education: Office of Special Education and Rehabilitative Services

Paul Jefko: Mr. President, Congress established this agency in the 1979 Department of Education Organization Act. It consolidated a number of programs, such as the preference given to blind persons to operate concessions on federal property and to provide educational material for the blind. Earlier in 1969, the Congress had established the Helen Keller National Center to provide services to the deaf and blind.

President Jefferson: Why does the federal government provide services to the blind and deaf?

PAUL: The 1935 Social Security Act provided additional aid to the needy blind. Laws since then provide the same aid to the deaf. Later, The Individuals with Disabilities Education Act gave money to the States to educate disabled individuals. In 2004, Congress passed the Assistive Technology Act helping disabled persons obtain communication devices. That concludes the agency history.

JEFFERSON: What devices can help the deaf hear and the blind see?

PAUL: For example, hearing aids fit in the ear to increase the loudness of speech. (Shows a hearing aid) Devices such as large print books and Braille books help the blind to read. (Shows a Braille Book) To summarize, the main mission of the agency is to ensure the disabled have equal access to education, employment, and community living.

JEFFERSON: Interesting. The Federal government provides funds to the States to educate its handicapped. Why don't the States do this for themselves?

PAUL: To ensure conformity across the nation. Congress has determined that a blind person in Mississippi should have the same opportunities as a blind person in New York. Continuing...this agency has several subordinate offices. The Office of Special Education Programs provides funds to States, Universities and non-profit organizations to develop education programs for disabled children. The National Institute on Disability and Rehabilitation Research funds studies into inclusion, social integration, employment, and independent living of disabled individuals.

JEFFERSON: So, the object here is to ensure a person with a missing limb has the same opportunity as one who has no such handicap. No one in Congress saw that providing this aid takes the responsibility from the individual, his or her family, charities, and the States to provide this assistance?

PAUL: I am sure they did, but voting against such aid would give the Congressman the reputation of an uncaring person that could be used against him or her in the next election.

JEFFERSON: You do not think the people will elect a parsimonious Congressman?

PAUL: Not if he is portrayed as an Ebenezer Scrooge.

JEFFERSON: Who?

PAUL: Wait! Let me check with our staff. I'm sorry. The reference was to a fictional work published after your time about a greedy, uncaring old miser. It has retained its popularity even today because of the image it portrays.

JEFFERSON: A greedy miser is not the image of one who wishes to protect the taxpayers' purse. Please continue.

PAUL: The Rehabilitation Services Administration funds efforts to help individuals get employment and live independently. The agency also funds the American Printing House for the Blind, the National Institute for the Deaf, and Gallaudet University, a private non-profit college for the deaf. What do you think about this agency, Mr. President?

JEFFERSON: There is no special authority in the Constitution for federal involvement nor is there a national defense or general welfare issue. Therefore, this agency is unconstitutional. Abolish the agency and terminate existing contracts for the convenience of the government.

PAUL: Thank you, Mr. President. Let us now turn our attention to an independent agency of the US, the Export-Import Bank.

Segment 40 - Independent Agency: Export-Import Bank of the United States

Paul Jefko: Mr. President, Congress established this bank during the Great Depression to help reduce unemployment, raise incomes, increase demand for US goods and services and increase industrial production. The Bank was chartered in the District of Columbia to help finance exports and imports between the US and other Nations. It has served under various Departments until it became an independent agency in 1945.

President Jefferson: How does it increase demand for US goods and services?

PAUL: The bank originally provided loans to the Soviet Union, needing consumer goods, but with no spare work force to manufacture them. On the other hand, we had a surplus workforce willing to manufacture the goods for them. After World War II, loans were provided to European countries to pay for US goods they needed for postwar reconstruction. Since then, Congress has required the agency to provide loan guarantees and insurance rather than funds.

JEFFERSON: How does a loan guarantee and insurance work?

PAUL: A guarantee means the bank will repay the loan if the borrower defaults. Insurance acts the same way except the lender pays a fee to the government to guarantee the loan payment. The Bank is a government corporation chartered by Congress to fund sales commercial lenders are unable or unwilling to provide. It also provides subsidies to US companies facing unfair competition with foreign firms subsidized by their countries.

JEFFERSON: So, the government backs suspect loans. If the private market does not want to fund them, they must not be very good.

PAUL: The main purpose of the Bank is to create and sustain US jobs by financing exports to international customers. Many projects are too large for a private lender to handle. For example, the bank has financed fertilizer plants,

132

bridges, jet aircraft, and locomotives along with military aircraft and communications. Mr. President what do you think of this agency?

JEFFERSON: No specific authority exists for this function. It does not provide national defense nor does it provide for the general welfare.

PAUL: What should be the next steps?

JEFFERSON: Halt all loans not committed. Maintain all loans currently in place until liquidated. Then, abolish the agency.

PAUL: Thank you, Mr. President.

Segment 41 - Department of the Treasury

Paul Jefko: Mr. President, as you recall, the Congress established the Treasury Department in 1789 after which the first Secretary submitted reports to Congress that laid the foundation for the financial structure of the Nation. Besides financial responsibilities, the Department oversaw the Supervising Architect of the Treasury, the Coast Guard, and the Bureau of the Budget. It held these three functions until 1949, 1967, and 1939 respectively.

President Jefferson: Why were they taken away?

PAUL: Congress realized some federal government functions support all the Departments and chose to make them independent so they would not be beholden to one Department. That is the case with the Architect and the Budget Bureau. On the other hand, the Coast Guard had evolved from its traditional revenue cutter role to a public safety, navigation guardian, and law enforcement agency.

JEFFERSON: Since the navigable rivers and seacoasts are the responsibility of the federal government, that seems appropriate.

PAUL: Consequently, the Guard moved to the newly established Department of Transportation in 1967. But as the early nation grew, Congress created more duties for the Treasury Department. For example, in 1862, a Bureau of Internal Revenue was created to collect an income tax to pay for the Civil War. In 1863, Congress created the Comptroller of the Currency to issue paper money and supervise the banking system.

JEFFERSON: What happened to the Second Bank of the US established for this purpose?

133

PAUL: Because it incurred the wrath of President Andrew Jackson, Congress did not renew its charter.

JEFFERSON: Andrew Jackson became President? I didn't think he could even read.

PAUL: Actually, he strengthened your Democratic Republican Party and is considered one of the strongest Presidents in our history

JEFFERSON: Will wonders never cease. You said the Comptroller of the Currency created paper money? Did it become worthless like the Continental dollars issued by the Continental Congress?

PAUL: Actually not. The Greenbacks, as they were known, were used to pay the salaries of civil servants and soldiers during the Civil War. They were Treasury Notes promising to pay specie on demand. Issued under a Congressional order to borrow $250,000,000 on the credit of the US, they financed the war. The US began using the Notes to pay all its bills and people began to use them as currency in paying their own debts.

JEFFERSON: So, they were actually backed by the Federal Treasury and held their value.

PAUL: Yes. Although the nation had periodic economic panics, everything went well generally until 1931, when a banking crisis forced over 1,000 banks to close leaving depositors with no funds. In 1933, the incoming President declared a bank holiday, closing all banks. During the bank holiday, the Comptroller of the Currency examined the books of the remaining banks and allowed them to reopen, if solvent, or have their assets liquidated, if not.

JEFFERSON: What would happen to the depositors when the government liquidated their bank's assets?

PAUL: They lost their money. To avoid this problem in the future and to maintain public faith in the banking system, this function was made permanent and given to the Federal Deposit Insurance Corporation, insuring bank deposits in national banks up to a certain amount. In the 1980's, Savings and Loans institutions collapsed across the country, similar to the Banks in the 1930's.

JEFFERSON: So, the taxpayer now bails out a bank that is run poorly and defaults on its depositors?

PAUL: No. Each bank, to obtain the insurance and be able to advertise to depositors that they carry the insurance, must pay a regular premium to the Federal Deposit Insurance Corporation, which uses it to fund insolvent bank depositors. So...that sums up the history of the Department. The original Departmental mission was to manage government revenue. Currently, its agencies include the Internal Revenue Service, which collects all revenue from personal and corporate income, excise, estate, gift, and employment taxes.

JEFFERSON: What are employment taxes?

PAUL: They are taxes withheld from the wages of workers to fund the Social Security and Medicare program we discussed earlier. Another bureau, the Financial Management Service pays the governments bills, collects non-tax debts, and provides financial reports. The Alcohol and Tobacco Tax and Trade Bureau collects taxes on alcohol, tobacco, firearms, and ammunition. The Bureau of the Public Debt sells Treasury securities.

JEFFERSON: I know we discussed this agency earlier. But, why do we have a separate tax agency for alcohol, tobacco etc.

PAUL: It enforced the Volstead Act, in the 1920's prohibiting the production, sale, and distribution of alcoholic beverages.

JEFFERSON: How was that constitutional?

PAUL: The 18th Amendment gave Congress the authority.

JEFFERSON: The people of the US amended the Constitution to restrict their freedom to drink wine or beer?

PAUL: Well, it did not prohibit the drinking or possession. Just the manufacture, transport, or sale. In any event, the Amendment was repealed by the 21st Amendment. So, we can all drink again in the US. Moving on...the Federal Financing Bank gives loans to government agencies for expenses not covered by appropriations. The US Mint produces, sells, and protects the coinage and financial assets of the nation.

JEFFERSON: The Federal Financing Bank loans money to government agencies? Whatever for?

PAUL: A number of federal agencies have authority to issue bonds to the public. What has happened is the agencies issuing bonds compete with each other for the interest rate. If the government issues too many bonds at one time, the interest rates on all will increase and add further debt to the US Treasury. The Federal Financing Bank buys these securities and reissues them in a manner that will not flood the market.

JEFFERSON: That seems wise.

PAUL: Also, other agencies need to make capital improvements but do not receive appropriations from Congress. The US Postal Service is financed strictly by stamp sales. Fees from other government agencies fund the General Services Administration. They both borrow from the bank to fund their capital improvements and pay back the bank from stamp sales or fees respectively. Continuing...The Bureau of Engraving and Printing prints Federal Reserve Notes, passports, homeland security materials, military identification cards, and Naturalization Certificates.

JEFFERSON: What is a Federal Reserve Note?

PAUL: It is the successor to the Greenbacks I mentioned before. They serve as legal tender for all debts and are backed by the full faith and credit of the US government. We are almost finished. The Office of the Comptroller of the Currency and the Office of Thrift Supervision we discussed earlier. The Financial Crimes Enforcement Network prevents money laundering and terrorist financing and the Office of Foreign Asset Control enforces economic sanctions on hostile states, nationals, and organizations.

JEFFERSON: Money laundering?

PAUL: Money made in illegal enterprises is put into legitimate businesses to disguise its origin.... That concludes the Treasury organization. We'll look into its agencies later.

JEFFERSON: I look forward to it

PAUL: This concludes the 6th program in this series. We will return next week for another discussion with President Jefferson. On behalf of President Jefferson, I wish you a good evening.

Program # 7

Paul Jefko: Good evening, welcome to part 7 of our program: 'They Are Here', where we continue our discussion with President Thomas Jefferson on the contemporary US government. Tonight, we begin our discussion with on the Department of State with the first Secretary of State.

Segment 42 - Department of State

Paul Jefko: But, before we look at State, many people may not know it, but your personal library was the basis for the Library of Congress. Can you tell our viewers how that came about, Mr. President?

President Jefferson: Not quite as you intimate, but I did have a hand in it. The Library was established in 1800 when President Adams signed the act of Congress and ordered books from London for the use of the Congress. Two years later, I signed a bill that allowed the hiring of a librarian. But during the War of 1812, the British burned the Capitol and its library. I offered my personal book collection to replace that which had been destroyed and Congress accepted.

PAUL: For those of us who have visited or used the resources of the Library, we are grateful for your hand in establishing this world class library. Mr. President, as you recall, Congress created the Department of Foreign Affairs, later the Department of State in 1789. Besides handling foreign affairs, its responsibilities included establishing a mint to coin money, overseeing the Great Seal of the United States and conducting the decennial Census. During the 19th century, the mint and the census were transferred to other agencies.

JEFFERSON: Yes, at one point, the State Department did things not specifically related to foreign affairs.

PAUL: These days, the Department strictly focuses on foreign policy and its implementation. Some policies included the purchase of Alaska from Russia in 1867. Other examples included the Bretton Woods Conference leading to the establishment of the United Nations. The Marshall Plan reconstructed Europe after World War II. After the Vietnam War, détente with the Soviet Union and outreach to Communist China became our diplomatic goals.

JEFFERSON: What is the United Nations?

PAUL: The United Nations or UN was established after World War II to encourage international cooperation and world peace. Almost every sovereign nation is a member of the General Assembly. A Security Council, made up of the largest countries, makes decisions to ensure peace, including armed intervention. Moving on...The Department's organization consists of Bureaus organized by geographical location and by function.

JEFFERSON: Who is on this Security Council?

PAUL: It has permanent members China, France, Russia, United Kingdom, and United States and ten non-permanent members elected by the General Assembly to serve a two-year term. Returning to the State Department...Its geographic bureaus include: European and Eurasian Affairs, Western Hemisphere, African Affairs, East Asian and Pacific Affairs, Near Eastern Affairs, and South and Central Asian Affairs.

JEFFERSON: How many nations are there in the world?

PAUL: 193 nations. (Shows a map of the world) Other State department bureaus deal with special issues. The Bureau of Overseas Building Operations manages the embassies, consulates and missions. The Bureau of Diplomatic Security protects personnel, information, and property at overseas posts. The Office of the Chief of Protocol assists the President on diplomacy etiquette. The Office of Foreign Missions provides services for foreign diplomats, monitors their activities in this country, and assures their treatment is in line with ours in their country.

JEFFERSON: Are we assuming foreign diplomats spy on our activities?

PAUL: Well, some do, but that is not the purpose of the Office of Foreign Missions. The Office ensures a foreign diplomat is treated as well as or as poorly as our diplomats to his or her country. But mostly, the Office aids foreign diplomats in administrative requirements such as licensing their motor vehicles, taxation, customs, property, and travel. Continuing with the organization...The Bureau of Consular Affairs issues passports.

JEFFERSON: Excuse me. What you are saying is if France does not exempt our ambassador from taxation, then we do not exempt France's ambassador to the US?

PAUL: Not necessarily. Reciprocal agreements between nations set down the privileges of the embassy staff. This office will enforce them here and strive to enforce them in the reciprocating country. Moving on...The Bureau of International Narcotics and Law Enforcement Affairs helps combat the worldwide illegal drug trade. The Office to Monitor and Combat Trafficking in

Persons coordinates US actions in the international struggle against slavery, sexual exploitation, and involuntary labor. The Bureau of Educational and Cultural Affairs brings together students and professionals to build better relationships between countries.

JEFFERSON: Sexual exploitation?

PAUL: Yes. Individuals will entice a vulnerable girl from a poor country to a rich country with the promise of a job. When she arrives in the rich country, she finds she is now a prostitute whose wages go to the person who brought her over.

JEFFERSON: Why doesn't she seek the protection of the law?

PAUL: In many cases, she is illegally in the country and will be jailed or deported if she announced her plight. Sometimes, she is murdered to prevent her going to the police.

JEFFERSON: Is there much of this going on?

PAUL: Human trafficking to include slavery, sexual exploitation and involuntary labor generates $32 billion a year worldwide.

JEFFERSON: (Staring and silent).

PAUL: Moving on...The Bureau of International Information is the propaganda arm of the US. The Bureau of Population, Refugees and Migration helps refugees around the world. The Bureau of Economic, Energy and Business Affairs promotes US economic interests internationally. The Bureau of Oceans and International Environmental and Scientific Affairs integrates these matters into US foreign policy.

JEFFERSON: Where do these refugees come from?

PAUL: They may be escaping a war in a foreign country or escaping political persecution.

JEFFERSON: Why and how do we get involved in other countries' affairs?

PAUL: Many organizations assisting the refugees are charitable groups. The US government provides funds to them for this purpose. Continuing...the Bureau of Verification, Compliance and Implementation ensures compliance with arms agreements. The Bureau of Democracy, Human Rights and Labor generates reports on human rights practices in the world.

JEFFERSON: Why do we care about internal practices of other countries?

PAUL: Did you not write in the Declaration that among these rights are 'life, liberty, and the pursuit of happiness"?

JEFFERSON: I am not talking about human rights. I am talking about our interference in the affairs of other sovereign nations. Why do we care if an Arabian satrap has a harem of 1000 women? Or if he imprisons those who disagree with his rule? If those who are oppressed wish to free themselves, that is their business, not ours. As long as it does not affect our security, let us leave them alone as we wish to be left alone.

PAUL: Because modern society sees certain behaviors as repugnant. That is why we have international organizations to develop and enforce certain values.

JEFFERSON: Let me say something first. State Department functions are only constitutional if they develop or implement treaties approved by the Senate, help regulate commerce with foreign nations or protect federal property overseas.

PAUL: That is a reasonable set of criteria. We will recall it as we review the State Department agencies later. Let us now turn to a major agency of the federal government that provides funds for its operations.

Segment 43 – Department of the Treasury: Internal Revenue Service

Paul Jefko: Congress established the Office of Commissioner of Internal Revenue under the Revenue Act of 1862 to collect a temporary income tax to support the Civil War. Congress repealed the tax in 1872 but reenacted it in 1894. However, the Supreme Court declared it unconstitutional as the Constitution prohibits a direct tax. Subsequently, the Sixteenth Amendment to the Constitution, adopted in 1913, states: "The Congress shall have power to lay and collect taxes on incomes, from whatever source derived, without apportionment among the several States, and without regard to any census or enumeration."

President Jefferson: Why weren't the Revenue Acts of 1862 and 1872 also declared unconstitutional?

PAUL: In Springer vs. US, the court held the writings of James Madison

140

and Alexander Hamilton asserting direct taxes are only "capitation or poll taxes and taxes on lands and buildings, and general assessments, whether on the whole property of individuals or on their whole real or personal estate. All else must, of necessity, be considered as indirect taxes." Since a tax on income is not on the whole estate but only a part, it is an indirect tax.

JEFFERSON: How then did the court call the 1894 Tax Act unconstitutional? Did that Act prescribe a different type of income tax?

PAUL: The later court ignored the earlier Springer decision and determined any tax on property was a direct tax. Therefore, income from property such as rent or sales was not subject to taxation unless apportioned by the federal government. The decision, of course became moot after the 16th Amendment was passed. After its ratification, the first income tax returns were required in 1913.

JEFFERSON: What is a tax return?

PAUL: Everyone in the US who earned a certain income level had to submit a form annually showing his or her income, the appropriate taxes due and include payment (Shows a copy of a Form 1040).

JEFFERSON: You mean I have to list all my income for the year and submit it to the federal government? That is not their business; that is my private business.

PAUL: Not according to the tax acts passed since the 16th Amendment…Continuing…the IRS Restructuring and Reform Act of 1998 organized the IRS around customer groups. That covers the history. Let us look at the mission.

JEFFERSON: What do you mean customer groups?

PAUL: The Internal Revenue Service affects four main customers. Wage and Investment customers receive income primarily from wages or investments. Members of the Small Business and Professional group earn their living in retail or services. Corporations and large businesses constitute the third group. And organizations who generate income but are Tax Exempt because they provide a public service or are government entities created by states or local governments comprise the fourth group.

JEFFERSON: I do not understand the last group. Please explain.

PAUL: For example, a State may want to build a toll road and it establishes an agency to issue bonds to fund the construction to be paid back from the tolls on the road. That agency may earn income from that road but it may be exempt from federal taxes because it serves a public not a private purpose. What do you think of this agency, Mr. President?

JEFFERSON: It is definitely constitutional as an extension of the express power to lay and collect taxes including the XVI Amendment on income taxes.

PAUL: Thank you Mr. President. We will now review the organization and functions of a major Army agency.

Segment 44 – Department of Defense: US Army Corps of Engineers

Paul Jefko: As you recall, Mr. President, the Continental Congress established the Army Corps of Engineers in June 1775 to fortify Boston. Constitutionally, you established the Corps in 1802. Prior to the War of 1812, the Corps fortified New York Harbor. The Corps was heavily involved in mapping and construction during the Mexican, Civil and World Wars.

President Jefferson: I remember I sent Corps officers to survey the Arkansas and Red Rivers.

PAUL: They have always been involved in US water resources. In 1863, the Corps was tasked to conduct a Great Lakes Survey. During the Civil War, the Corps built bridges, forts, and batteries, constructed roads, and destroyed enemy supply lines. Prior to World War II, the Corps received the military construction mission previously held by the Army Quartermaster Corps. The 1936 Flood Control Act authorized the Corps to conduct flood control projects.

JEFFERSON: Why? Was there a national flooding problem?

PAUL: Serious floods in the Mississippi and Ohio Rivers around that time caused severe property damage, but the impetus for the projects was to provide employment during the Great Depression. The agency later became the lead federal agency for flood control, hydropower, and recreation. It had earlier been given the mission of improving navigation on the Mississippi and Ohio Rivers.

JEFFERSON: So, the flooding was nationwide?

PAUL: Not really. Most flooding was in the Ohio River basin. Returning to its mission...during the Cold War, the Corps managed construction projects for America's allies overseas. Since 1980, the Corps assisted the EPA in its Superfund program. That is the basic history. The Corps has over 38,000 civilian and military staff and is the world's largest public engineering, design and construction agency.

JEFFERSON: What is the Superfund program?

PAUL: A law giving the Environmental Protection agency the authority to compel cleanup of land contaminated with hazardous substances. Summing up the Corps' mission today, they plan, design, build, and operate navigation locks and dams, flood control structures, beach nourishment and navigation dredging. They also design and construct military facilities for the Army, Army Reserve, Air Force, Air Force Reserve and other Defense and federal agencies.

JEFFERSON: So, they are the main building arm of the federal government.

PAUL: It seems that way. They also design and construct projects for coastal protection, flood protection, hydropower, ports, and water supply.

JEFFERSON: To me, their duties are for national defense and to assist trade, but several are dubious.

PAUL: But there's more. They also clean up hazardous waste on former military installations and reestablish wetlands. Their current projects include Everglades Restoration, Superfund Cleanup and Military Base Realignment and Closure. The Corps maintains 694 dams and 75 hydroelectric facilities and supports disaster relief through preparedness and emergency response. They also provide advice and support to front line commanders during wartime.

JEFFERSON: I am anxious to give you my opinions on these issues.

PAUL: Here is your chance. What do you think of this agency, Mr. President?

JEFFERSON: All the work done for the Army is constitutional if not longer than a 2-year period. None of the work for the Air Force is constitutional because the Air Force is not constitutional. Work for other federal agencies is constitutional if the agency's work is constitutional. All their work for foreign governments is constitutional if part of a Senate approved treaty. All their navigation work including operating locks and dams, dredging, and port improvement is constitutional as it affects interstate trade. However, none of their work in flood control, hydropower, recreation, beach nourishment, coastal protection, water supply, and disaster relief is constitutional, as the Constitution does not authorize the missions. Neither is it a national defense or general welfare issue.

PAUL: What should be the next steps for this agency?

JEFFERSON: Review all work in support of the Army and terminate those projects lasting longer than two years. All work for the Air Force will be terminated. Terminate all work for unconstitutional federal agencies or programs. All work for foreign governments not part of a treaty will be terminated. Terminate all civil projects not directly involved in navigation. All programs supporting disaster relief will be terminated.

PAUL: What about all the structures the Corps operates for the projects you terminated?

JEFFERSON: Offer them to the States or local governments as appropriate. Perhaps the private marketplace would care to operate them. If no takers arise, demolish them and return the area to its natural state.

PAUL: Thank you, Mr. President. Let's consider another Defense Agency.

Segment 45 - Department of Defense: National Reconnaissance Office

Paul Jefko: Mr. President, another Department of Defense agency is the National Reconnaissance Office established in 1961 to create an orbiting satellite system over the Soviet Union to monitor its activities. The agency was secret until 1992 when the Cold War ended and a new defense strategy had to be developed. One is to monitor terrorist camps. It was a major tool in the hunt for Osama Bin Laden.

President Jefferson: Who was he?

PAUL: If you recall our discussion of the attack on 9/11, Bin Laden was the founder and leader of Al Qaeda, a global militant Islamic terrorist organization, which attacked New York City. US forces tracked him down and killed him ten years later. Continuing...the agency mission is to design, build, and operate US spy satellites.

JEFFERSON: We discussed this earlier. The satellites see things on the earth in detail and send pictures by radio to the ground where they are analyzed to help protect our national security. Correct?

PAUL: Right on target, sir. (Shows photo of earth from satellite.) Although its operations are classified, its launches are public. It has stations on the ground receiving information from satellites and provides it to the requesting agency.

What do you say about this agency?

JEFFERSON: Very easy. Providing for common defense makes it constitutional.

PAUL: Thank you, Mr. President. We'll take a small commercial break before discussing nuclear security.

Commercial Break

Segment 46 – Department of Energy: National Nuclear Security Administration

Paul Jefko: In the 1940's and 1950's, two spy scandals pointed to the need for special security for our nuclear program. A husband and wife team, Julius and Ethel Rosenberg, provided secrets about the US atomic bomb project to our enemy, the Soviet Union. Later, in 1999, the US indicted a scientist named Wen Ho Lee for providing nuclear weapons secrets to China. At the time, the Department of Energy produced all nuclear weapons.

President Jefferson: Why did not the Department of Defense control the weapons?

PAUL: Well, Defense does control the weapons. However, the Energy Department produces them. Studies have indicated problems in the Department. A report after the Wen Ho Lee episode said the Department was a cynical organization with a disregard for authority and a pattern of denial compromising national security. Classified materials were left unattended, nuclear materials were poorly tracked and the Department was hostile to security issues.

JEFFERSON: So, the report caused the establishment of this agency?

PAUL: Yes. The organization has six offices. Defense Programs maintains nuclear warheads. Nuclear Nonproliferation works with former Soviet Union republics to safeguard nuclear weapons and fuel under their control. Naval Reactors provides the nuclear propulsion plants for Navy vessels. Emergency Operations has teams to minimize radiological outbreaks here or overseas. Infrastructure and Environment upgrades, rebuilds, and cleans up NNSA facilities and Nuclear Security protects personnel, facilities, nuclear weapons, and government information from threats.

JEFFERSON: Tell me about these nuclear warheads.

145

PAUL: I told you earlier about the atomic bomb and its operation. Various ways exist to transport the bomb to where you want it to explode. We can drop it from an aircraft as we did over Japan in WW 2. Nowadays, we place it on top of a rocket and fire it to its target. Since it is the head of the rocket, it is called the warhead. (Shows picture of ICBM taking off) Continuing…in fulfilling its missions, the agency manages 11 laboratories. They include the Naval Reactors Facilities in Idaho, Pittsburgh and Schenectady manufacturing nuclear propulsion systems for the Navy; Los Alamos National Laboratory, a key research center for nuclear weapons; Sandia National Laboratories assembling and dismantling nuclear warheads; the Kansas City Plant producing non-nuclear components for nuclear warheads; the Y-12 National Security Complex producing uranium for warheads and Savannah River complex providing nuclear material for warheads.

JEFFERSON: How is uranium produced for the warheads?

PAUL: Less than 1% of pure uranium can be used for bombs. The first step is to take rough uranium ore and extract the uranium. Then the bomb material, U235, is extracted from the pure uranium with centrifuges. If that clears up your understanding, what do you think of this agency?

JEFFERSON: It is constitutional for general defense of the nation.

PAUL: Thank you, Mr. President. Let us now look at an agency of the Transportation Department.

Segment 47 – Department of Transportation: Federal Transit Administration

Paul Jefko: Mr. President, during the 1950's, Congress passed a law allowing railroads to discontinue passenger service if they wished. Many railroads, who found passenger service not cost effective, discontinued it on some intercity rail lines but mostly on commuter rail lines within cities. Consequently, the 1961 Omnibus Housing Act funded demonstration projects to solve urban transportation problems.

President Jefferson: I believe we discussed this before. Why did the federal government have authority to force a railroad to provide transportation where it did not want to?

PAUL: In the late 19th century, western farmers were convinced railroads abused their privileges. In areas served by one railroad, the company charged what it wished knowing the farmer and other customers had no alternative.

146

Congress created the Interstate Commerce Commission to regulate the railroads, including the authority to determine who provided service over what lines.

JEFFERSON: The Commission had authority only over railroads crossing state boundaries, correct?

PAUL: No. The Supreme Court has said it was impracticable to define intrastate as distinct from interstate for railroads crossing state lines. Traffic and cargo used the same lines, equipment and employees for interstate or intrastate transactions. Therefore, all rail traffic was under control of the federal government's regulatory authority. Later, authority was granted to approve railroad company mergers, construction of new lines and abandonment of old lines.

JEFFERSON: Railroads then have ceased to be private businesses.

PAUL: Yes, that is a valid statement. It had a dramatic effect. With the advent of the air industry and the interstate highway system, the rail passenger business became less profitable and many railroads wanted to get out of the business and concentrate on freight only. One of the costlier rail lines transported persons each day from their homes to the city for work.

JEFFERSON: Why was passenger traffic less profitable?

PAUL: With the rise of the automobile, people drove themselves, because it was cheaper. Later, air travel was quicker. That particularly affected short, commuter lines, which attracted fewer customers as workers began to drive themselves to work. In 1962, President Kennedy asked Congress for federal funds for mass transportation. Congress analyzed the problem and, based on President Kennedy's request, passed the Urban Mass Transportation Act of 1964 creating the Urban Mass Transportation Administration.

JEFFERSON: How widespread are these commuter lines?

PAUL: Almost every major city in the US has one or more lines. For example, the New York City subway system serves over 8 million passengers a week. The mission of the Federal Transit Administration is to provide grants and technical advice to local public transit systems. These systems can be buses, subways, light rail, commuter rail, monorail, passenger ferries, trolleys, inclined railways and people movers. Mr. President, what do you think of this agency?

JEFFERSON: Since no specific authority exists in the Constitution for these programs and no general welfare issue arises, the agency is unconstitutional.

147

PAUL: What should the Congress do next?

JEFFERSON: Halt all grants to States and abolish the agency.

PAUL: Thank you, Mr. President. We will now move to a major health Department.

Segment 48 – Department of Health and Human Services: Center for Disease Control and Prevention

Paul Jefko: During World War II, malaria was a big problem for our troops in the South Pacific. The Army established the Malaria Control in War Areas Program to help mitigate the problem. After the war, that group became the Communicable Diseases Center, reporting to the US Public Health Service with the mission to control and eradicate malaria in the US. Their program to spray DDT in 6.5 million homes in mosquito-plagued areas eliminated the risk.

President Jefferson: What do mosquitos have to do with malaria?

PAUL: Some background first. Microscopic organisms cause many diseases by entering the body via your mouth, nose, ears etc. But sometimes they come in through your skin if an agent can penetrate it. The mosquito, as you know, 'bites' your skin, leaving an itchy red welt. What it actually does is use a tubular proboscis to penetrate your skin and suck out blood for its nourishment. (Shows a drawing of a mosquito on human skin)

JEFFERSON: I am familiar with the mosquito and its habits.

PAUL: Sorry. But you may not know that, while the mosquito sucks out your blood it can transmit disease microorganisms under your skin. One of these mosquitoes, the Anopheles type carries the protozoan causing malaria. The cinchona bark you are familiar with keeps the protozoan under control but does not eliminate it. If you stop taking the quinine from the cinchona tree, you will have further bouts of malaria. Since the source is the mosquito, science developed DDT, Dichlorodiphenyltrichloroethane, effective in killing all sorts of insects.

JEFFERSON: How is DDT used?

PAUL: When sprayed on the walls of homes where mosquitoes thrive and on the mosquito nets used to cover sleeping areas, it kills them. Because of DDT, no malaria occurs in the US.

JEFFERSON: I have never had a malaria attack, but I know General Washington and James Monroe had attacks.

PAUL: After this success, the Center developed a vaccine against influenza. In 1969, the Center built a biocontainment laboratory to protect scientists working with deadly microorganisms. By 1977, smallpox was eradicated globally. We eliminated polio from the Western Hemisphere in 1994. Rubella was conquered in the US in 2005.

JEFFERSON: What is a vaccine?

PAUL: Again, more background. The human immune system consists of various structures, agents and processes protecting against disease. If you come down with smallpox, for example, the body summons these agents, normally occurring in the bloodstream to attack the invasive agent causing the disease. Eventually, the body either defeats the invader or succumbs to it and dies.

JEFFERSON: But if you become ill with smallpox and survive, you will not become ill with it again, am I right?

PAUL: Yes, because the body has developed a defense protecting it in the future from similar attacks. The smallpox inoculation you are familiar with provides the body a mild form of the disease it can easily defeat but the agents defeating the disease remain to protect the body when a real infection arises. The Center has developed many vaccines to prevent diseases deadly in your time.

JEFFERSON: Such as?

PAUL: Chickenpox, Diphtheria, Influenza, Measles, Mumps, Whooping Cough, Polio, Rabies, Tetanus, to name a few. The Center's mission is to protect public health and safety by controlling and preventing disease, injury and disability. The Center focuses on infectious diseases, food borne illnesses, environmental health, occupational safety and health, health promotion and injury prevention. Consequently, it constantly monitors infections disease outbreaks, bioterrorism and environmental hazards. What do you think about this agency?

JEFFERSON: It is constitutional as it provides for the general welfare. However, the user should repay the taxpayer for all the vaccines and drugs developed with taxpayer dollars.

PAUL: Thank you, Mr. President. Our next item is an agency that began before your administration.

Segment 49 - Department of Homeland Security: United States Coast Guard

Paul Jefko: As you recall, Mr. President, Congress established the US Revenue Cutter Service in 1790 to collect import duties and prevent smuggling. Since there was no navy until 1798, the Cutter Service had the only ships protecting the US coast. After creating the Navy, Congress passed a law placing the Cutter Service under the Navy during wartime. On that basis, the Cutter Service served in the War of 1812, the Mexican-American War and the Civil War.

President Jefferson: Yes, unfortunately during the war of 1812, the Navy did not have enough ships to defend our country.

PAUL: In 1915, Congress merged the Cutter Service with the US Lifesaving Service and renamed it the Coast Guard. In 1939, the Coast Guard was assigned the Lighthouse Service and in 1946, Congress added the Bureau of Marine Inspection and Navigation. It later moved from the Treasury to the new Department of Transportation. Over time, the Guard was assigned various duties including rescuing Cuban refugees fleeing from Communist Cuba, and interdicting drug shipments.

JEFFERSON: What was the Lifesaving Service?

PAUL: The Service began in 1848 to help sailors and merchant seamen whose ships had run aground or were in danger of sinking. Moving on...today, the Guard also cleans up oil spills in water and enforces the Clean Water Act. After 9/11, the Guard was placed under the Department of Homeland Security.

JEFFERSON: The Clean Water Act?

PAUL: Yes, the Act prohibits the dumping of toxic substances into US navigable waters. As for the Guard's organization, it has a slew of missions. The Guard provides port, waterway and coastal security to thwart terrorist attacks. It maintains defense readiness to support naval operations, intercepts illegal immigrants attempting to reach the US, provides search and rescue operations on the sea to those in distress and provides and maintains navigation aids to ensure proper traffic flow.

JEFFERSON: So, the Guard is part of the national defense. Why then is it not placed under the Navy?

PAUL: I think the Navy projects its military might in the blue water of the oceans and the Coast Guard works on the brown water of the coast. Also, much of the Guard's mission is non-defense since it, for example, enforces international fishing laws, provides ice breaking services to promote navigation and commerce, sets safety standards and inspects vessels, responds to oil and chemical spills and prevents illegal dumping and importing invasive plant and animal species.

JEFFERSON: So, its main role is to regulate interstate and international maritime trade.

PAUL: Correct, but it also intercepts sea and air transport of illegal drugs to the US. What do you think about this agency, Mr. President?

JEFFERSON: All of the functions except drug interdiction are constitutional, in my opinion. Illegal drug interdiction is a State issue not authorized by the federal constitution.

PAUL: What should be the next steps Congress takes?

JEFFERSON: Eliminate illegal drug interdiction from the federal agenda and pass legislation to establish user fees for the navigation services provided instead of taxing the populace.

PAUL: Thank you, Mr. President. We will now look at another agency of Homeland Security.

Segment 50 - Department of Homeland Security: US Customs and Border Protection

Paul Jefko: Mr. President, the Tariff Act of 1789, I am sure you are familiar with, authorized the collection of duties and taxes on imports as a revenue source for the new federal government. Congress created The Customs Service to collect these duties. In an unrelated development, various states had passed immigration laws after the Civil War. To consolidate these actions under federal government authority, the Immigration Act of 1891 set up a Superintendent of Immigration in the Treasury Department to admit, process or reject immigrants.

President Jefferson: Were the States not doing a good job that the federal government had to step in?

PAUL: Not that so much. The Supreme Court in 1875 declared a State could not pass laws on immigration because the Constitution provides this specifically to the federal government. To fill this vacuum, laws were passed by

Congress to handle this. Later, immigration control moved in 1903 to the new Department of Commerce and Labor.

JEFFERSON: Why Commerce and Labor?

PAUL: Because immigration provided a key labor source for American industry. However, there were limits as Congress passed laws early in the 20th century to limit immigration. For example, a quota system was established in 1921 to limit immigration. In 1924, Congress created the Border Patrol in the Department of Labor to prevent illegal immigrants entering the US. The Border Patrol eventually became the Immigration and Naturalization Service.

JEFFERSON: Why did the Congress limit immigration?

PAUL: There was prejudice against certain ethnic groups. Although companies brought Chinese workers here in the 19th century to construct railroads, specifically in the West, the inhabitants of that area wanted to ship them back when the work was done. The Protestant population considered Irish and German Catholic immigrants who came here in the mid-19th century to work in the new textile mills or to become farmers in the mid-west undesirable.

JEFFERSON: Why Irish immigrants?
PAUL: Over 1 million died due to a potato famine while others, specifically the young, left for the US. In the late 19th and early 20th century, immigrants from eastern and southern Europe were said to carry diseases, were also Catholic, and spoke quite different languages. Congress limited immigration on a proportional basis to groups already here. For example, if 1 percent of the US population in 1920 was Polish, only 1% of those allowed to immigrate to the US in any year from Poland would be 1%.

JEFFERSON: Well, since the vast percentage of the US population came from the British Isles, then the vast majority of new immigrants had to come from there. Was there a large immigration from Britain?

PAUL: No, because there was not a great desire in Britain for immigration to the US. So, the ones who wanted to immigrate could not, and the ones that could were not interested. In 1940, the Immigration and Naturalization service was transferred to Justice from Labor. In 2003, the non-tax collection aspects of the US Custom Service and the enforcement arm of the Immigration and Naturalization Service were combined and placed under the new Department of Homeland Security. That covers the history of this agency. To summarize its organization, it employs 45,600 federal agents and officers that prevent terrorists, weapons, illegal drugs and animals and diseased plants from entering the US and protects American businesses from intellectual property theft.

JEFFERSON: Intellectual Property Theft?

PAUL: Companies have secrets enabling them to exploit their inventions. We have laws in this country to prevent a person from stealing another person's patented or trademarked ideas. In some overseas areas, counterfeit products are produced carrying a company name but are not made by that company. What do you think of this agency?

JEFFERSON: Almost everything is constitutional as part of general defense, specific power of naturalization and protection of writings and discoveries. However, the stopping of illegal drugs is not a defense issue or for the general welfare, nor is it a specific power authorized to the federal government. That is a State issue.

PAUL: What should the US government do next?

JEFFERSON: Cease operations dealing with drug interdiction.

PAUL: Thank you Mr. President. We will now review the Missile Defense Agency.

Segment 51 – Department of Defense: Missile Defense Agency

Paul Jefko: Mr. President, this agency was created in 1984 as the Strategic Defense Initiative Organization to create a space-based shield against nuclear missile attack. By 1987, it was tasked with including a ground-based weapons system. After the Cold War ended, the agency was refocused on defending against short-range missile attack, stressing theater defense rather than North American defense.

President Jefferson: Explain these nuclear missiles.

PAUL: A missile is a large rocket with a system guiding it from the ground to its destination, and a warhead with a nuclear bomb that can destroy a city. (Shows video of ICBM at takeoff) Since the US and the Soviet Union had many of these missiles, the idea of a shield against them was popular. Since the Cold War ended, the name of the agency changed to the Ballistic Missile Defense Organization.

JEFFERSON: So, we develop rockets to kill our enemy that the enemy duplicates. Then we have to develop a defense against them. And it goes on and on.

PAUL: Isn't that the history of the world? Anyway, in 2002, the agency name was changed to its current one with a new mission to defend the US, its forces overseas, its friends and allies against ballistic missiles of all ranges at all flight phases: boost, ascent, midcourse and terminal.

JEFFERSON: So, the US is fully protected from missile attack?

PAUL: That is hard to tell, since all this is classified. What should we do with this agency?

JEFFERSON: Although I see its necessity, I doubt its effectiveness. But, I must conclude the agency to be constitutional as it provides defense of the country.

PAUL: Thank you, Mr. President. We will move back to the Department of Labor and its biggest agency.

Segment 52 – Department of Labor: Employment and Training Administration

Paul Jefko: Mr. President, Congress established this agency in 1975 to promote job training and development. In 1981, the Office of Trade Adjustment Assistance moved to the agency.

President Jefferson: Didn't we discuss this before?

PAUL: Yes, as part of our discussion on the Department of Labor. The agency provides job training, employment and labor information and income maintenance to the States and their local governments.

JEFFERSON: The federal government finds jobs for people?

PAUL: Yes, as employment was determined to be a national issue. Typically, $8 Billion in grants go to States and local governments for this purpose.

JEFFERSON: None of these functions is constitutional as the Constitution does not specifically delineate them nor are they in support of general defense or general welfare. They only benefit the unemployed.

PAUL: What should we do with this agency?

JEFFERSON: Abolish it and save the taxpayer the $8 Billion.

PAUL: Thank you, Mr. President. Back to Defense, sir.

Segment 53 – Department of Defense: Defense Information Systems Agency

Paul Jefko: Congress established the Defense Communication Agency in 1960 to implement the Automatic Voice Network, the Automatic Digital Network and the Automatic Secure Voice Communications Network. Congress later tasked it with developing the satellite communication network for DOD. In 1971, it was given the mission of developing the Emergency Communications Network for the WMCCS.

President Jefferson: What are these networks? Wimics?

PAUL: These were military communication systems. The Voice Network allowed military voice communication, the Digital Network sent information and the third network encrypted communication. For example, the agency set up systems allowing Special Military Forces to call in air strikes from horseback in Afghanistan. In 2003, the President received voice, video and data communication capability in real time.

JEFFERSON: What is real time?
 PAUL: The President can talk with any world leader on a screen face to face. He can send documents and talk directly with no delay, or in 'real time'. The agency's offices include Strategic Planning, which handles spectrum issues and spectrum technologies, Network Services to support the products and services of the agency…

JEFFERSON: I know what a spectrum is. What does this have to do with communication?

PAUL: You are thinking of one part of the electromagnetic spectrum, the visible light color spectrum. (Shows a chart of the electromagnetic spectrum) Energy vibrates according to a specific frequency of cycles per second. Our eyes are able to detect energy vibrating at 430 to 790 trillion cycles per second, visible light. Radio, which we discussed before, vibrates at slower frequencies at the billions of cycles per second. Obviously, someone has to dole out portions of the spectrum to prevent transmitter interfering with another.

JEFFERSON: Transmitter interfering?

PAUL: Yes. Two people talking at the same frequency is like trying to understand someone in a room full of shouting people. Each transmitter is provided a specific frequency so that does not occur. Although the Federal Communication Commission, which we will discuss later, has the ultimate authority on this, encrypted communications problems have cropped up. That's what this agency does.

JEFFERSON: Are you saying our ears, like our eyes, also detect parts of the spectrum.

PAUL: Sound vibrations are a good example of the workings of the electromagnetic spectrum. However, sound differs. The electromagnetic spectrum does not depend on the environment it operates in. Radio waves and light waves, unlike sound waves, can be sent in a vacuum. They do not require a medium to transfer their energy. Sound requires a medium, that is, air, to transmit itself.

JEFFERSON: Really! Why?

PAUL: Because sound is the result of the disturbance of molecules. No molecules exist in a vacuum to be disturbed. Your ears are sensitive to molecular vibrations like the vibrations of a tuning fork. But the tuning fork is a good example of how all energy is transmitted. What is your opinion?

JEFFERSON: Since it provides communications for the defense of the nation, its work is constitutional as long as the agency it supports is constitutional. Remember that, in my opinion, the Air Force as a separate military organization is unconstitutional. Therefore, any work for that department is also unconstitutional.

PAUL: Thank you, Mr. President. It is that time again. We have concluded the 7th program in this series. President Jefferson will return next week for more discussion on our government. On behalf of President Jefferson, I wish you a good night.

Program # 8

Paul Jefko: Good evening, ladies and gentlemen and welcome to part 8 of our program: 'They Are Here', where we discuss the current US government with our distinguished guest, President Thomas Jefferson.

Segment 54 – Department of Homeland Security: Federal Emergency Management Agency

Paul Jefko: Before we start, Mr. President, you founded the University of Virginia. Can you tell us why that was so important to you?

President Jefferson: Certainly. Although I had graduated from the College of William and Mary in my native Virginia, it was a state supported institution that had required religious training and deemphasized scientific study. I believe that Virginia needed a college that would be liberal in its teachings and provide practical training for its students. I also hoped that other states would send their students to drink of the cup of knowledge. Two years ago, President Monroe, Madison and Chief Justice Marshall met at Rockfish Gap and determined to establish the University of Virginia at Charlottesville. I am happy that the Commonwealth chartered the University early this year. I look forward to insuring its success.

PAUL: You may not know it sir, but the University of Virginia is not only a successful site of higher learning, the United Nations designated it the only college World Heritage Site. I am sure all the graduates of that eminent institution who have tuned in tonight to listen to your comments are grateful to you for their education. But, moving on…If you recall, Mr. President, the Congress in 1803 extended the time the merchants in Portsmouth, New Hampshire had for providing tariff monies because of disastrous fires at their port. That event was the first time the federal government became involved in disaster response. In the 1930's the Reconstruction Finance Corporation was established to provide loans for repair of public facilities after a natural disaster.

Jefferson: I beg to differ. Portsmouth received a delay in providing tariff collections because of a fire. The Congress did not provide money to rebuild the port. That was a private and State issue. Now you say the federal government provides loans to repair public facilities owned by a State or local government?

PAUL: That is correct. In 1968, Congress provided flood insurance to homeowners and in 1974 gave the President the authority to declare disasters and authorize funds for disaster recovery. In 1978, the Congress created FEMA and tasked it with coordinating with 22 federal agencies to handle disaster response. It absorbed Civil Defense responsibilities as well as the Federal Insurance Administration, the National Fire Prevention and Control Administration, the National Weather Service, the Community Preparedness Program, the Federal Preparedness Agency of GSA and the Federal Disaster Assistance Administration of HUD.

JEFFERSON: National Fire Prevention and Control?

PAUL: In the 1970's there was an apparent national fire problem. The office was set up to provide training to State and local fire officials. In any case, FEMA became part of the Homeland Security Department in 2003.

JEFFERSON: What does managing an emergency have to do with homeland security?

PAUL: Good question. The agency mission is to coordinate response to disasters overwhelming local and state resources. To receive assistance, the State Governor must declare a state of emergency and request the President to declare a disaster. Besides disaster recovery, FEMA has experts and funds for rebuilding by providing low interest loans to individuals. It also provides disaster preparedness funds to local communities.

JEFFERSON: So, if a disaster affects only one state, the federal government can still provide loans to an individual?

PAUL: That is correct. Funds rebuild homes, businesses and public facilities, clear debris, repair roads and bridges, restore water, sewer and other utilities, and provide flood insurance. What do you think of this agency, Mr. President?

JEFFERSON: No authority exists in the Constitution for this mission, as it is a State responsibility and not a national defense or general welfare issue.

PAUL: What should Congress do?

JEFFERSON: Abolish the agency.

PAUL: Thank you, Mr. President. Let us now review another independent agency.

Segment 55 – Independent Agency: The Environmental Protection Agency

Paul Jefko: Mr. President, during the 1950's, a concern arose that human activity had a bad impact on the environment. A book, <u>The Silent Spring</u>, brought notice to Americans on the unintended impact pesticides have on the environment. In 1969, the National Environmental Policy Act of 1969 created a Council on Environmental Quality, reporting to the President.

President Jefferson: Are we talking about arsenic?

PAUL: Well, we used arsenic and other chemicals as pesticides up until the mid-20th century. Scientists came up with a better pesticide called DDT. However, it was discovered that it also prevented seabirds from reproducing. Anyway, this act required an environmental impact statement for all major federal actions that affected the environment.

JEFFERSON: What constitutes an environmental impact statement?

PAUL: It has four parts: Purpose and Need for the Proposed Action; Description of the Affected Environment; Range of Alternatives to the proposed action; and an analysis of the impacts of each alternative on threatened or endangered species, air and water quality, historic and cultural sites, local community and costs. In 1970, Congress centralized all federal environmental responsibilities in EPA.

JEFFERSON: All right, after you prepare this statement, what happens?

PAUL: It provides the basis for any lawsuits by those who do not want the project built.

JEFFERSON: If no one files a lawsuit, then the project gets built?

PAUL: Yes. The idea ensures that the public and private interests get their input on a federal project. Even if Congress has appropriated money for it, it still must go through this process. Some projects are delayed for years as they proceed through the court system. Continuing...the EPA's first accomplishment banned DDT. A more controversial action occurred in 2011 when the EPA began regulating greenhouse gases under the Clean Air Act.

JEFFERSON: What are greenhouse gases?

PAUL: The two greenhouse gases that you are familiar with are carbon dioxide and methane. They were not a problem in your time because Earth's

159

population was much less, and the widespread burning of fossil fuels had not begun. The problem is that these gases can affect the average Earth temperature causing disasters such as rising sea levels, super storms, droughts, floods etc.

JEFFERSON: Fossil fuels, what are they?

PAUL: You are familiar with coal as a fuel, one major fossil fuel. The two others are petroleum and natural gas or methane. We use all three as fuel in our time that generates carbon dioxide when burned and raises the level of that gas in our atmosphere. Carbon dioxide retains heat from the sun and contributes to elevated temperatures at the earth's surface, melting glaciers and polar ice that can cause sea levels to rise.

JEFFERSON: You explained earlier about floating ice at the earth's poles. Tell me more.

PAUL: Both the north and south poles of the earth are covered with ice. In the last 100 years, the surface temperature on the earth has risen ½ a degree. The heat increase resulted in melting of that ice resulting in a 6-inch rise in sea levels. In addition, since weather is caused by temperature variations on the earth, higher temperatures seem to cause more violent storms as well as flooding and droughts. The subject is controversial because a sizable portion of the populace believes the science is spurious.

JEFFERSON: What do the scientists say?

PAUL: Although scientists all agree that the temperature of the earth has risen, and that the change is caused by burning of fossil fuel, the popular press disagrees. That is why the EPA is so controversial. The EPA mission is to protect human health and the environment by developing and enforcing regulations having the force of law. It has offices that regulate energy efficiency, air quality, climate change, pollution, pesticides, toxic substances, solid waste, emergency response to spills, and water pollution.

JEFFERSON: That seems to cover much of the activity of the American people.

PAUL: Their efforts have resulted in an improvement of the environment since the EPA founding, but many people do not remember how bad it was. Now they view the EPA as an agency that interferes with business and hinders development. It has an office of Enforcement and Compliance that directs and reviews regulation enforcement.

JEFFERSON: Let me get this straight. The EPA develops regulations that have the force of law. Why did Congress give them this power?

PAUL: This is actually how Congress legislates these days. Congress became too busy to write specific laws that cover every possible detail. In other cases, Congress determined that specialists at the agency were better prepared to develop the detailed applications of statutes to fit problems as they arise. Remember that these regulations cover air and water. Anything that can pollute those two areas the EPA controls. So, Mr. President, what do you think of this agency?

JEFFERSON: No specific authority appears in the Constitution for these functions. They do contribute to the general welfare of the nation only in those areas that cross State lines. I believe that air pollution and water pollution regulations are constitutional as they affect the entire nation or at least more than one State at one point or another. But those laws that deal with land need to be looked at to determine whether they really affect the nation's general welfare.

PAUL: What should be our next procedures Mr. President?

JEFFERSON: Abolish the laws regarding energy efficiency, solid waste and pollution that occur on land solely in one State.

PAUL: Thank you, Mr. President. Our next topic will be the FBI.

Segment 56 – Department of Justice: Federal Bureau of Investigation

Paul Jefko: Mr. President, in 1896, the National Chiefs of Police Union established the National Bureau of Criminal Identification to provide its members information to help identify known criminals. In 1908, the US Attorney General set up a Bureau of Investigation to enforce the Mann Act, known otherwise as the White Slave Traffic Act. During WW I, the Bureau investigated sabotage and enemy espionage.

JEFFERSON: The White Slave Traffic Act?

PAUL: As women engaged in the work force in the early 20th century, young girls were kidnapped or coerced into prostitution. The Mann Act made it a federal crime to transport a woman across state lines for immoral purposes. Continuing…in 1924, the Bureau absorbed the functions of the National Bureau of Criminal Identification and later developed a fingerprint identification system and DNA testing procedure to provide evidence in a criminal trial.

JEFFERSON: Fingerprinting?

PAUL: Yes, the curves and whorls on your fingertips are unique and can identify you if you leave a print of your fingers at a crime scene. (Shows a picture of a fingerprint form)

JEFFERSON: Tell me, if I entered a person's home without his consent, robbed him and left a fingerprint in his home, how could they know it was my fingerprint?

PAUL: Well, the government first needs to have your fingerprints on file. Any person, who is arrested, works for the federal government or the military has their fingerprints taken and stored in a searchable file. A print on file matching a print at a crime scene identifies the criminal. Fingerprints are strong evidence at a criminal trial and confirms the person was at the crime scene.

JEFFERSON: Doesn't this violate the Fifth Amendment in that the defendant provides evidence against himself?

PAUL: There have been several Supreme Court cases ruling this out. The justices ruled that only testamentary evidence, that is, from the defendant's own mouth, cannot be compelled. A person can be required to take a blood alcohol test for example to prove a drunken driving conviction...Returning to the history of the FBI...after several name changes it assumed its current name in 1935 under the Department of Justice.

JEFFERSON: Returning to the fingerprint issue...if my fingerprints are not on file, I cannot be convicted because of a fingerprint.

PAUL: Not necessarily. If you leave a fingerprint on something, it can be admitted as evidence if someone testifies you were the one leaving the print. It can therefore be compared with a print at the crime scene. Moving on...the FBI created its Public Enemy listing in 1953 encouraging the populace to look out for wanted criminals. After the Munich Olympic Game hostage crisis, the Bureau set up a Hostage Rescue Team.

JEFFERSON: What was the Munich Olympic Game?

PAUL: I assume you are familiar with the ancient Greek Olympic Games highlighting athletic events?

JEFFERSON: Yes, in fact, in France in the last century, they held L'Olympiade de la République with the same events the ancient Greeks competed in. They also used the Olympiade to introduce their metric system.

PAUL: Well, since the late 19th century, the world has hosted an Olympic

162

Games every four years at various locations inviting competitors from all countries who wish to send their athletes. In one games, held in Munich, Germany, Islamic terrorists took Israeli athletes hostage and killed them when an attempt was made to rescue them.

JEFFERSON: Who are Israeli athletes?

PAUL: A Jewish nation called Israel resides on the same land described in the Bible as Israel. The Islamist terrorists believe the Jews took the land from the Arabs and want Israel destroyed.
JEFFERSON: Did the Jews seize the land?

PAUL: The Israelis say no, but room for disagreement exists. Anyway...the FBI has two missions. It investigates all federal crimes and serves as a counter espionage agency. It has 56 field offices and 400 resident agencies in the US. Some crimes it investigates are: public corruption, civil rights violations, hate crimes, human trafficking, police abuse, attacks on family planning clinics, antitrust crimes such as price fixing, and bid rigging, bankruptcy fraud, corporate securities fraud, identity theft, organized crime, art theft, bank robberies, cargo theft, crimes against children, cruise ship crime, Indian country crime, jewelry theft, murder for hire, retail theft, vehicle theft, and gang violence.

JEFFERSON: Many of these crimes seem to be the province of the States. Are there federal laws authorizing the FBI to investigate State issues?

PAUL: The FBI only enforces federal laws but some states can call them in for their expertise. Mr. President, what do you think of this agency?

JEFFERSON: The agency is constitutional for those federal laws that are constitutional. I believe some crimes you related are not federal, for example, public corruption of state and local officers, police abuse, art theft, bank robbery, crimes against children, jewelry theft, murder for hire, retail theft, vehicle theft, or gang violence. If you want to say the crimes you mentioned affect interstate trade and therefore come under federal jurisdiction, that interpretation can apply to all crime. Congress should review federal criminal laws and eliminate those that the States can handle.

PAUL: Thank you, Mr. President. Let us turn now to another Department: Commerce.

Segment 57 - Department of Commerce

Paul Jefko: Mr. President, Congress established this agency in 1903 as the

163

Department of Commerce and Labor to promote American business, create jobs, promote economic growth, encourage development and improve American living standards. In 1913, the Department split into the Department of Labor and Department of Commerce. Included in the Department was the Lighthouse Service, the Coast and Geodetic Survey, the Steamboat Inspection Service, the Census, Standards, Navigation, Fisheries, Foreign and Domestic Commerce and the Bureau of Corporations.

President Jefferson: Bureau of Corporations? States issue corporate charters.

PAUL: Corporations in the late 19th century had become very powerful and some had worked to acquire monopolies in certain areas that restricted interstate trade. The Bureau was set up to investigate these illegal corporate practices. Besides these initial functions, Commerce has acquired additional duties through the years. It absorbed the Patent and Trademark Office in the 1930's. In 1940, the Weather Bureau was transferred from the Department of Agriculture and later the Civil Aeronautics Authority replaced the previously established Bureau of Air Commerce.

JEFFERSON: The Weather Bureau?

PAUL: Yes. It accumulates weather data and uses it to predict the weather. It has stations throughout the US collecting the data and sending it to the headquarters for analysis. A station is even located north of your home in Charlottesville. Continuing...In 1949, the Department subsumed the Public Roads Administration. In 1958, the Civil Aeronautics Authority was abolished. In 1966, Congress moved the Bureau of Public Roads to the new Transportation Department and the National Oceanic and Atmospheric Administration was created in 1970.

JEFFERSON: How does the Bureau predict the weather?

PAUL: Well, I'm not an expert, but it seems weather patterns move from west to east. (Shows a chart of a US weather pattern) So, as a general rule, rain in Kentucky today will probably arrive in Virginia tomorrow. Of course, prediction models today use very sophisticated measurements of atmospheric pressure, wind speed, cloud cover and historical data to forecast weather up to a week in advance...Besides the Weather Bureau, the Department later added Economic Analysis, Minority Business Development, Economic Development, International Trade Administration and Export Administration.

JEFFERSON: What is minority business development?

PAUL: During the Civil Rights era in the mid-1960's, the Congress

164

decided to assist those minorities that were traditionally discriminated against by providing grants to stimulate their entry into business...To summarize, the Department's functions include gathering economic and demographic data for business and government decision making; issuing patents and trademarks and setting industrial standards; promoting US exports, enforcing international trade agreements; regulating export of sensitive goods and technologies; forecasting the weather, conduct oceanic and atmospheric research; managing living marine resources, formulating telecommunications and technology policy; fostering minority business development and promoting economic growth in distressed communities.

JEFFERSON: This is certainly more than what the Constitution means when it says 'regulate commerce'.

PAUL: We will give you a chance to look at these agencies in more detail later. But for now, Mr. President, we will look at one of the main reasons Congress established the Homeland Security Department, the Transportation Security Administration.

Segment 58 - Department of Homeland Security: Transportation Security Administration

Paul Jefko: Mr. President, this agency is a key element of the Homeland Security Department. The agency was an outgrowth of the 9/11 attacks and was specifically set up to protect air travel after that attack. Congress originally established the agency under the Department of Transportation and ordered it to hire security screeners at 450 airports within 12 months. In 2003, it was transferred to the Department of Homeland Security.

President Jefferson: What security was in place prior to the 9/11 attacks?

PAUL: The airline itself had security in place to prohibit normal weapons on the aircraft. But the 9/11 hijackers carried box cutters, small knives, they used as weapons. They were also allowed on board even though they did not have proper identification. In response, the TSA now has the responsibility for security of all air, highway, rail, bus, and mass transit travel, plus pipelines and ports. TSA personnel oversee the most important element, air travel, by screening passengers at airport terminals but some private security companies operate the system at some airports under TSA supervision.

JEFFERSON: What does it do, search everyone?

PAUL: Yes. All persons wishing to travel by air must submit to a baggage search and they must walk through a metal detector.

JEFFERSON: A metal detector?

PAUL: A device that can tell whether you have any metal on your person, obviously a search for a weapon. (Shows photo of metal detector at airport)

JEFFERSON: People do not object to being searched?

PAUL: Some do and loudly complain. But they can travel by other means. Continuing...TSA offices have varied functions. Intelligence and Analysis analyzes information on transportation networks. Transportation Threat Assessment and Credentialing oversees the key programs. Security Operations oversees day to day operations. Transportation Sector Network Management evaluates security vulnerabilities. Law Enforcement places air marshals on airliners and uses dogs to sniff out bombs. And, Global Strategies works with other countries on security.

JEFFERSON: Dogs sniff out bombs?

PAUL: Dogs can track wild game or a fugitive with their sense of smell. TSA trains dogs to search out explosives. What do you think about this agency?

JEFFERSON: All are constitutional as it applies to the general defense of the nation. However, Congress should provide for a user fee to recover the costs from the user of the transportation.

PAUL: Thank you, Mr. President. Let's now go back to an agency of the Department of Defense.

Segment 59 – Department of Defense: United States Special Operations Command

Paul Jefko: Mr. President, recall Roger's Rangers during the French and Indian War and Francis Marion known as the Swamp Fox in the American Revolution. They led what we call guerilla raids on enemy forces. During the American Civil War, a group called Mosby's Raiders destroyed railroads, captured supplies and raided the headquarters of Union armies. During World War II, these 'Special Forces' became more sophisticated.

President Jefferson: Do not forget 'Morgan's Rifles' from Virginia whose tactics included killing the British Army's Indian guides and then its officers to create confusion. He was heavily criticized for these ungentlemanly methods.

PAUL: Well, until recently, most special operations were considered unfair. In World War II, the Devil's Brigade fought against larger forces while Darby's Rangers scaled the cliff at Pointe du Hoc on D-Day. In the Pacific, the Alamo Scouts attacked a Japanese prison camp in the Philippines and freed American prisoners. The Office of Strategic Services operated in Europe and Japan organizing local resistance and sabotage operations. The Army created the Special Forces in 1952 to conduct guerilla warfare.

JEFFERSON: So, these forces are troops trained in certain tactics for special missions.

PAUL: You might say that. The Navy created the SEALS teams to do special operations in maritime environments. Not to be outdone, the Air Force formed the Air Commandos. Congress established this agency to integrate all special operations forces in response to a botched rescue of American hostages in Iran. In 2005, the Marines were added to the group. The US has used this command heavily since then, especially in the war on terrorism.

JEFFERSON: It seems everyone wants to benefit from the largesse provided to these operations.

PAUL: That seems so. The command has authority over any operation combining at least two services. Strength figures are 26,000 for the Army, 8,900 for the Navy, 19 units for the Air Force, and 2500 for the Marines. What is your opinion of this command, Mr. President?

JEFFERSON: The US Navy and Marines participation in this agency is constitutional. Army's participation cannot be authorized for more than two years, while the Air Force participation is unconstitutional.

PAUL: What should the next steps be?

JEFFERSON: First, as I related earlier, either place the Air Force under the Army or Navy, amend the Constitution to allow a separate Air Force, or the Air Force must be abolished. Congress must also establish a system to authorize expenditures for the Army for this function on a biennial basis.

PAUL: Thank you, Mr. President. We will stop here and take a break for a word from our sponsor.

Commercial Break

Segment 60 – Judiciary: US Courts

Paul Jefko: Mr. President, the Judiciary Act of 1789 established the structure of the Supreme Court with a Chief Justice and five Associate Judges. It also established district and circuit courts. In 1881, Congress established a court of appeals for each district. As States entered the Union, the Congress created additional courts. In 1990, Congress gave the Supreme Court administrative authority over the federal courts.

President Jefferson: So, we now have another layer of judges between the trial courts and the Supreme Court. Why?

PAUL: Currently, the Supreme Court receives 10,000 cases on appeal each year. They only act on 100. Obviously, without an intermediate level of courts, injustice would occur. Moving on…As you know, Congress can establish two different types of courts, article 3 courts and article one courts. Article one court judges have fixed terms and cannot render final judgments on life, liberty and property rights.
JEFFERSON: Yes, a useful distinction.

PAUL: Article 3 judges serve for life and can rule on life, liberty and private property rights. The Supreme Court term begins on the first Monday in October. Each side in a case argued before the court is allowed 30 minutes and up to 24 cases can be argued in one year.

JEFFERSON: That time allowed for argument is not necessary. In my experience, the justices decide on the briefs presented to them and the discussions with the other justices before they even hear an oral argument.

PAUL: Questions do pop up during those hearings, though. But more on the procedure…Supreme Court justices review 130 petitions weekly. In May and June, the court decides on the cases to be tried in the next session. Ninety-four federal districts hold trials. Special courts exist for International Trade and Federal Claims. Each district also has a bankruptcy court to liquidate business assets. A US Sentencing Commission develops sentencing guidelines for US federal courts.

JEFFERSON: Sentencing guidelines?

PAUL: Yes. To ensure crimes are punished in a common manner through the nation, guidelines have been developed to provide a sentence based on the level of the offense and the criminal history of the offender. What do you think about this court system, sir?

JEFFERSON: All are constitutional as the Congress has the authority to set up its court system under Article 3 and Article 1.

PAUL: Thank you, Mr. President. We will now turn to an agency that may intrigue you, the National Science Foundation.

Segment 61 – Independent Agencies: National Science Foundation

Paul Jefko: Mr. President, rubber was very important to our national defense in World War II. However, the source of natural rubber was in areas controlled by our enemy. Although synthetic rubber had been invented in the 19th century, its production was nil because of the high cost.

President Jefferson: I realize rubber removes pencil marks, but why was rubber so important to the War Department?

PAUL: Its greatest use was in transportation, for automobile tires, hoses, gaskets, and belts as well as in medical gloves. Without rubber, the Army literally cannot move. As long as natural rubber was available, there was no incentive in the marketplace to develop synthetic rubber. Although a crash program by the US government in World War II did produce the synthetic rubber needed by the military, the problem drove legislators to look at a more effective approach to scientific research.

JEFFERSON: Obviously, the appropriate persons did not realize rubber was a significant material to national defense. They did not foresee this problem?

PAUL: At the time, a few universities and private corporations conducted federal research. A number of federal agencies including the defense agencies awarded contracts for various scientific projects in their area of interest. As it happened, if you received one contract to perform a study, you were more likely to receive other related contracts. Therefore, research was conducted in very few areas on a scattershot approach. Senator Kilgore of West Virginia, in response, advocated a research organization to conduct basic and applied research based on economic and social goals.

JEFFERSON: How about military needs?

PAUL: The establishment of the Defense Department gave rise to research for military defense needs. No agency addressed non-military requirements systematically. Kilgore's opponents thought his ideas were socialistic that took research out of the hands of the scientist. A man named Vannevar Bush came up with the idea that the government conduct only basic research owned by the researcher and not the government.

JEFFERSON: We are back to socialism again and at the time you mentioned, the big threat was communism, a heavier version of socialism. Do I have it right?

PAUL: You are right on the money, sir. The National Science Foundation as established was akin to Bush's approach. The Foundation funds basic research and education in all non-medical science and engineering. The director, his or her deputy and the 24 members of the National Science Board are appointed by the President and confirmed by the Senate. Of 42,000 proposals it receives annually, it funds 28%.

JEFFERSON: But the government does not own any of this taxpayer-funded research?

PAUL: Unclear. Apparently, the research is available to the public, meaning anyone could use the information.

JEFFERSON: By the way, how can 24 persons review 42,000 proposals a year?

PAUL: They have more staff than the 24. They have 150 scientists on staff coordinating the proposals with outside scientists to conduct the review. The agency has seven divisions: Biological; Computer and Information Science and Engineering; Engineering; Geosciences; Mathematical and Physical; Social Behavioral and Economics; and Education and Human Resources. It also has several offices for special purposes.

JEFFERSON: We have looked at other agencies providing grants to perform research. Is any scientific research done without the taxpayer paying for it?

PAUL: In a recent year, the government conducted 31% of scientific research. However, the research the government conducts is basic, while corporations conduct applied research to generate profits. Continuing with its special offices…Cyberinfrastructure obtains all the computer tools required for the researchers. Polar Programs conducts basic research in the Arctic and Antarctic. Integrative Activities manages the research programs.

JEFFERSON: What type of research is conducted in the Polar Regions?

PAUL: They have permanent camps there to study an active volcano, glaciers and core drilling projects. (Shows photo of scientists at base camp) Moving on…International Science and Engineering is a liaison point for all the science and engineering communities. In a recent budget year, the agency spent $6 Billion in research and $1 Billion in education. What do you think of this agency, Mr. President?

JEFFERSON: Although no specific authority exists for this agency, it contributes to the general welfare of the nation and is thereby constitutional. Congress should ensure the federal government retains the ownership of the research to ensure any applications fund the cost of the basic research. The federal government under the Constitution has no business spending taxpayer dollars to fund research and then give it away. There must be compensation.

PAUL: Thank you, Mr. President. Returning to the Department of Health and Human Services...

Segment 62 - Department of Health and Human Services – Health Resources and Services Administration

Paul Jefko: Mr. President, Congress merged the Health Resources Administration and the Health Services Administration in 1982. It now has four divisions, Health Professions; Health Maintenance Organizations and Resources Development; Health Care Delivery and Assistance; and the Indian Health Service.

President Jefferson: So, the federal government has an agency to provide medical services to the American people?

PAUL: Yes, but only to the uninsured, isolated or medically vulnerable. Grants are given to organizations to provide health care to the uninsured, people with AIDS, pregnant women, mothers and children and to train health professionals in rural communities, oversee organ donations, prepare against bioterrorism, compensate those harmed by vaccination, and maintain information on malpractice, waste, fraud and abuse.

JEFFERSON: Organ donation?

PAUL: Yes. A person may donate a bodily organ to transplant into a needy person.

JEFFERSON: You mean if I have heart trouble, I can get a new heart from someone?

PAUL: Yes, but not only hearts but lungs, kidneys, livers, pancreas',

171

corneas, skin, bone marrow and other organs. The agency also operates community health centers in cities and rural areas. They spent $2.5 Billion in a recent year for care to 17 million patients. What is your opinion of this agency, Mr. President?

JEFFERSON: None of the functions is specifically authorized in the Constitution. Under the rubric of general defense of the nation, preparing against bioterrorism is constitutional, but all other functions do not pertain to the general welfare of the nation but only a certain slice of the population and are thereby unconstitutional.

PAUL: What should the next steps be?

JEFFERSON: The States should be offered the opportunity to assume these services for their citizens if their constitutions allow, after which the agency will be abolished. Transfer anti-bioterrorism functions to the Department of Homeland Security.

PAUL: Thank you Mr. President. We will now review an agency in the Department of Energy.

Segment 63 - Department of Energy: Office of Environmental Management

Paul Jefko: Mr. President, during the Cold War, the US produced tens of thousands of nuclear warheads. Producing these weapons in 16 facilities in Nevada, Tennessee, Idaho, Washington and South Carolina generated huge amounts of nuclear radioactive waste. As an example, the waste includes 52,000 tons of spent radioactive fuel, 91 million gallons of waste from plutonium processing, tons and tons of plutonium, 500,000 tons of depleted uranium, and millions of contaminated tools, clothing and 265 million tons of uranium tailings.

President Jefferson: How does this affect people?

PAUL: A person exposed to this stuff at high doses can incur burns, experience nausea, vomiting, unconsciousness and death. Over time, even low doses can cause cancer. Three facilities have contamination estimated to cost $155 Billion to clean up. This agency was set up in 1989 to handle the problem. It has 134 projects at nine sites in Washington, Idaho, New Mexico, Tennessee, Kentucky, Ohio, South Carolina and New York.

JEFFERSON: So, I estimate cleaning up the remaining six sites will cost

$300 billion?

PAUL: I do not have that information. It may be less because the three sites I mentioned were the worst sites. Sixteen sites have already been decontaminated. They treat the radioactive liquid into a stable form, place nuclear material in a safe location, dispose of low level wastes, decommission facilities and remediate soil and ground water.

JEFFERSON: Why do we have all these problems?

PAUL: During World War II, they were not concerned about the collateral problems of what they did. They tried to make a bomb before their enemies did. Now we clean up their mess. They have 34,000 contractor employees on this work. What do you think about this agency?

JEFFERSON: Since this contamination is located on federal property, the Congress's authority to do so is constitutional.

PAUL: Thank you, Mr. President. Now let us turn to Federal Prisons.

Segment 64 – Department of Justice: Federal Bureau of Prisons

Paul Jefko: In 1891, Congress passed the Three Prisons Act authorizing the construction of three penitentiaries under supervision of the Justice Department General Agent. In 1907, Congress abolished the position and transferred the Prisons to the Superintendent of Prisons and Prisoners. In 1930, the Bureau of Prisons was set up to administer 11 federal prisons. 10 Years later, there were 24 facilities with 24,360 inmates.

President Jefferson: Why are there so many prisoners?

PAUL: In the 1920's, organized crime began to circumvent the prohibition laws. That resulted in many federal prosecutions and convictions. Because of the dangerous nature of these prisoners, high security prisons were built to ensure an escape proof facility. New sentencing guidelines in the 1980's also increased the number of federal prisoners. In 1999 there were 136,000 federal prisoners supervised by 10,000 employees.

JEFFERSON: What crimes do these people commit?

PAUL: Many have violated federal drug laws. Some were terrorists, spies, or fraudsters. Bank robbers are also violators of federal law. Today, the bureau

173

has 116 facilities, 6 regional offices, a headquarters, 2 training centers and 22 community corrections offices. It also has a federal execution center in Indiana. In a recent year, this agency cost $5.6 Billion. What do you think?

JEFFERSON: The agency is constitutional as the enforcement of federal powers may require prosecuting and punishing violators.

PAUL: Thank You, Mr. President. Back to the Department of State…

Segment 65 – Department of State: President's Emergency Plan for AIDS Relief

Paul Jefko: Mr. President, a study commissioned by President Bush warned that the HIV pandemic affected US national security. Based on that, Congress passed the Global AIDS Act of 2003 that established the State Department Office of the Global AIDS Coordinator. They renewed it in 2008 to make it the basis of US global health efforts. The plan provides antiretroviral treatment to HIV infected people in poor international areas to prevent new infections and provide care to infected people.

President Jefferson: You have mentioned AIDS and HIV before. Obviously, this illness is serious. Tell me about it.

PAUL: HIV had at one time a 100% death rate. If you contracted the virus, you were destined to have at most 9 years to live.

JEFFERSON: How does one acquire the disease?

PAUL: You can get it through sexual intercourse with an infected person, sharing a needle with an infected person and it even can be transmitted from mother to fetus.

JEFFERSON: What are the symptoms?

PAUL: It appears at first to be influenza accompanied by a rash but it can, without treatment, cause cancer, pneumonia and other illnesses that eventually kill the infected person. You see, AIDS attacks the body's immune system so normal illnesses the body easily fights off, become serious and even fatal. In order to fight the disease in foreign countries, 75% of funds purchase and distribute drugs, while 15% goes for care to individual with HIV/AIDS.

JEFFERSON: Where did this disease originate? It does not appear in my time.

PAUL: Scientists believe it originated with chimpanzees in Africa. They have a similar illness that seems to have jumped to humans. What do you think about this agency, Mr. President?

JEFFERSON: The federal government has special authority to regulate commerce with foreign nations and general authority to provide for the common defense. This agency, if it implements part of a foreign treaty, can provide the assistance described if the Senate deems it necessary to the national defense. It is constitutional under those conditions.

PAUL: What should be done?

JEFFERSON: If no treaty exists, this program needs to be abolished.

PAUL: Thank you, Mr. President. It is time to look at the agency that manages our forests.

Segment 66 - Department of Agriculture: US Forest Service

Paul Jefko: In 1876, Congress created the Office of Special Agent in the Department of Agriculture to assess the quality of the forests in the US. This office expanded into the Forestry Division in 1881. In 1891, the Forest Reserve Act gave the President the power, through the Department of Interior, to establish timberland reserves to protect them from thieves and profiteers. Congress established the current Forest Service in 1905 under the Department of Agriculture.

President Jefferson: In heaven's name, why is the federal government concerned about timber theft?

PAUL: A business group in Los Angeles, California was concerned about ranchers and miners cutting down timber in the San Gabriel Mountains. They believed it harmed the watershed. Without adequate forest cover, rainfalls caused flooding.

JEFFERSON: So, a problem in California required the federal government to seize land?

PAUL: Well, much of the forest resources set aside west of the Mississippi were federal owned land. East of the Mississippi, forest reserves were set aside by purchasing private land.

JEFFERSON: I understand the federal government should protect its own property, but it can do that without designating it a special forest reserve.

PAUL: True.

JEFFERSON: And the federal government has no business buying land from private owners just to preserve it. Local and State law enforcement have the authority to protect private property.

PAUL: You have a point, but besides protecting the forests, the service sells timber as needed by the national economy. The agency currently manages 155 national forests and 20 national grasslands totaling 193 million acres. Each forest has a Forest Supervisor. These forests supply half the country's prime construction material. The agency has seven regional research stations and a Forest Products Laboratory. They conduct research on usage, quantitative measures, forest management, environment, inventory and analysis.

JEFFERSON: The government is in the business of selling timber?

PAUL: Yes. Moreover, in a recent year, $2 Billion was spent for forest fire preparedness and suppression, and $1 Billion for resource restoration. Mr. President, what should we do with this agency?

JEFFERSON: No enumerated power in the Constitution allows the federal government to own land except for use as building sites for government or military purposes. Certainly, no authority exists to operate federal lands as a source of raw material. Research on forest material is as valid as research conducted in medicine and science for the general welfare of the nation. All other activities are unconstitutional. By the way, Congress should obtain patents for all research paid for with taxpayer dollars on behalf of the American people. They should share in any benefits from the discoveries.

PAUL: What should the next steps be?

JEFFERSON: The agency should offer the land to the State where it lies. If not accepted, put the land up for sale on a 10-year scheme to eliminate the land inventory. Any land unsold shall be left untouched to return it to its natural condition. If forestland is needed for research purposes, it can be leased, not purchased from the owners. However, patent and license any research for the benefit of the American people.

PAUL: Thank you, Mr. President.

Segment 67 – Department of Homeland Security: US Immigration and Customs Enforcement

Paul Jefko: Mr. President, immigration in this country was not a problem until the late 19th century when waves of European and Asian immigrants came into this country.

President Jefferson: Why did immigration become such a problem? It never was in my time.

PAUL: In your time, the travel cost from Europe or Asia to the US limited the number of persons traveling here. Most were artisans or businessmen who had skills or money useful to our growing country. Early America had a labor shortage. As travel by ship became cheaper, brokers in the US promoted America as the land where jobs were available. In the mid-19th century, the source of immigrants shifted from England and Germany to Irish escaping the potato famine and southern Europeans escaping poverty.

JEFFERSON: Potato famine?

PAUL: The Irish working class and poor lived on potatoes as their staple diet. Beginning in 1845, a blight killed over two thirds of the crop causing mass starvation. During this period, about 1-2 million Irish emigrated to the US. These immigrants were Catholic and threatened the Protestant culture of the US. Some Americans became concerned that these immigrants posed health hazards. Still others were concerned that they took jobs from natural born Americans. Consequently, States passed laws to regulate this influx until the Supreme Court ruled the federal government had exclusive authority in this area.

JEFFERSON: Have immigrants become a problem in the US?

PAUL: They were very ambitious in politics, especially in larger cities. From early in the 20th century, Irish became mayors, governors and even senators in many areas. President Kennedy was elected in 1960 though he was Irish and Catholic. These days, very little if any anti-Irish sentiment exists in the US. At the time, however, the Congress set up the Superintendent of Immigration within the Treasury Department who built the Ellis Island Immigration Station in New York Harbor to approve incoming European immigrants. The Basic Naturalization Act in 1906 established the Bureau of Immigration and Naturalization.

JEFFERSON: So, all immigrants come through New York now?

PAUL: Not any more. Ellis Island was closed as an immigrant processing

177

station in 1954. Now immigrants arrive mostly by aircraft and the agency processes them upon arrival at any international airport in the US. Back to the origins of this agency…The first limits on immigration occurred after World War I. Illegal immigration began at that time and the US Border Patrol was established in 1924 to stop it. The Border Patrol doubled in size during World War II to keep enemy aliens out of the US.

JEFFERSON: How are these illegal immigrants entering the US?

PAUL: Two ways. Some enter here as tourists and just stay. Unless arrested for a crime, they can escape detection for years. The other way is to cross the border from Mexico to the US. In 1965, Congress gave INS the authority to prosecute corporations and individuals hiring illegal aliens. The agency enforces over 400 federal laws. Its Arms and Strategic Technology Investigations Unit works to protect military weapons and sensitive technology from falling into the hands of terrorists and hostile nations. The Detention and Removal Operations Unit locates, arrests and deports illegal immigrants and operates 16 detention-processing centers.

JEFFERSON: 16 processing centers! How many illegal immigrants are there?

PAUL: Almost 12 million persons illegally live in the US. In a recent year, 392,000 were deported. Continuing with the agency structure…Intelligence collects, analyzes and distributes data for use by the Department. International Affairs investigates immigration and customs violations, manages visa security and international visitors.

JEFFERSON: If a person comes here legally on a visa, why is it difficult to deport them?

PAUL: Once they are here, they can move anywhere. Documents can be forged to provide them proper identification. Some employers will hire them knowing they are illegal because they can pay them a lower wage. Continuing…Investigations looks into immigration crime, human rights violations, human smuggling, narcotics and weapons smuggling, financial crimes, cybercrime and export enforcement.

JEFFERSON: Human smuggling?

PAUL: Yes. Organizations smuggle people across the US border for a fee. What do you think of this agency?

JEFFERSON: Since the Constitution provides the federal government with the authority over immigration and naturalization, all the functions of this agency are constitutional except some functions of the Investigations Division. Control of human rights violations are a state matter as are financial crimes.

PAUL: What should be the next steps?

JEFFERSON: Any functions relating to human rights violations or financial crimes must be the province only of the States. Terminate the federal role.

PAUL: Thank you, Mr. President. That concludes our program for this week. President Jefferson and I will return next week for further chat on our government. On behalf of President Jefferson, I wish you a good night.

Program # 9

Paul Jefko: Good evening, ladies and gentlemen and welcome to part 9 of this Series: 'They Are Here', where we converse with our nation's third President, Thomas Jefferson.

Segment 68 - Department of Energy: Office of Science

Paul Jefko: Mr. President, our viewers may not know of your keen interest in agriculture. Can you tell us a bit about your passion in this area?

President Jefferson: Yes. Our farmers were not very efficient in my day. They felt it was cheaper to buy another acre of land than fertilize the acre they had. I developed a seven-year plan that would provide the crops we needed and also fertilize the soil. I also had our hands plow in contours around the hills to conserve rain water and prevent soil from washing down the hill. And, I must confess to smuggling rice out of Italy which I provided to the farmers of South Carolina.

PAUL: Well, we won't let the Department of Homeland Security know. But to continue our discussion, Mr. President, after World War II, the federal government had to deal with the atomic bomb it had developed. Congress established the Atomic Energy Commission (AEC) and transferred atomic research to it from the War Department. Later, when other energy applications became feasible, the Congress abolished the AEC and put in its place the Energy Research and Development Administration (ERDA) to consider all energy sources.

JEFFERSON: What are these other energy sources?

PAUL: Some are solar, geothermal, fossil fuels and energy conservation. Faced with a fossil fuel crisis in 1977, Congress created the Department of Energy and placed in it ERDA along with the other energy agencies throughout the government.

JEFFERSON: What was the fossil fuel crisis?

PAUL: The world runs on fossil fuels, specifically coal, oil and natural gas. Vast quantities of oil are located in the Middle East, specifically Saudi Arabia. Although the US has its own oil reserves, the large supplies in the Mid-East began to be imported to the US beginning in the 1960's. During the Yom

Kippur War between Israel and Egypt in 1973, the US provided weapons to the Israelis. The Arab nations objected and placed an embargo on oil to the US and other countries in Western Europe.

JEFFERSON: I am very familiar with embargoes. Was this one successful?

PAUL: For a while, the lack of fuel damaged the US economy. After the US negotiated an agreement between Israel and Syria, another combatant, the embargo was lifted. After that crisis, the Office of Energy Research, to manage Energy R&D and non-weapons labs, was established under this Department. The Department changed its name to the current one in 1999 to denote it as the primary agency for scientific energy research. Its offices include Advanced Scientific Computing Research, Basic Energy Sciences, Biological and Environmental Research, Fusion Energy Sciences, High Energy Physics and Nuclear Physics.

JEFFERSON: So, this research is necessary for national defense?

PAUL: That was its original purpose as the US considered the Arabs to be using oil as a weapon. It has 10 laboratories including the Princeton Plasma Physics Lab, the Stanford Linear Accelerator, the Argonne and Fermi National Accelerator, the Great Lakes Bioenergy Research Lab, and ahem, the Thomas Jefferson National Accelerator. The agency supplies 40% of the total funding for physical science research in the country. What do you think of this agency, Mr. President?

JEFFERSON: Although no specific authority lies in the Constitution for this function it provides research benefitting the general welfare of the country and is thereby constitutional.

PAUL: Thank You, Mr. President. Let's look at another Independent Agency.

Segment 69 – Independent Agencies: United States Agency for International Development

Paul Jefko: Mr. President, after World War II, the US was worried the Soviet Union would exploit the war-ravaged Western European economies and turn them Communist. US and European Leaders set up the International Monetary Fund and the World Bank to provide loans to countries needing assistance in economic development. In addition, the Marshall Plan also provided funds to help European countries rebuild their countries.

President Jefferson: How bad was the devastation?

PAUL: Well, millions of people were homeless, and the European economy had collapsed due to destruction of its industrial infrastructure. (Shows photos of Berlin in 1945) Most major European cities had been bombed, and transportation structures such as railways, bridges and docks had been destroyed. Millions in refugee camps relied on food from the US. Aid programs later expanded. In 1957, Congress created the Development Loan Fund to provide loans to foreign countries other US government agencies could not or would not take on. In 1961, Congress passed the Foreign Assistance Act consolidating the loan functions of the Development Loan Fund, the currency functions of the Export Import Bank and agriculture distribution functions of the Agriculture Department.

JEFFERSON: Why were we providing assistance in 1961, 16 years after the end of the war?

PAUL: Because the Cold War caused us to compete with the Soviet Union for the allegiance of vulnerable countries. Other aid programs begun were loan guarantees to US companies doing business overseas. Today, this agency administers all foreign non-military aid, operating under direction of the President, Secretary of State and the National Security Council.

JEFFERSON: But the Cold War has ended. Why are we still providing this assistance?

PAUL: Because the US considers foreign aid, along with military action and diplomacy, as the third leg of the national security stool. The aid is in the form of technical assistance, training, scholarships, food, disaster relief, infrastructure construction, small business loans, budget support, and credit guarantees. AID has 18 offices in Asia, operates in seven countries in the Middle East and North Africa, and has 23 field and three regional offices in Sub Saharan Africa. In a recent year, the following countries received over $1 Billion in aid: Afghanistan - $3 billion; Israel - $2 Billion; Egypt - $2 Billion; Iraq - $2 Billion; Jordan - $1 Billion; Pakistan - $1 Billion; Kenya - $1 Billion; South Africa - $1 Billion; and Colombia - $1 Billion.

JEFFERSON: I have not heard of half of these countries. Whom do we contend with over these countries?

PAUL: In vulnerable areas without the basics of life, terrorists can establish themselves, as Al Qaeda did in Afghanistan. The US does not want other countries to become a haven for terrorist activity aimed at the US.

JEFFERSON: Although not specifically authorized in the Constitution, the aid is part of the national defense if directed so by Congress and therefore constitutional.

PAUL: Thank you, Mr. President. Let us continue on this program with an Agriculture agency.

Segment 70 – Department of Agriculture: Natural Resources Conservation Service

Paul Jefko: Congress established the Soil Erosion Service under the Department of the Interior in 1933. Upon its transfer to the Agriculture Department in 1935, it became the Soil Conservation Service. In 1994, it got its current name. The agency sets up individual soil conservation practices and creates locally elected conservation officials to help farmers reduce sediment and pollution from cropland runoff. The Food Security Act of 1985 required farmers to use established conservation measures or lose eligibility for other agriculture programs.

President Jefferson: Help me understand the problem the farmer faced.

PAUL: Remember our discussion of the Dust Bowl of the 1930's. (Shows video of dust bowl) Farmers plowed land having minimal topsoil and minimal rainfall. The plowing methods used made the soil subject to wind erosion. The soil literally blew away. The agency mission was to help farmers conserve their soils. In addition to soil, its new mission since 1994 encompasses all natural resources including water, air, plants and animals.

JEFFERSON: It appears these farmers were not very smart. They should have known the land was too arid to plant crops by simply feeling the soil.

PAUL: That is true, but, in any case, the agency currently provides advice to farmers, private landowners and managers. Its purpose is to conserve natural resources on private lands by cooperating with local and state agencies.

JEFFERSON: So, we now have one place for a farmer to get information from the federal government about his entire assets?

PAUL: Yes. The Environmental Quality Incentives Program provides grants and advice to install conservation practices on agricultural land. The Conservation Stewardship Program provides payment for conservation performance. Recipients include farmers, ranchers, landowners, agricultural companies, environmental groups and policy makers.

JEFFERSON: Instead of the bad farmer having to sell his farm to a better farmer, we provide information and cash to bad farmers to improve their practices.

PAUL: I think the family farm is an honored icon in American history. Besides, the farmer would probably have to sell to an agribusiness.

JEFFERSON: What is that?

PAUL: They are corporations who own thousands of acres and hire farmers to till and harvest their crops. What do you think of this agency?

JEFFERSON: No specific authority exists in the Constitution for providing funds to encourage soil conservation as it is not a national defense issue nor is it a general welfare requirement because only a small number of citizens benefit. Abolish this agency along with its mission.

PAUL: Thank you Mr. President. We now look at an agency that was established under your administration.

Segment 71 – Department of Commerce: National Oceanic and Atmospheric Administration

Paul Jefko: Mr. President, Congress created this agency in 1970 to consolidate several existing agencies: The US Coast and Geodetic Survey, which you know of, created in 1807, the Weather Bureau, and the Bureau of Commercial Fisheries. The agency provides weather alerts, charts the seas and the skies, protects the ocean and coastal resources and researches the environment. It has 300 uniformed service members as part of a commissioned officer corps.

President Jefferson: Why are they in uniform? Is it a military organization?

PAUL: Well, during the Civil War, civilians performing this duty could have been arrested and executed as spies, so the Congress decided to establish a separate Corps and uniform for them. The personnel could be transferred to the military services in wartime. Today, its offices include the National Environmental Satellite, Data and Information Service, which manages environmental satellites, provides information from them and performs research.

JEFFERSON: What do environmental satellites do?

PAUL: They mostly track severe storms such as hurricanes and cyclones. The National Marine Fisheries Service assesses fish stocks, enforces fishing regulations and advocates sustainable fishing methods. The National Ocean Service mitigates coastal and ecosystem hazards. The National Weather Service provides weather, hydrologic and climate warnings and forecasts.

JEFFERSON: This weather information. Who benefits from it?

PAUL: Many businesses, airports, road crews, cities and towns, communication companies and others use this information. You might consult the Weather Service if you plan a picnic. Continuing…the Office of Marine and Aviation Operations operates ships and aircraft for research purposes. The Office of Oceanic and Atmospheric Research researches environmental phenomena, new technologies and provides the information to consumers and businesses. What do you think of this agency?

JEFFERSON: Although there is no specific authority in the Constitution for these activities, the general welfare clause provides authority to conduct all of the functions of this agency, since they benefit the vast majority of the American population.

PAUL: Thank you, Mr. President. We now move on to the US Mail.

Segment 72 – Independent Agencies: United States Postal Service

Paul Jefko: The US Post Office was a source of political influence as postal workers were numerous and those who supported the winners in elections received jobs. Although the Constitution gave Congress the power to establish post roads, the Congress designated existing roads as postal roads but did not construct any new ones. Subsequently, navigable waterways were designated postal roads in 1823 and railroads in 1838.

President Jefferson: Has Congress ever authorized any postal road construction?

PAUL: Congress never passed a law authorizing construction of post roads, but they have constructed interstate highways under other legislation. Anyway…by 1828, 7,500 post offices had 30,000 federal employees. In 1845, mailers were charged fees based on weight and distance.

JEFFERSON: Mailers were charged? The receiver paid postage in my day.

PAUL: That changed in 1847, when the Post Office began selling postage stamps. You bought the adhesive stamps from the post office and placed them on the letter you wanted delivered. International Parcel Service was established in 1887 and Domestic Parcel Service in 1913. In 1918, airmail service was provided at a higher price, but the extra price was abolished in 1975 when airmail became a routine service. In 1930, letter carriers began residential and commercial customer delivery.

JEFFERSON: The postal employee delivers mail from house to house?

PAUL: Yes, sir. Each residence has a mailbox for receipt of mail. Currently, the US Postal Service is an independent agency with 522,000 workers and 212,000 vehicles. It has exclusive access to letterboxes in the US but competes on an equal basis with private package delivery services. Its revenue comes from postage and postal products only. A Board of Governors appointed by the President and confirmed by the Senate governs the agency. The Board chooses the Postmaster General and his Deputy.

JEFFERSON: If private delivery services exist, why does the Postal Service provide a competing service?

PAUL: The Postal Service has a monopoly on first class letter service and is allowed to compete on parcel delivery, but none of the money received from its first-class monopoly can be used to supplement its package delivery service. The USPS has contracts with passenger airlines to transport 450 million pounds of mail annually and leases 100 aircraft and 18 hubs in the US. What do you think of this agency?

JEFFERSON: This is constitutional: a specific authority provided in the Constitution.

PAUL: Thank you, Mr. President. Let's return to the Native American.

Segment 73 - Department of Health and Human Services: Indian Health Service

Paul Jefko: Mr. President, in 1921, the Snyder Act established Federal Indian Programs. In 1955, 2,500 employees, 48 hospitals, 18 health centers, 62 treatment stations and 13 school infirmaries were transferred from the Bureau of Indian Affairs to the new Indian Health Service.

President Jefferson: Is providing health care part of a treaty with these tribes?

PAUL: No, because the Snyder Act provided citizenship to any Indian born within the US.

JEFFERSON: Why did Congress do this?

PAUL: To thank the thousands of Indians who had enlisted and fought for the US in the First World War. The first mission of the agency was to survey and document the health status of the American Indian and Alaskan Native population. The goal was to raise the health of the federal recognized Tribes and Alaskan Natives. Five hundred and fifty-seven recognized tribes live in 35 states. The agency has 12 area offices and 163 Tribal Service Units.

JEFFERSON: Interesting. At the time, did the US provide health care to any other person living in America?

PAUL: Only veterans.

JEFFERSON: But all Indians receive this care, not just Indian veterans.

PAUL: That is correct. Part of it was also the guilt the country felt over taking Indian land and forcing them to move onto reservations. Continuing... Tribes control 54 % of the total budget. A Special Diabetes Program for Indians provides exams, medications, therapies, nutrition education and physical fitness. Thirty-two percent of Indians have periodontal disease and 67% have untreated tooth decay. Suicides are 60% greater than the national average.

JEFFERSON: The program has been in existence for how many years?

PAUL: Almost 90.

JEFFERSON: And still severe health problems remain. The program does not seem very effective.

PAUL: You have a point. The agency's budget is $4 Billion annually. What is your opinion, Mr. President?

JEFFERSON: The Congress has the authority under the Constitution to set rules for citizenship. Therefore, the Snyder Act is constitutional. However, I see no authority allowing the federal government to raise the health of the Tribes and Alaskan Natives, without a treaty. The programs neither help our national defense nor provide for the general welfare. If not considered part of a tribe under treaty, the individual Indian is just another citizen with the same rights and responsibilities. The individual Indians not assimilating into our culture must fend for themselves.

187

PAUL: What would you do?

JEFFERSON: This agency should be abolished.

PAUL: Thank you, Mr. President. We will now review another health agency.

Segment 74 - Department of Health and Human Services: Substance Abuse and Mental Health Services Administration

Paul Jefko: This agency changed a lot as it originated as the Narcotics Division in the Treasury Department in 1929. In 1930, it became the Division of Mental Hygiene, the National Institute of Mental Health in 1949, the National Institute on Alcohol Abuse and Alcoholism in 1970, renamed the Alcohol, Drug Abuse and Mental Health Administration in 1973 and its current name in 1992. The mission is to reduce illness, death, disability and cost to society from substance abuse and mental illness.

President Jefferson: How widespread is mental illness in the US?

PAUL: It depends on how you define it. Serious mental illness interferes with or limits an individual's life activities and affects about 4% of the national population.

JEFFERSON: So, it is not a general welfare problem?

PAUL: No. The agency has three centers: Substance Abuse Treatment provides vouchers for drug and alcohol abusers; Substance Abuse Prevention has programs to prevent illegal drug use and underage alcohol and tobacco use; and Mental Health Services removes obstacles to treatment and helps families deal with mental disorders. Its Office of Applied Studies surveys Drug Use and Health. What do you think of this agency?

JEFFERSON: There is no special authority in the Constitution for this agency to provide vouchers for drug and alcohol treatment, preventing use of illegal drugs and underage alcohol and tobacco and helping families with mental disorders. And, there is no general welfare issue as it helps only drug and alcohol abusers and those with mental disorders. Underage tobacco and alcohol use is the province of the family.

PAUL: What should the next steps be?

188

JEFFERSON: Abolish the agency.

PAUL: Thank you, Mr. President. I mentioned the next agency in our earlier discussions and postponed our analysis until now.

Segment 75 – Independent Agencies: Board of Governors of the Federal Reserve System

Paul Jefko: As you recall, Congress established two national banks, in 1791 and 1816 respectively, both going out of business when their charters expired. You also know the only currency issued by the federal government in your time was minted coin. However, private banks throughout the country issued bank notes people used as paper currency. Depending on the financial strength of the issuing bank and economic conditions, the value of these notes varied.

President Jefferson: Yes, some were valued less than the paper and printing.

PAUL: In fact, some notes were not backed with any hard money. The federal government, chastened by the Continentals issued during the American Revolution, refrained from issuing bank notes. However, when the Civil War required more revenue, Congress passed the National Banking Act of 1863 allowing national chartered banks to issue banknotes backed by the US government promise of redemption in specie.

JEFFERSON: I remember Congress redeemed the Continentals around 1790 with Treasury bonds at 1% of value.

PAUL: Even though there was a stable currency in the US issued bank notes, panics and bank runs continued because state banks did not keep an adequate amount of specie. In response, Congress passed the Federal Reserve Act of 1912 establishing a Federal Reserve Board of five members appointed by the President. The mission of the Federal Reserve was to maintain the integrity of the currency and regulate the banking system.

JEFFERSON: The Great Depression occurred after that time, if I recall your narrative, so it did not accomplish its mission.

PAUL: That is correct. Excessive speculation after World War I led to a stock market crash causing the worst depression in US history. When 10,000 banks failed, many blamed the Federal Reserve for not acting quickly enough.

JEFFERSON: The agency charged with regulating the banks seemed to have missed the mark.

PAUL: Part of the problem was that knowledge of the economics of money and banking was limited at that time. Research and experience has made governmental responses much more effective since then. During the Depression, Congress passed the Glass-Steagall Act separating commercial and investment banking and placed national banks under Federal Reserve control. After World War II, the Employment Act required the Federal Reserve to promote maximum employment as an added duty.

JEFFERSON: Why was that added?

PAUL: Economists believed monetary policy helped manage the business cycle, the up and down movement of the economy, to diminish high levels of unemployment occurring periodically. Since then, although there were mild recessions in economic activity, there were no depressions with high levels of unemployment. Notable, in 1999, the Glass-Steagall Act was repealed.

JEFFERSON: Why?

PAUL: Certain interests thought the act stifled trade and development and clamored for less regulation.

JEFFERSON: So, the people did not realize the regulations they hated actually protected them?

PAUL: It seems memories are short. Organizationally, the Fed is the US central bank. It conducts monetary policy, regulates banking institutions, maintains the financial system, and provides financial services to banks, the government and foreign institutions. The Fed has 12 Federal Reserve banks in Boston, New York, Philadelphia, Cleveland, Richmond, Atlanta, Chicago, St Louis, Minneapolis, Kansas City, Dallas and San Francisco.

JEFFERSON: So, we have a national bank with various branches.

PAUL: That is correct. Also, the Reserve has a Federal Open Market Committee buying and selling government securities, managing bank reserve requirements and adjusting the discount rate to control inflation and maintain monetary policy. National chartered banks are required to hold stock in the Federal Reserve Bank of their regions.

JEFFERSON: The private banks own the Federal Reserve banks?

PAUL: Only symbolically. They cannot sell their stake in the Federal

190

Reserve Bank. After a 6% capital investment payment to member banks annually, the federal government receives all the profits from its businesses.

JEFFERSON: How does the Federal Reserve control inflation?

PAUL: When the FOMC wishes to control inflation, it restricts the money supply by selling government bonds and raising reserve requirements. The interest rate also can be raised or lowered to either control inflation or enhance employment. The Federal Reserve Board also sets margin requirements for purchasing securities.

JEFFERSON: All these policies can control the value of the national currency?

PAUL: Yes. The Board also enforces federal laws on consumer credit such as the Truth in Lending Act, the Equal Credit Opportunity Act, the Home Mortgage Disclosure Act and the Truth in Savings Act. What do you think of this agency?

JEFFERSON: The Constitution specifically allows the federal government to regulate the value of its currency. On that basis, selling government bonds and raising reserve requirements is an acceptable function if it works. Setting the interest rate to control inflation is also an acceptable function. As part of its authority to borrow money, it can also buy and sell government securities and set margin requirements for those securities. However, it can only set reserve requirements and discount rates for those national institutions. For those institutions only lending within a state, the Federal Reserve has no authority. Nor does it have any authority to enhance employment. That is a function of the individual. The Acts cited for enforcement should only apply to interstate businesses.

PAUL: What are the next steps to be taken?

JEFFERSON: Eliminate reserve requirements for banks lending only within a state. The Fed should not consider employment in its decisions. Its policies should only be to inhibit inflation.

PAUL: Thank you, Mr. President. Before we turn to our next agency, let us stop here for an important word from our sponsor.

Commercial Break

Segment 76 – Department of Health and Human Services: Centers for Medicare and Medicaid Services

Paul Jefko: Mr. President, under President Johnson, Medicare was established and placed under the Social Security Administration, while Congress placed Medicaid under the Social and Rehabilitation Service of the Health, Education and Welfare Department. Medicare provides health care to the elderly while Medicaid provides health care to children, and low income, elderly, blind and disabled Americans. In 1972, Medicare was authorized for those under 65 with disabilities.

President Jefferson: Haven't we already discussed this agency?

PAUL: We previously discussed the Medicare and Medicaid Programs, but not the organization tasked to administer the programs. In 1977, Congress established the Health Care Financing Administration under the Department of Health, Education and Welfare to coordinate Medicare and Medicaid. Later, the HMO Act provided grants and loans to private health maintenance organizations to provide health care directly to Medicare recipients.

JEFFERSON: There is no need to go on about this. I have already said this was unconstitutional.

PAUL: I understand. The State Children's Health Insurance Program was established in 1997. Medicare Part D for drugs came along in 2003. The agency directly administers Medicare and provides grants to States to administer Medicaid, and the State Children's Health Insurance Program.

JEFFERSON: Why doesn't the federal government either administer both or let the states administer both?

PAUL: Since Medicare is paid from payroll taxes, the federal government collects and disburses payments. Tax dollars fund Medicaid with no payment from patients. Some States limit the benefits provided to their citizens to hold down Medicaid costs. The federal government provides 50% of the cost of the Children's Health Insurance Program and provides guidelines for administration. The agency also develops nursing home standards and oversees Healthcare.gov. What do you think of this agency?

JEFFERSON: As I said earlier about these programs, no specific authority exists in the Constitution for this function. It also does not affect the national defense nor the general welfare as it only helps the poor and elderly. It is unconstitutional.

PAUL: What should be done?

JEFFERSON: I have already spoken earlier: abolish Medicare and Medicaid. A phased in plan for elimination minimizes the effect on those who obtain unconstitutional benefits from this agency.

PAUL: Thank you. Mr. President. Let us return to the Defense Department.

Segment 77 - Department of Defense: Defense Advanced Research Projects Agency

Paul Jefko: Mr. President, concerned by the Soviet launch of Sputnik, President Eisenhower established the Advanced Research Projects Agency in 1958 to develop projects expanding the frontiers of technology beyond military needs. In 1960, the President centered its mission on defense against ballistic missiles, detection of nuclear tests and counterinsurgency. In the 1970's it received its current name and focused on energy, information processing and tactical technology.

President Jefferson: This agency does research on new military weapons?

PAUL: Well, it does a little more than that. Beginning in 1973, it worked on all military items, not just weapons. It has helped develop the Global Positioning System, the Internet, speech recognition, robotics, armor and anti-armor, infrared sensing, high-energy lasers, antisubmarine warfare, cruise missiles, advanced aircraft and advanced computing. They even work on interstellar travel. The agency works in small teams on projects lasting 2 to 4 years. Each team has a project manager tasked with a problem.

JEFFERSON: That is a lot to absorb. Can you explain each item you mentioned?

PAUL: The Global Positioning System uses the satellite system we have already talked about to locate any place on the earth. The Internet allows any communication device to communicate with another. Speech Recognition allows a machine to hear and interpret human speech. Robotics use machines to perform a human function. Armor protects against missiles and bombs. Infrared sensing allows a soldier to see an enemy soldier in the dark.

JEFFERSON: How is that done?

PAUL: Remember when we discussed the electromagnetic spectrum and the wavelengths of light? Well, a portion of the spectrum our eyes cannot detect as visible light, known as infrared, lies below the red portion of the light spectrum and are actually heat waves. The infrared sensor device, looking like large spectacles, detects these heat waves and converts them to a light we can see. (Shows photo of infrared image)

JEFFERSON: Amazing.

PAUL: Continuing…High-energy lasers use light as a weapon to destroy incoming missiles. The remainder are self-explanatory. Six offices direct the work of the project managers: Defense Sciences, Information Processing, Technology, Information Exploitation, Microsystems Technology, Strategic Technology, and Tactical Technology. What is your opinion, Mr. President?

JEFFERSON: Although there is no specific authority in the Constitution for this agency, it does have
constitutionality as it has been deemed by Congress to provide for the general defense of the nation.

PAUL: Thank you, Mr. President. Our next agency is a large part of our Agriculture Department.

Segment 78 – Department of Agriculture: Farm Service Agency

Paul Jefko: Mr. President, during the Great Depression, Congress established the Resettlement Administration to relocate farmers from depressed areas to more profitable farming areas. Later, the agency merged with the Agricultural Adjustment Administration, providing loans to farmers in return for their limiting crop production, and added the Farmers Home Administration, insuring loans to farmers made by other lending institutions.

President Jefferson: Why were farmers given loans to decrease planting?

PAUL: At the time, there was surplus food production. In some cases, the production cost was higher than the price achieved in the market, forcing many farmers into bankruptcy.

JEFFERSON: Normally, the farmers would lose their land or take it out of production eventually leading to fewer crops and livestock available in the market increasing their price. Isn't that the method occurring throughout history?

PAUL: Yes, but the huge number of bankruptcies during the Depression threatened the existence of the family farm and the agricultural output of the nation. Over 750,000 farms were lost between 1930 and 1935...Continuing...the agency transformed again as it became the Commodity Stabilization Service paying farmers to take land out of production and even later renamed the Agricultural Stabilization and Conservation Service.

JEFFERSON: So, instead of letting the farmer decide to take land out of production, the taxpayer pays the farmer to do so.

PAUL: I think the problem was the farmer would not voluntarily take land out of production. He would plant and hope for the best.

JEFFERSON: If it costs more to plant and harvest than the farmer received in sales, he would stop planting.

PAUL: I see your point, but he would not stop planting, he would probably go bankrupt.

JEFFERSON: And then his farm would be sold to a better farmer.

PAUL: Actually, it would probably be sold to a land developer who would build houses on it.... Anyway, the current agency combined the mission of the latter agency with the Farmers Home Administration and the Federal Crop Insurance Corporation. The mission of the agency is to implement farm conservation laws.

JEFFERSON: Crop Insurance?

PAUL: Yes, a farmer can purchase insurance to reimburse him or her for losses resulting from natural disasters...To implement all these programs, Congress set up a locally controlled system. All the qualified farmers in a county elect a county committee to oversee these programs. The committee selects a County Executive Director who manages a Service Center in each county. The county hires the Service Center employees but the federal government pays their wages.

JEFFERSON: I do not understand. Why is a taxpayer in Richmond paying for a county employee in Pennsylvania?

PAUL: I believe it provides local control. The County Executive Director has the power to hire and fire to maintain better service to the farmers. Each Service Center is a central site paying out farm commodity loans and purchases, farm ownership and operating loans, the conservation reserves, disaster assistance and support to the Commodity Credit Corporation.

JEFFERSON: So, we have a complete welfare system for the farmer similar to that provided to the elderly and children. How much is this costing the taxpayer?

PAUL: $13.7 billion in direct payments annually. What do you think of this agency?

JEFFERSON: No express authority exists in the Constitution for providing loans to farmers or to pay them for not planting crops. The program is not necessary for national defense and since it only helps farmers, it is not providing for the general welfare.

PAUL: What should we do?
JEFFERSON: First, no further loans shall be made or extended. Sell all current loans if possible to private lenders. Those that cannot be sold will be managed until liquidated. Payments for not planting will cease over a 10-year period to minimize disruption. Reduce the amount paid each year by 10% until all payments are stopped. Along with reducing payments, the farmer may increase his planting in proportion. After 10 years, the agency will be abolished.

PAUL: Thank you, Mr. President. We should look at an important national defense organization now.

Segment 79 – Department of Defense: Defense Threat Reduction Agency

Paul Jefko: Mr. President, after the end of the Cold War, both the US and the Soviet Union agreed to dismantle most of their nuclear, biological and chemical weapons to prevent their falling into the wrong hands. In 1991, the START 1 Treaty bound the US and the former Soviet States to cut the number of nuclear weapons in half by 2001.

President Jefferson: I assume the Senate approved the treaty?

PAUL: Yes. Later in 1998, three agencies were combined to establish this agency and meet the requirements of the START 1 Treaty: The Defense Special Weapons Agency, The On-site Inspections Agency and the Defense Technology Security Administration. Its three main tasks are inspection, disarmament and technology development. It also provides combat support to the US Strategic Command to counter weapons of mass destruction.

JEFFERSON: How many workers are in this agency?

PAUL: With 200 civilian and military staff, it inspects foreign stockpiles of weapons and leads foreign inspections of US stockpiles.

JEFFERSON: Such a small staff for such a large task.

PAUL: Well, most of the weapons are located in a small number of locations. Unless there is a major problem, the inspection process is routine. It also develops technology for bunker busting bombs, blast resistant facilities, chemical and biological countermeasures, and bomb and nuclear material detection. What do you think of this agency?

JEFFERSON: Since this is part of an international treaty, the process set up is constitutional as is the agency.

PAUL: Thank you, Mr. President. That ends this week's program. Tune in next week for the final program with President Jefferson. On behalf of President Jefferson, I wish you a good evening.

Program # 10

Paul Jefko: Good evening, ladies and gentlemen and welcome to the final part of this Series: 'They Are Here', where we discuss our current government with the author of the Declaration of Independence, Thomas Jefferson.

Segment 80 – Department of Commerce: US Census Bureau

Paul Jefko: Mr. President, one of the most popular foods that current Americans enjoy is Macaroni and Cheese. I understand that you are the proponent of this culinary delight.

President Jefferson: This is an old dish in Italy. I encountered it in Paris and in Italy while I was ambassador to France. When I was Secretary of State, I asked our ambassador in France to buy a macaroni extrusion machine but it did not prove suitable. For those times I served the dish at Monticello, I used imported macaroni.

PAUL: As a Mac and Cheese lover, Mr. President, I thank you personally for bringing that dish to America…but to continue our discussion on government, you oversaw the first census conducted in 1790, a head count asking for the head of the family and the number of persons in each home, designated as either free white males over 16, free white males under 16, free white females and all other free persons and slaves. Changes have occurred since then. For example, the 1810 census required the census taker to actually visit the citizen's home.

JEFFERSON: Yes, we were concerned about the accuracy of the 1800 census.

PAUL: The 1830 census used standard forms for the first time. The Bureau added questions to obtain social statistics in 1870. The 1890 census used the Hollerith hole punch system. In 1902, the Bureau became permanent and moved under the Interior Department. The next year it moved to the Commerce and Labor Department. In 1937, the Bureau conducted a special census on employment. For 1980, the Bureau designated an 'M' Night to count persons who were homeless, ate in soup kitchens, and slept in transit terminals.

JEFFERSON: Are there that many homeless persons, a special time is

198

designated to count them?

PAUL: On any given night, there are over 600,000 homeless. Similarly, on T night, census takers counted permanent residents in hotels or motels. All census data became available on the Internet in 1997. Although the Bureau uses statistical sampling for much of its information, the Supreme Court ruled an actual head count must determine Congressional representation. The agency also conducts the American Community Survey, the US Economic Census and the Current Population Survey used to allocate $400 Billion in federal funds.

JEFFERSON: Explain the reason for the Current Population Survey.

PAUL: The Congress provides some federal funds to the States for particular purposes. The survey determines the method of allocating the funds for each State. For example, providing unemployment relief to a State depends on the unemployment rate in that State. One more item…The agency also publishes the Statistical Abstract of the US and has since 1878. What do you think of this agency, Mr. President?

JEFFERSON: Since the Constitution requires a decennial census, this activity is constitutional and its ancillary functions of other surveys are constitutional as information for the Congress.

PAUL: Thank you, Mr. President. We now return to the Agriculture Department.

Segment 81 - Department of Agriculture: Foreign Agricultural Service

Paul Jefko: The Foreign Agriculture Act of 1930 gave diplomatic status to agricultural commissioners who negotiated tariff reductions and gathered information on markets for agricultural goods. Congress gave the mission to the newly established Foreign Agricultural Service. Later President Roosevelt transferred the overseas staff to the State Department while its headquarters office remained in the Agriculture Department as the Office of Foreign Agricultural Relations.

President Jefferson: Correct. All diplomatic personnel are subject to the Secretary of State.

PAUL: During World War II, the agency handled food aid, analyzed food availability in Allied countries and in 1953, was reconstituted under the current name. The Market Development Cooperator Program was created in 1955 to

199

increase agreements with groups representing specific agricultural commodities.

JEFFERSON: What are groups representing agricultural commodities?

PAUL: Organizations representing food producers, such as the North American Blueberry Council or the American Soybean Association.

JEFFERSON: What benefits do these associations obtain from this program?

PAUL: Well, the agency helps them market their goods overseas...Continuing, in 1961, Congress merged the Commodity Stabilization Service with this agency to manage export credit and foreign food aid. Its main mission today is to develop markets for US agricultural products overseas, negotiate international trade agreements and collect statistics and market information. It has several programs. The Export Credit Guarantee Program funds US agricultural exports.

JEFFERSON: It funds our exports?

PAUL: Yes, sir. The Market Access Program reimburses private companies for their marketing costs.

JEFFERSON: Hold on. We reimburse private companies for the costs of selling their products?

PAUL: Yes, sir.

JEFFERSON: And the American taxpayer pays for this?

PAUL: Yes, Sir...Moving on, the Foreign Market Development Program funds nonprofit associations to remove market obstructions. The Emerging Markets Program provides assistance to promote US agricultural products in emerging markets. The Quality Samples Program assists private firms to furnish samples of agricultural products to foreign importers. The Technical Assistance for Specialty Crops Program funds projects addressing sanitary issues affecting US exports.

JEFFERSON: Do American agricultural products face much competition overseas?

PAUL: Well, the main food producer in the world is China, but it also has the largest population. I am not sure how much they export. Moving on...The Dairy Export Incentive Program provides cash to dairies allowing them to sell their product at a lower price. The Facility Guarantee Program finances the establishment of agricultural facilities in emerging markets.

JEFFERSON: The taxpayer funds the building of facilities in other countries to support our farmers?

PAUL: Yes. It makes export of our farm products more efficient. The General Sales Manager Online Program enables exporters and banks to submit online documentation for CCC credit.

JEFFERSON: We now provide subsidies to farmers along with children, the elderly, Indian tribes and veterans.

PAUL: We are not finished. The Sugar Import Program provides a level field for sugar imports. The Dairy Import Program enforces tariffs and quota for dairy imports. The Food for Progress Program provides commodities to developing countries expanding free enterprise. What do you think of these programs, Mr. President?

JEFFERSON: None of the programs enhance the general welfare or strengthen national defense. That being said, the only constitutional programs come under Congressional authority to regulate commerce with foreign nations and the power to tax. Those programs include the Sugar Import Program, the Dairy Import Program, the Tariff schedule and the Food for Progress Program.

PAUL: What should be the next steps?

JEFFERSON: The remainder of the programs should be abolished.

PAUL: Thank you, Mr. President. Let us now turn to Drug Enforcement.

Segment 82 – Department of Justice: US Drug Enforcement Administration

Paul Jefko: Mr. President, President Johnson created the Bureau of Narcotics and Dangerous Drugs to combat recreational drug use in America. Its focus was on marijuana and narcotics. Another agency, the Office of Drug Abuse Law Enforcement controlled depressants, stimulants and hallucinogens. In 1973, both offices merged to form the current agency. Its main mission was to reduce narcotics sale and distribution in the US.

President Jefferson: How widespread was this problem?

PAUL: It costs the US $193 billion annually in crime, lost productivity and health care. In 1975, the agency concentrated its efforts on major drug traffickers. Because of the demand for illegal drugs in the US, drug cartels emerged in Colombia. President Reagan sent military advisors to Latin America to combat them. Congress also allowed the seizure of property of those persons convicted of drug dealing. Although the agency has done little to stem drug operations, both the President and Congress continue to fund and expand the authority of the agency.

JEFFERSON: Why?

PAUL: No President wants to admit defeat. And, no other alternative exists. It resembles any other law enforcement we have. We fund police to solve murders even though we know we will never eliminate the crime…Continuing, besides international drug smuggling, synthetic drugs were produced in the US and legal prescription drugs were sold on the black market.

JEFFERSON: Synthetic drugs?

PAUL: Yes, our knowledge of chemistry has enabled some scientists to produce artificial opioids and cannabinoids along with new drugs made from natural substances. Moving on…The Office of Intelligence provides information leading to drug seizures and arrests. The Office of Aviation provides photographic reconnaissance. The Domestic Cannabis Eradication/Suppression Program targets marijuana cultivation.

JEFFERSON: The States should be equipped to handle these problems.

PAUL: True. But currently, some States have legalized the production and sale of marijuana.

JEFFERSON: Exactly, since drug use is a State issue.

PAUL: But other agency functions like the Demand Reduction Program provide the public information on the dangers of illegal drugs. The Office of Diversion Control seeks to limit controlled drugs from entering the black market. The Foreign Cooperative Investigations Program works with foreign governments to combat drug cartels. Forensic Sciences provides scientific support to drug agents. Computer Forensics Program obtains information from drug offenders' computers.

JEFFERSON: Let us go back to the crux of the matter. Crime, health and productivity can be handled by State and local law enforcement and private employers.

PAUL: The 21st century differs from the 18th, sir. Much of this crime is organized and even international. The Organized Crime Drug Enforcement Task

Force provides a venue for DEA, FBI, ICE, ATF, US Marshals, IRS, Coast Guard, Justice Criminal Division, Tax Division and US Attorneys.

JEFFERSON: I disagree. No enumerated power allows the federal government to disallow recreational drug use within the US. Authority does exist however to prevent drug smuggling if Congress declares drugs to be illegal contraband. Moreover, no authority can be found in the Constitution for the following programs: The Aviation Program within the US, The Domestic Cannabis Eradication/Suppression Program, The Demand Reduction Program, The Office of Diversion Control, and The Organized Crime Drug Enforcement Task Force. All other agency programs are constitutional. The only role the federal government has in this area is the prevention of drug smuggling. Once the drugs are here, or if they are produced domestically, the States have the responsibility for their control if they wish. However, no national defense issue, or general welfare issue exists.

PAUL: What should we do?

JEFFERSON: The agency should be abolished. Customs agencies should handle any enforcement issues.

PAUL: Thank you, Mr. President. We will now look at the Native American once again.

Segment 83 – Department of the Interior: Bureau of Indian Affairs

Paul Jefko: Mr. President, as you know, Congress in 1789 put all Native American relations under War Department control. And, under your administration, Congress established a Superintendent of Indian Trade within the War Department to maintain the fur-trading network. Later, in 1824, Secretary of War John C Calhoun created a Division of Indian Affairs within the War Department without Congressional authorization.

President Jefferson: Well, he and I differed on the role of the federal government. No wonder he disregarded the Constitutional authority of Congress. Did they impeach him?

PAUL: No, he got away with it. In fact, in later years, he became a States Rights champion and referred to you as his mentor. In any case, the Division was transferred to the Department of Interior when it was formed in 1849 and given its current name in 1947. Throughout its history, the Bureau conducted a number of bad policies that did not help Native Americans. For example, it took native children and placed them in boarding schools to assimilate them into European culture.

JEFFERSON: Really! How?

PAUL: Their hair was cut and American clothing was provided to them. They were not allowed to speak their native languages and they were given English names and forced to attend church services. They were also given vocational training. To manage tribes and fur trading, the agency supported corrupt tribal leaders. The agency forced the Indians onto reservations where they had to live.

JEFFERSON: I believe assimilation aids survival of the Indian. However, placing the children in boarding schools does not seem as effective as providing them schooling in our culture and customs in their own areas. I also believe citizenship to be another way to assimilate the tribes. What has happened to them?

PAUL: Those policies I described destroyed the Indian culture and made them wards of the State. Other legislation gave them American citizenship, and allotted reservation land held in common to individual Indians to encourage them to take up farming. The system did not work as many natives did not want to farm and instead sold their allotment to white settlers or faced foreclosure when they did not pay state taxes.

JEFFERSON: Why didn't the Indian wish to farm his own land?

PAUL: In some cases, the land was not suitable for farming, while in others the native wanted to maintain his hunter-gatherer type culture. By 1934, when the allotment system was abolished, 138 million acres of Indian land in 1887 had dwindled to 48 million acres. Today, the Bureau manages 55 million acres held in trust for Native Americans, Tribes and Alaska Natives. Moving on…some programs managed by the agency include Trust Fund Management distributing funds from timber sales, and agricultural and oil leases on 11 million acres.

JEFFERSON: So, the agency sells timber and agricultural products on behalf of the tribes? Why aren't the tribes doing it for themselves?

PAUL: Apparently, some feel the Indians cannot handle their own money. Moving on…The Federal Acknowledgement Program processes tribal petitions for recognition. The Indian Education Program operates 184 schools and 27 colleges. The Natural Resources Program protects water, water rights, fish, parks, forests, agriculture and range. The Law Enforcement Program enforces federal and tribal law on reservations.

JEFFERSON: What do these schools and colleges teach?

PAUL: A similar curriculum to any other college except for its emphasis on Indian Studies. A student can obtain a degree in a Science, but can also train in the manual trades. What are your opinions on this agency, Mr. President?

JEFFERSON: Congress does have authority to declare the Indians American citizens and under treaty provide lands to the tribes. They also have authority to manage the lands given to the tribes. In effect, as long as Indian/White relations are done under a federal treaty, all is constitutional. On the other hand, even though I favor the policy, unless there is a treaty to provide schooling to the Indian, there is no constitutional basis for it.

PAUL: Thank you Mr. President. Next up is the National Park Service

Segment 84 – Department of Interior: National Park Service

Paul Jefko: Mr. President, Congress established national parks and monuments and assigned them to the Department of the Interior to manage. In 1916, Congress set up the current agency under Interior to handle the national parks and monuments. In 1933, Congress transferred the Civil War historic sites from the War Department to this agency. At the same time, the sites managed by the Agriculture Department and around the National Capital were also transferred.

President Jefferson: Why do we have national parks?

PAUL: The first park was Yellowstone Park, established in 1872 in the State of Wyoming. The site was so unusual, having geysers, hot springs and other natural beauty, Congress wanted to protect it from the private exploitation they saw at Niagara Falls. Since then, Congress has added new parks periodically. After 1966, the Congress added National Lakeshores, National Recreation Areas and National Heritage Areas to the list of properties that could be established.

JEFFERSON: Of course, this requires the federal government to purchase the land for these parks.

PAUL: Of course. When this agency was established, it assumed control over 35 national parks and monuments. Fifty-six more were transferred in 1933. Today, the Service manages 391 areas covering 84 million acres. The agency manages all US National Parks, National Monuments, National Historic Landmarks and the National Register of Historic Places.

JEFFERSON: So, we establish one national park and then create the demand for more.

PAUL: You are correct. However, each category has a specific definition. Hence, a National Park is a large natural place, which allows no hunting, mining, logging or grazing. A National Preserve is similar to a National Park except hunting, mining, logging, and grazing are permitted. A National Recreation Area is an area emphasizing water-based recreation. A National Seashore is an area protected from private development.

JEFFERSON: Why do we want to protect it from private development?

PAUL: I do not know if you have ever been to Niagara Falls.

JEFFERSON: I have never been but I have an engraving of it by John Vanderlyn in my home.

PAUL: Well, as the industrial revolution spread in the late 19th century, mills and factories spread along the river flowing to the falls, and siphoned off water and reduced the flow. If you wanted to see the Falls, you paid a fee to view them to persons who owned property near the Falls. Consequently, New York established the site as a State Park to limit development and make it more accessible to the public.

JEFFERSON: Exactly. If the State wishes to establish a state park permitted by their State Constitution, it is fine.

PAUL: Other distinctions include a National Lakeshore similar to a National Seashore except it is located on the Great Lakes. A National River is protected from private development. A National Trail cannot have private development and has scenic or historic properties. A National Parkway is an auto motorway providing scenic travel protected from development. A National Monument designates an historic or scientific location.

JEFFERSON: Soon we will have nothing available for private development.

PAUL: Perhaps…A National Historic Site designates a site with a single historic feature. A National Historical Park designates a larger historical area than a historic Site. A National Memorial designates a spot commemorating an historic person or episode. A National Battlefield is the site of a battle. A National Cemetery is one of historic significance. The agency serves 270 million annual visitors.

JEFFERSON: I can see it is very popular.

PAUL: What are your thoughts on this agency?

JEFFERSON: No specific authority exists in the Constitution allowing the federal government to acquire land for national parks or to designate federally owned land as a national park. Since this agency does not provide for national defense nor does it provide for the general welfare of the country, it is unconstitutional.

PAUL: What should be done?

JEFFERSON: Offer each current park to the respective State for its ownership and operation. Those not accepted should then be offered to the general public or private owners for ownership and operation. If no one wishes to assume responsibility, the parks should be closed and the property sold as market conditions allow.

PAUL: Thank You, Mr. President. An agency in the Department of Justice is up next.

Segment 85 – Department of Justice: Office of Justice Programs

Paul Jefko: Mr. President, Congress set up the Law Enforcement Assistance Administration in 1968 to provide federal funds to State and local law enforcement agencies. In 1982 the Office of Justice Assistance, Research and Statistics replaced that agency which was further replaced by the current agency in 1984. The agency has several offices. The Bureau of Justice Assistance funds bulletproof vest programs for State and Local governments.

President Jefferson: Vests that are bulletproof? They must be heavy.

PAUL: They are 5 times stronger than steel and are flexible. (Shows pictures of an FBI agent wearing the vest)

JEFFERSON: Do they actually stop bullets?

PAUL: Yes, a bullet cannot penetrate the fabric but the projectile can still can cause severe bruising. Continuing…The Office of Juvenile Justice and Delinquency Prevention seeks to prevent gang violence. The National Institute of Justice provides grants for research into criminal justice. The Bureau of Justice Statistics provides assistance to local governments to improve their statistical abilities. The Office for Victims of Crime provides information on victim service agencies in the US.

JEFFERSON: The local police or sheriff normally assists crime victims. Why is the federal government involved?

PAUL: Law enforcement officials cannot provide legal services, counseling, financial assistance, emergency shelters and other items. One more branch, The Office of Sex Offender Sentencing, Monitoring, Apprehending, Registering and Tracking maintains information on sex offenders. What do you think of this agency, Mr. President?

JEFFERSON: The Constitution, under the 'necessary and proper' clause states the federal government can enforce its own laws and can provide the resources to do so. That does not mean the federal taxpayer can fund State and local law enforcement activities. Nor can it be involved in local law enforcement or assistance to non-federal crime victims.

PAUL: What shall we do?

JEFFERSON: Eliminate the Bureau of Justice Assistance, The Office of Juvenile Justice and Delinquency Prevention, the Disproportionate Minority Contact Initiative, the Bureau of Justice Statistics, and the Office for Victims of Crime. The National Institute of Justice's role in informing Congress is constitutional.

PAUL: Thank you, Mr. President. It is now time to turn to another independent agency.

Segment 86 – Independent Agencies: Millennium Challenge Corporation

Paul Jefko: Mr. President, the events of 9/11 prompted a defense and foreign policy review, since some believed our foreign aid did not go to those countries helping our national security. A competition was designed using 17 performance criteria for distributing foreign aid funds. The President established a board to evaluate projects using three broad categories: countries ruling justly, countries investing in people and countries providing economic freedom.

President Jefferson: And we assume if these countries meet those criteria, our funds will enhance our security?

PAUL: That is the idea. Countries denying human rights, lacking democracy, supporting terrorism and drug commerce and protecting international criminals are not eligible. What do you think of this agency?

JEFFERSON: There is no specific authority to provide this aid. However, under the common defense clause, the Congress may decide it helps American security. That being said, the agency seems to be devoted to 'global development' and not national defense. One may infer global development helps our national security but the link is tenuous and vague. Obviously, those countries denying human rights, lacking democracy, supporting terrorism etc., should not receive any aid under this program, but they are not anyway.

PAUL: Well, we have supported such nations in the past.

JEFFERSON: Really!

PAUL: Yes. During the Cold War, we supported dictators to keep their country from becoming 'tools' of Communist Russia.

JEFFERSON: Although I would hold my nose in providing aid to such countries, I see the assistance given can increase our national security. Consequently, I maintain that unless the aid provided by this agency bolstered our defenses, no constitutional basis for this agency exists.

PAUL: What should our next steps be?

JEFFERSON: Abolish the agency.

PAUL: Thank you Mr. President. Let's go to a commercial after which we will look at another agency under Health and Human Services.

Commercial Break

Segment 87 – Department of Health and Human Services: Food and Drug Administration

Paul Jefko: Mr. President, in 1883, the Department of Agriculture's Division of Chemistry investigated the adulteration and misbranding of food and drugs sold in the US. Later, a book by Upton Sinclair, The Jungle, exposed the unsanitary conditions in the meat packing industry leading Congress to pass the Food and Drugs Act of 1906. In 1930, Congress set up the agency as a bureau of the Agriculture Department.

President Jefferson: What unsanitary conditions existed?

PAUL: Moldy meat was used to make sausage after treatment with borax. Rats were rampant over the unprocessed meats stored in warehouses. Sometimes, dead rats were processed into the meats. Consequently, the public demanded new laws, to include pre-market review of all new drugs and banned false labeling. Later laws defined drugs requiring a doctor's prescription.

JEFFERSON: Why the emphasis on labeling?

PAUL: As in your day, there were patent medicine salespersons who peddled nostrums they said cured various illnesses. The new law required them to list the ingredients. The labeling requirement showed alcohol, cocaine, heroin and other opiates in the medicines that did nothing to cure sickness. In 1953, the agency was transferred to the Department of Health, Education and Welfare. In 1970, Congress put medical devices under agency authority. Today the agency has 5 regional offices, 20 district offices, 223 field offices, and 13 laboratories to regulate food safety, tobacco, dietary supplements, drugs, vaccines, blood transfusions, medical devices, radiation devices, cosmetics and veterinary products.

JEFFERSON: Why tobacco?

PAUL: Because scientific studies have proven tobacco use is a risk to health, is addictive and was marketed to children to attract a new addicted crop of adult customers...To meet these and all other regulatory requirements, its offices include the Center for Food Safety and Applied Nutrition, which regulates all food except meat, poultry and some egg products. The Center for Drug Evaluation and Research evaluates all new drugs before sale.

JEFFERSON: Wait. The problems birthing this agency were food issues, but this agency does not regulate meat, poultry and eggs?

PAUL: Its original mandate included meat, poultry and eggs, but when the agency was transferred out of the Agriculture Department, its meat, poultry and eggs inspections were left there...The Center for Veterinary Medicine regulates drugs used for pets and animals. The Office of Regulatory Affairs conducts inspections for all its areas. The Center for Biologics Evaluation and Research regulates human gene therapy, transplantations, genomics and DNA testing.

JEFFERSON: Human gene therapy?

PAUL: A disease treatment that replaces a nonfunctional or damaged gene with a functional one to correct a specific disease...The FDA's other offices include The Center of Devices and Radiological Health to regulate medical devices. The National Center for Toxicological Research gives advice on biological events. What is your opinion of this agency?

JEFFERSON: The Commerce Clause allows this agency to regulate all the items listed here.

PAUL: What should be done?

JEFFERSON: All food and drug establishments should be assessed a fee in lieu of taxpayer funding.

PAUL: Thank you, Mr. President. It is time to review the Mint.

Segment 88 – Department of the Treasury: United States Mint

Paul Jefko: Mr. President, the Coinage Act of 1782 authorized the establishment of the mint. And, as you recall, Congress established the first mint in Philadelphia in 1792. In fact, the Philadelphia Mint was the first building constructed under the Constitution. Other mints have been established since. Branch mints were set up in Charlotte, North Carolina and Dahlonega, Georgia to produce gold coins from local gold mines.

President Jefferson: I remember the discovery of gold in Carolina just before the turn of the century.

PAUL: Another gold find in Georgia began in 1828, larger than the Carolina find. New Orleans also had a mint but the US closed all the Southern mints during the Civil War. The New Orleans Mint reopened in 1879 but has since closed. The Treasury opened a mint in Carson City, Nevada to mint silver coins after a huge silver deposit discovery. A mint was also established in Manila, Philippines to provide coinage for the US colony there.

JEFFERSON: Why did we establish a mint in the Philippines?

PAUL: The Spanish had established one there in the mid-1800's. When the US took over the colony after the Spanish American War, we continued to mint coins there for local usage. They were based on the peso not the dollar. Currently four mints exist in Philadelphia, Denver, San Francisco and West Point. Finally, a bullion depository is located at Fort Knox, Kentucky. The Mint's mission is to produce, sell and protect the country's coinage.

JEFFERSON: How much coinage do we actually mint?

PAUL: Well, besides producing 11 to 20 billion coins each year, the Mint also produces foreign coins, has custody of the US bullion supply, and produces coins for collectors, and Congressional Gold Medals. Most coins are minted in Philadelphia. Denver also mints circulating coins but San Francisco produces Proof Coins and West Point produces the American Eagle coins.

JEFFERSON: What are Proof and American Eagle coins?

PAUL: Proof coins are normally the first ones minted of a new issue to check quality. (Shows a proof set of coins) However, these days, they mint proofs specifically to sell to coin collectors. American Eagle coins are gold, silver and platinum coins that can be used for circulation, but are really targeted for sale to collectors or investors since their true value depends on the price of the inherent metal, not their face value. In addition, a Mint Police Force protects the Mint and the assets at Fort Knox.

JEFFERSON: How many American Eagle Coins are minted?

PAUL: As an example, the Treasury minted and sold to collectors over 337 million silver Eagle coins. (Shows a Silver American Eagle coin) The mint is self-funded, as no taxpayer funds are used for its operations. What do you think of this agency, Mr. President?

JEFFERSON: This is constitutional as an enumerated power but only to coin money for circulation. The other benefits to collectors are not enumerated nor are they related to national defense or general welfare. Those are unconstitutional.

PAUL: What should we do?

JEFFERSON: Close the San Francisco and West Point Mints and desist from minting coinage not for circulation or for official congressionally authorized medals.

PAUL: Thank you, Mr. President. It is time to look at another Education agency.

Segment 89 – Department of Education: Office of Postsecondary Education

Paul Jefko: Mr. President, the Higher Education Acts of 1965 authorized this agency to aid disadvantaged children and college students. Federal Student Aid provides financial assistance to college students. Grant Programs assist Hispanic-Serving and Historically Black Colleges and Universities. The Fund for the Improvement of Postsecondary Education promotes reform, innovation and improvements.

President Jefferson: What are Historically Black Colleges?

PAUL: Institutions of higher learning established after the Civil War by northern religious missionary organizations to serve the newly freed black communities, mainly throughout the South....Continuing...Another Division of this Agency, Higher Education Programs researches minority issues in postsecondary education. The agency also publishes a list of accrediting agencies. What about this agency, Mr. President?

JEFFERSON: No specific authority can be found in the Constitution for any of these programs. They do not provide for the general welfare but apply only to those who plan to obtain postsecondary education. No national defense issue comes into play here. Therefore, all its programs are unconstitutional.

PAUL: What do we do?

JEFFERSON: Abolish the agency.

PAUL: Thank You, Mr. President. We now turn to the Defense Intelligence Agency.

Segment 90 – Department of Defense: Defense Intelligence Agency

Paul Jefko: Mr. President, until the Defense Intelligence Agency was established, each Military Department collected, analyzed and distributed intelligence for its own use, but the President tasked this agency to consolidate all intelligence functions for the entire Department. It has 17,000 employees stationed here and in 140 countries. It collects intelligence on foreign military forces, weapons of mass destruction, international terrorism, and narcotics trafficking.

President Jefferson: So, this is the place all our spies are supervised?

PAUL: Actually, 17 intelligence services exist in the US government, but this one provides national security via human intelligence gathering. It has a National Center for Medical Intelligence to collect information on foreign

213

diseases, environmental health risks, foreign health care systems and biological weapons. The Missile and Space Intelligence Center monitors foreign missile systems.

JEFFERSON: 17!

PAUL: Oh, yes. Shall I name them?

JEFFERSON: Please!

PAUL: The Director of National Intelligence, the Central Intelligence Agency, The Office of Intelligence and Counterintelligence in the Department of Energy, The Office of Intelligence and Analysis and Coast Guard Intelligence in the Department of Homeland Security, the Bureau of Intelligence and Research in the Department of State, the Office of Terrorism and Financial Intelligence in the Department of the Treasury, the National Security Agency, the National Geospatial-Intelligence Agency, the National Reconnaissance Office, Air Force Intelligence, Surveillance and Reconnaissance Agency, Army Military Intelligence, Marine Corp Intelligence Activity, Office of Naval Intelligence in the Department of Defense, the National Security Branch of the Federal Bureau of Investigation and the Office of National Security Intelligence of the Drug Enforcement Administration.

JEFFERSON: Amazing!

PAUL: And besides the functions I have described for this agency, its Defense HUMINT Service manages the agency's spies throughout the world and its National Intelligence University awards Bachelor and Master's degrees in Intelligence.

JEFFERSON: A college developing intelligence? I have made a pun.

PAUL: A very bad one sir. The agency also manages the Defense Attaché positions in 135 embassies. Finally, The Defense Counterintelligence and Human Intelligence Center runs covert operations against foreign agents. What do you think of this agency?

JEFFERSON: All are constitutional as part of the general defense of the nation.

PAUL: Thank you, Mr. President. Now comes Patents and Trademarks.

Segment 91 - Department of Commerce: US Patent and Trademark Office

Paul Jefko: Mr. President, as you know, the first Patent Act in 1790 established a Patent Board, consisting of the Secretary of State, Secretary of War and Attorney General. Later, Congress moved the responsibility to clerks in the Department of State. In 1881, Trademark Registration was added to its duties. In 1925, Congress transferred the office to the Department of Commerce. What do you have to say on this, Mr. President?

President Jefferson: This is specifically authorized in the Constitution and is therefore constitutional.

PAUL: Thank you, Mr. President.

Segment 92 - Department of Energy: Office of Energy Efficiency and Renewable Energy

Paul Jefko: Mr. President, Congress created the Office of Energy Conservation in the Department of the Interior in 1971. Four years later, it was renamed the Energy Research and Development Administration and two years after that was merged into the Federal Energy Administration under the new Department of Energy. President Reagan reduced the programs and renamed the agency the Office of Conservation and Solar Energy.

President Jefferson: Why the emphasis on energy?

PAUL: At the end of the 1960's, oil production in the US peaked, causing concerns over its impact. An embargo by the oil exporting countries in the 1970's caused severe dislocations in the US and world economy. After numerous reorganizations, it received its current name in 2001. The agency invests in high risk, high value research on energy efficiency and renewable energy. It has nine programs.
    1) Biomass to make ethanol competitive;
    2) Building Technologies for energy efficient building practices;
    3) Geothermal Technologies to reduce its cost to 3 cents per kilowatt-hour;
    4) Fuel Cells and Infrastructure Technologies to produce hydrogen storage and delivery;
    5) Industrial Technologies to reduce carbon production in manufacturing;
    6) Solar Energy Technology to research photovoltaics, concentrated solar and solar heating and lighting;
    7) Solar Decathlon Vehicle Technologies to promote non-pollution

215

vehicles;

8) Weatherization and Intergovernmental to help state and local governments, Indian Tribes and international agencies adopt renewable and energy efficient technologies; and,

9) Wind and Hydropower to research wind power in low wind areas and hydropower efficiencies.

JEFFERSON: Have these new ideas borne fruit?

PAUL: The federal government has set itself up as the basic research manager of the US. Private companies are supposed to take this basic research and apply it to resolve problems. In some cases, it is effective, in others not. For example, a number of wind farms were constructed with technology developed by the federal government. What do you think of this agency?

JEFFERSON: No specific authority exists in the Constitution for these programs. These programs do not provide common defense of the nation. Some may argue they contribute to the general welfare, but the connection is too vague. They are all unconstitutional.

PAUL: What should be done?

JEFFERSON: Abolish the agency.

PAUL: Thank you, Mr. President. Let's take a look at US Attorneys.

Segment 93 – Department of Justice: US Attorneys

Paul Jefko: Mr. President, as you know, the Judiciary Act of 1789 established the Office of Attorney General and the US Marshal Service. The Act required the President to appoint a prosecutor within each judicial district to prosecute crimes and offenses against the US and litigate civil actions where the US was a party. When Congress created the Department of Justice in 1870, the US Attorneys came under the supervision of the Attorney General.

President Jefferson: Why?

PAUL: As the number of attorneys and cases grew, there was too much for the President to supervise. Congress originally gave him a supervisor in the Treasury Department in 1820 for these attorneys, but the Civil War caused such havoc and confusion, Congress came up with the current system. Currently, there are 93 US Attorneys, one for each judicial district and one for Guam and the Northern Mariana Islands.

JEFFERSON: Guam and the Mariana Islands?

PAUL: We received Guam from Spain after the Spanish-American War. The Mariana Islands were a Japanese territory we acquired after World War II. Each district may have up to 350 lawyers and 350 more support staff. The President appoints all US Attorneys for four-year terms. The headquarters has three Divisions: Criminal, Civil and Tax, all self-explanatory. An Office of Legal Education trains federal, state, and local prosecutors and litigators on federal procedures. What do you think of this agency, Mr. President?

JEFFERSON: Although there is no specific authority for this agency, the necessary and proper clause allows the Congress to legislate to execute the powers it has. Obviously, to enforce the laws, it must have prosecutors. The three Divisions are thereby constitutional. Training state and local prosecutors on federal procedures is a necessary part of this enforcement power.

PAUL: Thank you, Mr. President. Next up, the Job Corps.

Segment 94 – Department of Labor: Job Corps

Paul Jefko: Mr. President, President Johnson established this agency as part of his War on Poverty. Early on, the agency's clientele had a high dropout rate and some hostility from the communities where the centers were located. Since that early start, the agency has helped over 2 million citizens and serves 60,000 youths annually. Although its opponents claim the program was inefficient, it still exists.

President Jefferson: Why inefficient?

PAUL: Some have said a 50% dropout rate is unacceptable. Others say the private sector can adequately provide these jobs and the training. However, the persons who come to the Centers have no marketable skills. One hundred and twenty-five Job Corps Centers in the US provide free education or vocational training up to 2 years to those 16 to 24 years old. Participants are provided housing and a monthly allowance.

JEFFERSON: Housing and spending money?

PAUL: If they have no money, they will not be able to work and attend training at the same time. However, each student must develop a Personal Career Development Plan focusing on the Health Professions, Construction, Culinary Arts, Business or Technology. Private contractors run 77% of the Centers. What do you think of this agency?

JEFFERSON: There is no specific authority for this agency in the Constitution nor does this agency provide for the general welfare or enhance national defense. It is unconstitutional.

PAUL: What shall we do?

JEFFERSON: Abolish the agency.

PAUL: Thank you. Mr. President. We now move again to the Agriculture Department.

Segment 95 – Department of Agriculture: Rural Development Housing and Community Facilities

Paul Jefko: Mr. President, we have touched on this agency before. It began as the Farmers Home Administration in 1946, giving loans and loan guarantees to farmers and low-income families in rural areas to construct or repair housing and assumed its current name in 1994. Focusing on those areas having no more than 20,000 people, the agency provides grants, loans and loan guarantees to individuals and organizations for buying, repairing or constructing homes or rental housing for farm workers and rural residents.

President Jefferson: Why only in rural areas?

PAUL: I do not have an answer to that, except Congress deemed it expedient. I will just say the agency provides funds for rental assistance and housing projects for the elderly or disabled or facilities such as libraries, schools and municipal buildings. The budget for rental assistance is around $1 billion annually. What do you think of this program?

JEFFERSON: There is no authority in the Constitution for this and since it provides no general defense of our nation or provides for the general welfare, it is unconstitutional.
  PAUL: What next?

JEFFERSON: All new agency activities should be stopped immediately. Manage all current loans until liquidated and sell them if possible. After liquidating all loans, abolish the agency.

PAUL: Thank you Mr. President. Let's hit the railroads.

Segment 96 – Independent Agencies: National Railroad Passenger Corporation

Paul Jefko: Mr. President, as the Great Depression waxed, passenger rail travel waned sharply. Although World War II troop movements increased traffic somewhat, by 1955 the losses to passenger railroad companies totaled $700 million. Railroad company mergers reduced the costs but competition from automobiles and the airlines further reduced rail passenger travel. After a number of rail companies declared bankruptcy, Congress passed and President Nixon signed the Rail Passenger Service Act establishing the National Railroad Passenger Corporation, known as Amtrak, to operate intercity passenger trains.

President Jefferson: If the service was not profitable, why keep it?

PAUL: No politician wanted to be the one who ended rail passenger service in the US. Amtrak was established as an experiment to give the system one more chance so the politicians could say they at least tried to save the system. The law allowed any intercity passenger carrier to procure stock in the new corporation with either cash or equipment donation. Those not joining were required to continue current service for five years after which the Interstate Commerce Commission had to approve any service reduction.

JEFFERSON: What is the Interstate Commerce Commission?

PAUL: It is a regulatory agency established by Congress in 1887 to ensure fair rates on interstate railroads, bus lines, truck lines, and telephone companies. When Amtrak was set up, twenty of the 26 rail companies joined. Although Amtrak merged trains, services and stations, it still required federal funding to continue.

JEFFERSON: How much federal funding?

PAUL: Although Congress has invested over $36 billion over the last 40 years, the Corporation still cannot pay its own way. Ticket sales pay for 85% of its operating costs. Currently, Amtrak operates 300 trains on 21,300 miles of track connecting 500 cities and towns in 46 states. In a recent year, it transported over 31 million passengers with 20,000 staff. Its operating costs were $2.2 Billion and its capital budget was $552 million. Mr. President, what do you think of this corporation?

JEFFERSON: The Constitution provides no specific authority to operate a railroad or other transportation system. Since transporting passengers is not a national defense or general welfare issue, this agency is unconstitutional.

219

PAUL: What should Congress do with this agency?

JEFFERSON: The agency should maintain its schedules for a year while attempting to dispose of its routes and rolling stock. After all are disposed of, the agency should be abolished.

PAUL: Thank you, Mr. President. Let us turn once again to Homeland Security.

Segment 97 – Department of Homeland Security: United States Secret Service

Paul Jefko: Mr. President, Congress established this agency in 1865 to suppress counterfeit currency. One-third of the currency at that time was counterfeit. After President McKinley was assassinated in 1901, it was given the mission of presidential protection. When Robert Kennedy was assassinated in 1968, Presidential and Vice Presidential candidates and nominees received protection. Combatting credit card and computer fraud were added in 1984.

President Jefferson: These duties do not seem to go together. What does counterfeit currency have to do with protecting the President?

PAUL: Nothing really. After McKinley was murdered, Congress looked for a current law enforcement agency to protect the President. The only other option was the Federal Marshals Service. Since the Marshals worked closely with the Judiciary Branch, it was not thought appropriate to add this extra burden. In 1998, the Service became responsible for security at designated national events.

JEFFERSON: Such as...

PAUL: Well, for example, every 4 years, the political parties gather for a convention to choose their Presidential candidate. Also, the President's State of the Union address to Congress, even the Super Bowl.

JEFFERSON: Super Bowl?

PAUL: Never mind. It's too hard to explain. Let us just say it is an athletic event treated as a national holiday. Continuing...in 2003, the Service was transferred to Homeland Security. It has 6500 staff. In summary, the agency protects the President, Vice President, the President Elect, the Vice President Elect and their immediate families, Former Presidents and their spouses, Children of former presidents until 16, visiting heads of foreign states or governments and spouses, official US representatives on special missions abroad, major presidential and vice presidential candidates 120 days before election and special national security events designated by the Secretary of Homeland Security.

JEFFERSON: That is much work for 6,500 people.

PAUL: Quite true. What do you say?

JEFFERSON: The constitution provides specific authority to combat counterfeiting and the general defense of the nation provides authority to protect the President and others as determined by Congress. All functions are constitutional.

PAUL: Thank You, Mr. President. Time to turn to the Department of State once again.

Segment 98 – Department of State: Bureau of Overseas Building Operations

Paul Jefko: Mr. President, this agency builds and manages our embassies and consulate buildings overseas. Attacks against our embassies in Tehran, Kenya and Tanzania caused the Department to reevaluate the security of all buildings overseas. Studies indicated over 85% of the embassies, missions and consulates did not meet security standards.

President Jefferson: What are some of the standards?

PAUL: Well, for example, each building must be at least 100 feet from the street to prevent damage from street bombings. Since most embassies are in cities, that is a problem. The new standards required constructing 50 new facilities while $140 million is used annually to enhance the physical security of the remaining facilities until they are replaced. This agency does that with four offices: Planning and Development, Real Estate and Property Management, Project Execution and Operations and Maintenance.

JEFFERSON: They all make sense.

PAUL: Most funds go to private construction and engineering firms. What do you think of this bureau?
JEFFERSON: There is no specific authority in the Constitution for constructing or purchasing buildings in foreign countries. However, under the clause regulating foreign commerce, we need structures for our representatives

221

to occupy when in intercourse with foreign governments. The agency is constitutional.

PAUL: Thank you, Mr. President. We turn now to fish and wildlife.

Segment 99 – Department of Interior: US Fish and Wildlife Service

Paul Jefko: In 1871, the Congress created the US Commission on Fish and Fisheries to determine the reasons for and solutions to the decline of food fish stocks in internal and coastal waters. In an unrelated action in 1885, Congress set up the Division of Economic Ornithology and Mammalogy in the Department of Agriculture to determine the role of birds in controlling agricultural pests and to map plants and animal distribution in the US.

President Jefferson: What caused the decline in fish stocks?

PAUL: There were various reports. One stated the mesh in fishermen's nets were too small and caught young mackerel too small for the market and were thrown back in the sea, dead. The Congress upgraded the Commission to the Bureau of Fisheries in 1903. In 1918, Congress passed the Migratory Bird Treaty Act to implement a treaty between the US and Canada to control migratory bird hunting.

JEFFERSON: Why are we concerned with migratory bird hunting?

PAUL: Are you familiar with the passenger pigeon?

JEFFERSON: Yes, they fill the sky near my home. They are considered good to eat by my servants.

PAUL: Well, they no longer exist.

JEFFERSON: Why?

PAUL: Men hunted them to extinction and destroyed their habitat to create farms. That is why Congress passed the Duck Stamp Act in 1934 requiring waterfowl hunters to purchase a federal hunting license. Specific hunting seasons and daily limits now are in place for hunters. Well, the fish people and the wildlife people were combined into the current agency and placed under the Interior Department in 1940.

JEFFERSON: Wait. You must have a license to hunt?

222

PAUL: Most States require hunting licenses to protect the wildlife stock or to obtain revenue. The only federal intrusion is for migratory birds and endangered species. Moving on…in the 1950's, the agency formed the Bureau of Commercial Fisheries and the Bureau of Sport Fisheries and Wildlife. In 1970, the Department of Commerce took over the Bureau of Commercial Fisheries, while the Bureau of Sport Fisheries and Wildlife assumed the current agency's name.

JEFFERSON: Were sporting fish stocks declining?

PAUL: No, but the object was to protect the areas where sporting fish are available for pleasure fishing. Adding to these protections, Congress passed the Endangered Species Act in 1973 to protect species from extinction. In the 1980's the Congress expanded the National Wildlife Refuge System. The Service enforces federal wildlife laws, protects endangered species, manages migratory bird flyways, restores fisheries, conserves and restores wildlife habitat, assists in international conservation efforts and provides funds to State fish and wildlife agencies.

JEFFERSON: The States can handle that responsibility.

PAUL: You may be correct. It has eight regional and 700 field offices in the US. Its major divisions include Habitat and Resource Conservation that protects, conserves and restores fish and wildlife resources. Environmental Quality focuses on pollution problems affecting fish and wildlife. International Affairs implements international treaties for species conservation and habitats. What about this agency?

JEFFERSON: There is no specific authority in the Constitution for these programs, except for commercial fisheries in navigable waters. Restoring and protecting commercial fisheries is constitutional per the Commerce Clause as interpreted by the courts. The other functions are not essential to national defense and do not contribute to the general welfare. However, if the Senate has approved an international treaty on these subjects, the program is permissible and constitutional.

PAUL: What should be done?

JEFFERSON: The agency must continue to enforce the international treaties under its purview. However, abolish the remainder. These are State responsibilities if they choose to accept them.

PAUL: Thank you, Mr. President.

223

Segment 100 – Department of Agriculture: Agricultural Marketing Service

Paul Jefko: Sir, this agency started in 1913 as the Office of Markets to standardize and grade eggs. It expanded in World War II to inspect and grade the food for our soldiers. In 1939, a major reorganization of the Agriculture Department merged this agency, the Bureau of Agricultural Economics, the Bureau of Animal Industry, the Bureau of Plant Industry, the Bureau of Dairy Industry and part of the Food and Drug Administration into one agency.

President Jefferson: So, from egg inspections we now inspect all animal products?

PAUL: True. After several name changes, it took its current name. The agency tests, grades and provides market news for Cotton, Tobacco, Dairy, Fruits and Vegetables, Livestock, Seed and Poultry. It has three main programs. The Microbiological Data Program monitors alfalfa sprouts, cantaloupe, spinach, tomatoes and lettuce for bacterial contamination. The Science and Technology Program manages the laboratories for the agency.

JEFFERSON: Market news?

PAUL: Reports include information on prices, volume, quality, condition, and other market data on farm products in specific markets and marketing areas. Continuing…the Transportation and Marketing Program provides money to States to improve marketing methods and provides information to the producers, shippers, exporters, rural communities, other government agencies and universities on the food transportation system. The agency spends over $1 Billion annually and employs more than 53,000 persons in the US and Mexico.

JEFFERSON: Why Mexico?

PAUL: They are there to monitor transportation of products between Mexico and the US. What do you think of this agency?

JEFFERSON: Certainly, the regulation of commerce requires a uniform standard for agricultural products, so the testing and grading is appropriate and constitutional. However, maintaining a market news service is out of line. Examining vegetables for contamination also is constitutional. However, providing money to States for improving their marketing or providing information on transporting products is not specifically authorized nor does it help the general welfare as it applies only to those in the transporting business.

PAUL: What should we do?

JEFFERSON: Eliminate the market news service and desist from giving States funds for improving their marketing practices and transportation problems. That is a private and state responsibility. Also, consider charging a fee to producers for inspecting vegetables.

PAUL: Thank you, Mr. President. That ends not only this week's program, but our entire series. I wish to thank President Jefferson for his hard work and cooperation on reviewing our current government considering his vast experience in the early days of our nation. On behalf of President Jefferson, I wish you a good evening.

www.ingramcontent.com/pod-product-compliance
Lightning Source LLC
Chambersburg PA
CBHW030430290526
45786CB00001B/225